LEGENDARY LOCALS

OF

UKIAH

CALIFORNIA

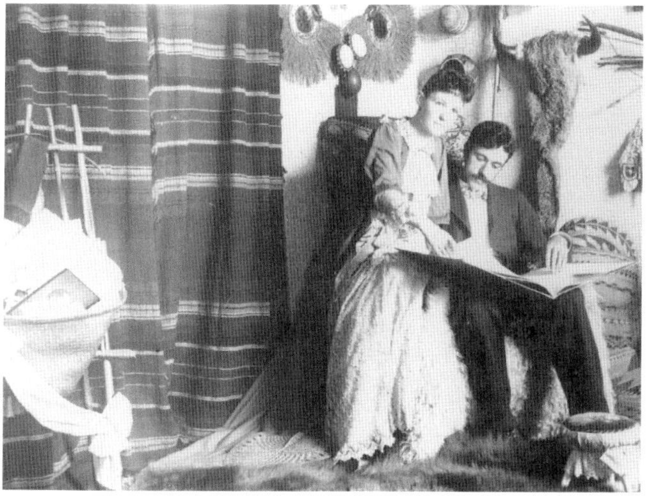

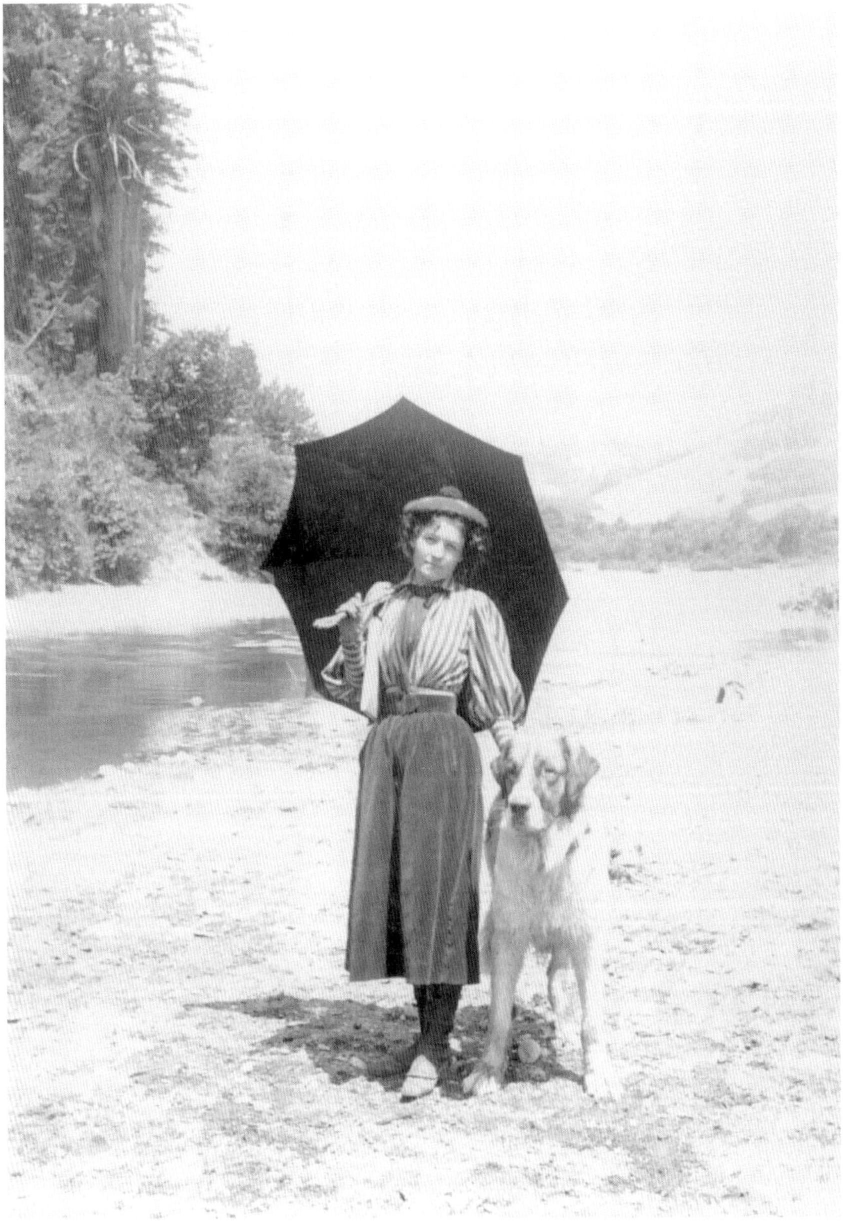

Grace Carpenter Hudson

Grace Carpenter Hudson, a native of Ukiah, was known throughout the world as a fine artist who depicted the Native American people—particularly the Pomo tribe of Mendocino County. (Courtesy of Grace Hudson Museum, photograph by A.O. Carpenter.)

Page 1: Dr. John Hudson

Dr. John Hudson, husband of Grace Carpenter Hudson, was recognized nationwide as an ethnographic expert. He was particularly well known for his research of the Pomo people and his impressive collection of their artifacts. (Courtesy of Grace Hudson Museum, photograph by George Wilcox.)

LEGENDARY LOCALS

OF

UKIAH

CALIFORNIA

DARLINE BERGERE

LEGENDARY LOCALS

ISBN 978-1-4671-0182-0

Legendary Locals is an imprint of Arcadia Publishing
Charleston, South Carolina

Printed in the United States of America

Library of Congress Control Number: 2014942212

For all general information, please contact Arcadia Publishing:
Telephone 843-853-2070
Fax 843-853-0044
E-mail sales@arcadiapublishing.com
For customer service and orders:
Toll-Free 1-888-313-2665

Visit us on the Internet at www.arcadiapublishing.com

Dedication

To Samantha Johnson Ilyin, a constant inspiration in my life, and my children, for the support they give me to face my challenges

On the Front Cover: Clockwise from top right:
Rich Petersen, prominent Mendocino County criminal attorney (Courtesy of Justin Petersen; see pages 122 and 123), Jan Cox, community activist (Courtesy of Porter Dinehart; see pages 116 and 117), Dr. E. John Gardner, prominent physician (Courtesy of Nancy Biggins; see page 15), Quinn Van Antwerp, actor (Courtesy of Laural Near; see page 81), Lyle Tuttle, internationally known tattoo artist (Courtesy of Lyle Tuttle; see page 91), Grace Hudson, artist (Courtesy of Grace Hudson Museum; see page 2), and John Parducci (Courtesy of Parducci family; see pages 54 and 55).

On the Back Cover: From left to right:
Shiloh Fernandez, actor (Courtesy of Sam Fernandez; photograph by Tyler Shields; see page 81), the Western band Riders in the Sky (Courtesy of Spencer Brewer; see page 79).

CONTENTS

ACKNOWLEDGMENTS

Special thanks are owed to my editor, Erin Vosgien, who was always there to assist me in every way and never lost patience with me—although she certainly had enough reason to. Thank you Erin, from the bottom of my heart. Many people contributed to production of this book, including Nancy Biggins, who shared her encyclopedic knowledge of Ukiah history and was always there with new information to spur me on whenever I felt the task of producing a book seemed impossible and overwhelming.

Members of the entertainment community who provided me with information include Spencer Brewer, Paula Samonte, Elena Casanova, Patrick Ford, Rowland Nielson, Will Siegel, Charlotte Everett, and a host of others—each of them leading me to the next. The School for the Performing Arts and Cultural Education (SPACE) gave me access to a wealth of photographs, as did Marvin Schenck and Sherrie Smith-Ferri from the Grace Hudson Museum. Ed Bold, Barbara, Colleen, Phil, and Ron at the Held-Poage Historical Library helped me ferret through many historical documents. Thanks also to John Mayfield, entrepreneur and philanthropist; Ralph and Susan Maize, who opened up their home to me to study photographs and ask questions; Carole Hester, who was always there with a helping hand and a good word; and the families who came to my rescue when I put out the frantic call for photographs of their relatives.

Finally, thanks to my son, Alexander Bergere, who assisted me with his computer expertise. He always encouraged me and told me to just keep writing and getting the pictures, saying that he would take care of "the easy part" and put it all together.

Ukiah is a terrific town, with terrific people who are always willing to share their knowledge and lend a helping hand.

INTRODUCTION

It is my hope that this book will instill in you a desire to learn more about the amazing people who have lived in this valley—the pioneers, the families who started businesses here, and the generations that followed. Ukiah is a blended community that celebrates its diversity, producing world famous athletics, musicians, spiritual leaders, and an internationally known tattoo artist who appeared on the cover of *Rolling Stone*. Very few towns can claim such a wide range of residents.

Ukiah is unique in the diverse backgrounds of its early settlers: the Pomo band of Native Americans, which included the Yokayo band, the Guidiville band, and the Pinoleville band; and the Cunningham and Thomas families, early farmers who settled in the area. Pear orchards were established and became a major contributor to the local economy. In the early 1920s, the local chamber of commerce began promoting Ukiah as "the Gateway to the Redwoods."

In the 21st century, Ukiah is even more diverse in its residents. While the logging industry has waned, the vineyards have multiplied. Large and small wineries have found a home here, as the weather is ideal for growing grapes. Tasting rooms abound, and the area sponsors many winery events, including the Taste of Redwood Valley, the Taste of Downtown.

Visitors can also enjoy the exhibits at the Grace Hudson Museum and tour the Sun House—the residence of Grace Hudson and Dr. John Hudson. Some of the finest collections of Pomo baskets and weavings in the country are displayed at the Grace Hudson Museum, which also hosts a number of special exhibits throughout the year. Local art galleries hold openings the first Friday of the month, providing not only exhibits of new artwork but music as well. The Ukiah branch of the Mendocino County Library holds a book sale in conjunction with these gallery openings.

Throughout the summer months, free concerts are held in Todd Grove Park on Sundays. The Ukiah Symphony, blues bands, Western musicians, and rock groups all play, thanks to the generosity and hard work of local musician and Grammy nominee Spencer Brewer. Summer also brings the Moonlight Movie Madness event, a six-week series of free movies held on Fridays at Alex Thomas Plaza. September is Ukiah's month for classic car buffs, however—hosting the weekend long Fabulous Flashback Car Show. On Friday evening, a sock hop is held at a local shopping center parking lot, and on Saturday, School Street is shut down to display dozens of classic cars from all over Northern and Central California, as well Oregon and Nevada. On Sunday, the event is closed out with a parade and Poker Run. October continues this fun with PumpkinFest, during which downtown streets are closed off and filled with musical acts, and art exhibits. Savings Bank sponsors the scarecrow contest at this true family event.

Ukiah remains an old-fashioned small town, where people ride their bicycles everywhere and can still hear the bell of the ice cream truck ringing on weekends. It is an ideal place for families raising their children, or for those looking for a bucolic environment in which to retire.

Ukiah is also home to the Vichy Springs Resort. Found on the outskirts of town, the resort was once visited by such famous people as Mark Twain, Robert Lewis Stevenson, and John L. Sullivan—who had his training camp there. It has also been said that Presidents Grant and Harrison were frequent visitors to the resort and its rejuvenating mineral springs baths.

People venture to Ukiah to fish, to taste the fine wines made there, and to hear the music and many don't go home. They find the valley so to their liking that they embrace the area and relocate, living in Ukiah to better enjoy all that it has to offer.

CHAPTER ONE

Well-known Personalities

Every town, large or small, has its heartbeat—the people whom everyone knows, whether they are a part of the business community, local government, or the town's myriad organizations. In Ukiah, these people keep the town on track by networking with one another to help make certain that things are running smoothly. One individual—or many—putting the building blocks together to form a plan, assist in a community need, or institute an endeavor that will benefit everyone. They come from all walks of life but share a common goal: the betterment of Ukiah. This chapter features a war hero, doctors, judges, Native Americas, a prominent figure in agriculture, those in government, and individuals who have dedicated their lives to helping Ukiah—whether by providing low-income housing or employment—and proving that it is a community that works together.

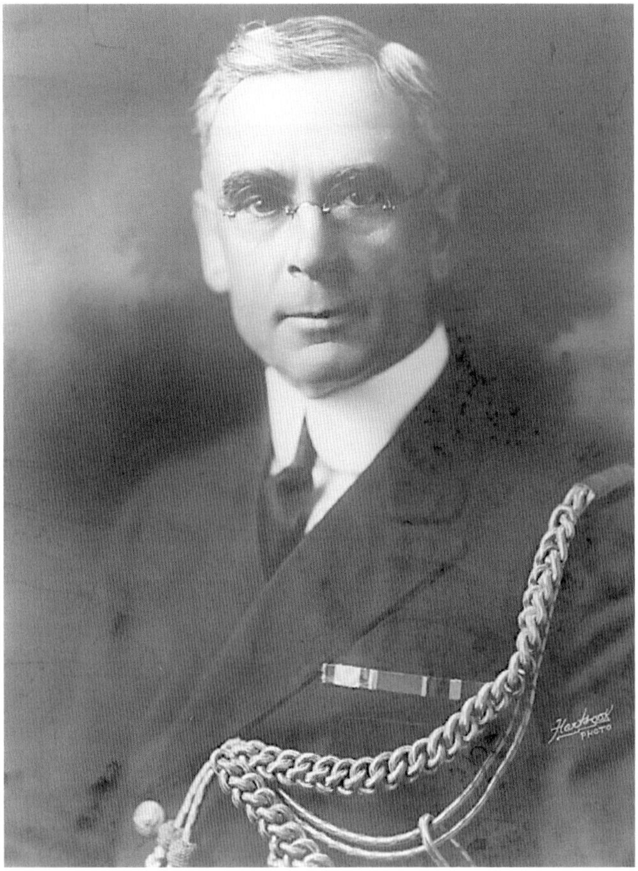

William Harrison Standley

Adm. William Harrison Standley of the US Navy was born in Ukiah in 1872. His grandfather operated a hotel in Ukiah, and at one, time his father, "Doc" Standley, served as Mendocino County Sheriff.

Standley graduated from the Naval Academy in 1895. During the Spanish-American War, he was assigned to the monitor *Monterey*. After the fighting with Spain ended, he served aboard the gunboat *Yorktown* in the Philippine Insurrection. In 1899, during this tour of duty, he earned a commendation for bravery after volunteering for a reconnaissance mission into enemy territory.

His next assignment took him to San Francisco, and the gunboat *Marietta*, in 1901. Later that year, Standley became the Officer in Charge of the craft. He went on to serve aboard a number of different ships, and in 1915, took command of the gunboat *Yorktown*.

Standley returned to the Naval Academy in 1916, working as an assistant to the Superintendent in charge of Buildings and Grounds. Under his direction, the new seamanship and navigation buildings were built at a cost of over $4 million.

His exceptional abilities led to his appointment as vice admiral in 1932. Before he retired in 1937, Standley often performed the function of acting secretary of the Navy. He was called back to active duty in 1941, after the attack on Pearl Harbor.

In 1942, President Roosevelt appointed Standley ambassador to the Soviet Union. Under his direction, vast amounts of military aid arrived in Russia to assist the nation in its fight against the Nazis. He held the post until the fall of 1943.

Standley was called to active duty again in 1944, where he served in the Office of Strategic Services until the fall of 1945. He retired to San Diego, California, where he resided until his death in October 1963. He is buried in Arlington National Cemetery in Arlington, Virginia. (Courtesy of Held-Poage Library.)

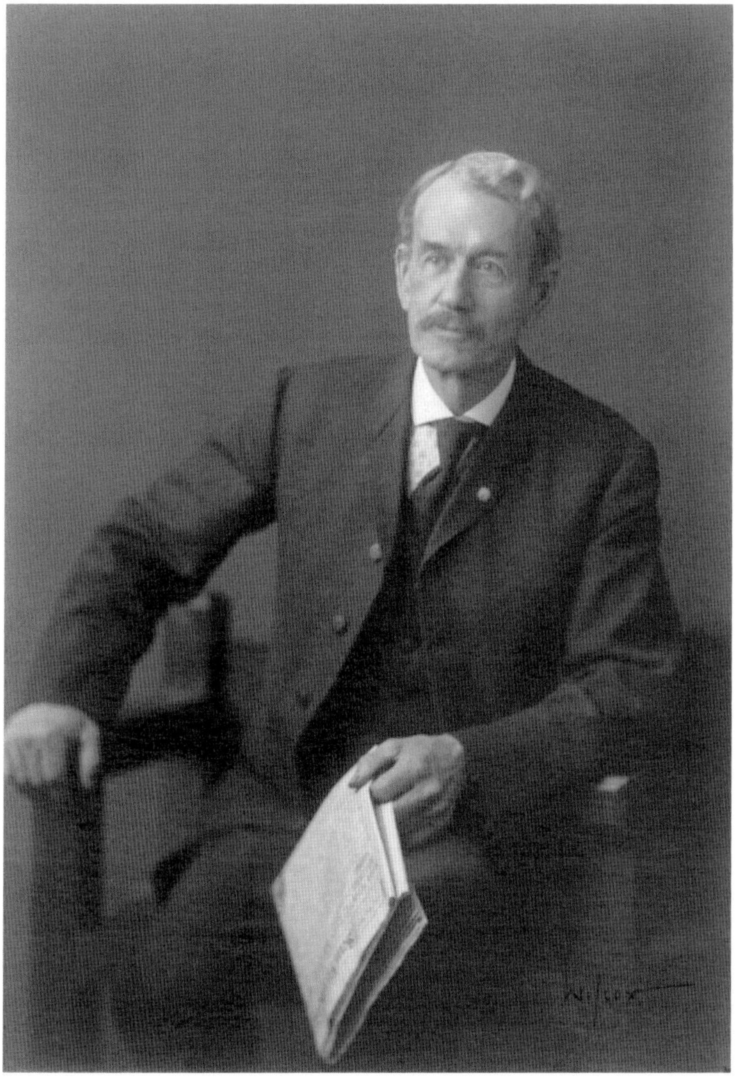

A.O. Carpenter

Born on the East Coast, Aurelius Ormando Carpenter moved with his family to the Kansas Territory in 1855. Both his mother and father were in the newspaper business, working as writers, editors, and publishers. After A.O. completed his basic schooling, he joined the abolitionist movement and fought alongside John Brown at the Battle of Black Jack. As he was recovering from the wounds that he suffered in the battle, a young woman helped to care for A.O. The woman, Helen McCowan Carpenter, fell in love with the young man, and they were married a few months later. In 1957, A.O. and Helen moved with her family to California, to join her brother who was mining in the state. Settling in Mendocino County's Potter Valley, A.O. farmed while Helen taught school. Reel, as he was sometimes known, started and co-owned the county's first newspaper, the *Mendocino Herald*. Over the next few years, he was affiliated with a number of newspapers, including the *San Francisco Fair Daily* and the *Ukiah City Press*.

After A.O. and Helen moved to Ukiah, he established a photography studio, which the family ran for over 40 years. Both he and Helen were very involved in both the white and Pomo communities, which is undoubtedly where Grace Carpenter Hudson developed the love of painting Pomo children for which she is so well known. (Courtesy of Grace Hudson Museum, photograph by George Wilcox.)

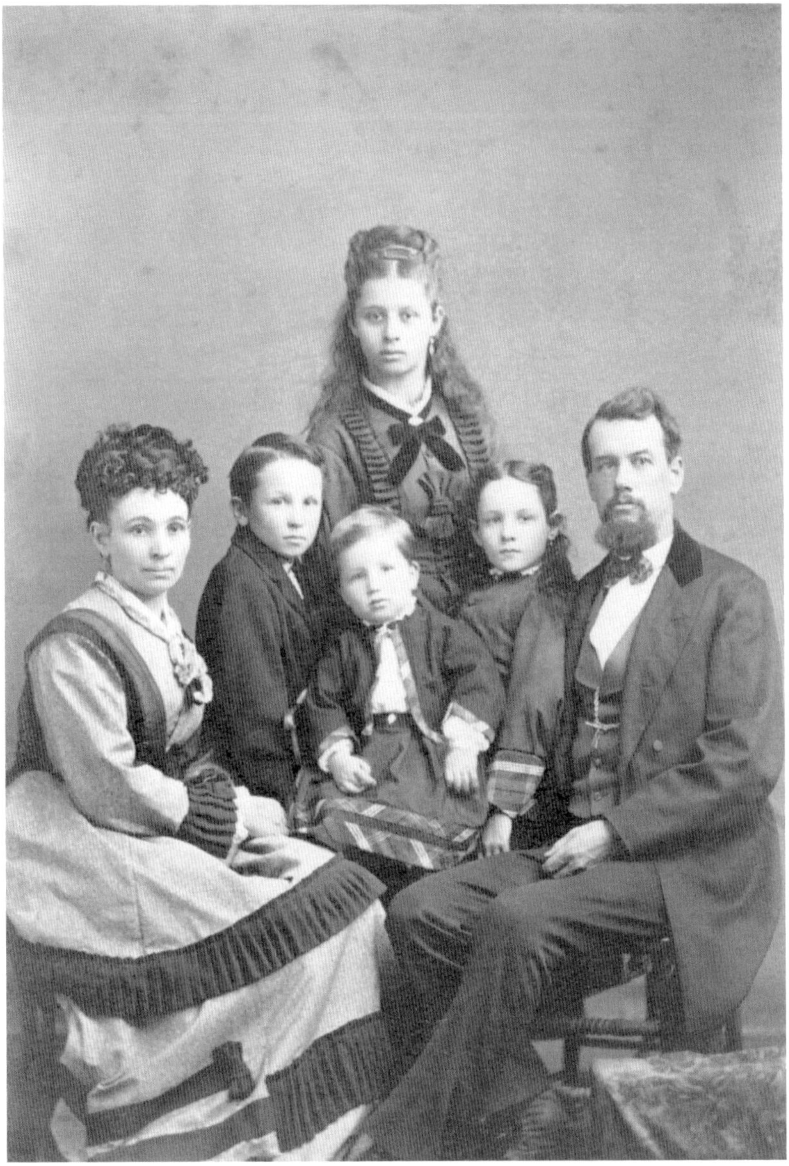

Helen McCowan Carpenter

Helen McCowan accompanied her husband to Ukiah Valley in 1859, travelling from the Midwest. Helen had earned a teaching credential from Bloomingdale Quaker Academy, and upon arrival in the Ukiah area, she applied for teaching credentials and became the first teacher certified by the new County Board of Education. She worked as an educator for the next decade.

Her twins, Grace and Grant, were born in 1865, and another son, Frank, was born in 1870. Although occupied with raising her children, Helen found time to assist her husband with his photography business. She was also quite active in several fraternal organizations, including the Order of the Eastern Star, and the Rebekah Lodge.

An amateur artist, Helen encouraged her children to explore their creative abilities.

She has many published works of her own, including poetry, stories, and music. (Courtesy of Grace Hudson Museum.)

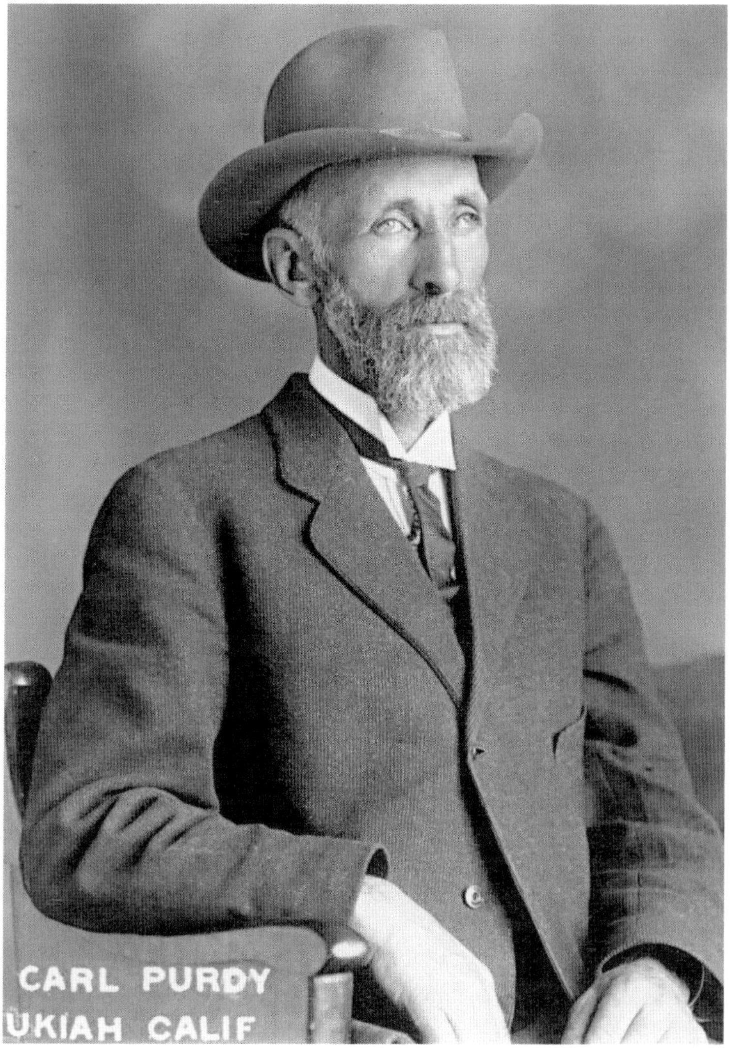

Carl Purdy

When daffodils appear in the spring, remember Carl Purdy. Born in the Midwest in 1861, Purdy moved west in 1865 with his family and arrived in Ukiah in 1870. From a young age, Carl was fascinated with the wildflowers he saw. As a young man, he became interested in birds and horticulture. Carl Purdy came from a military family, but because of an accident resulting in damage to his vision, following in the family tradition was not possible. He had already been accepted to West Point when the accident occurred.

He later became interested in biology, which resulted in him becoming a teacher. He was hired as a botany teacher at the Cottoneva School on the coast. His interest in botany led him to send for books from London, and information on plants for his classes. It was this passion for collecting native plants and bulbs that started him on the path to becoming a wholesale distributor—shipping bulbs and plants all over the world and becoming famous in his field. His experiments with Bartlett pears in the 1890s brought this fruit to Mendocino County.

In the late 1890s, Purdy met Luther Burbank, which resulted in a lifelong friendship. He continued collecting plants throughout his later years, until he was well into his 80s. Today, Carl Purdy Hall at the fairgrounds in Ukiah is named for him. (Courtesy of Held-Poage Library.)

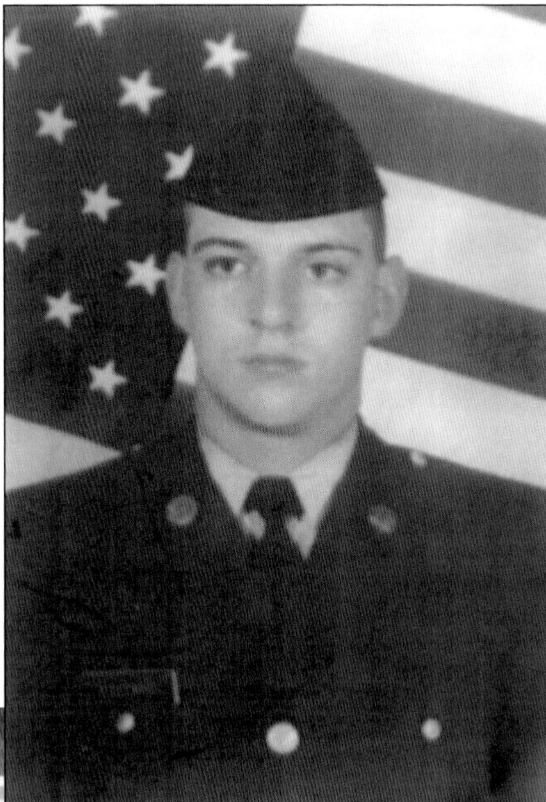

Sgt. Jason Buzzard

On a sunny day in June 2006, Jason Buzzard was laid to rest in his hometown of Ukiah. He was the first soldier from Mendocino County to be killed in the Iraq War.

A group from Ukiah met Jason in Sacramento to escort him home for the last time. CHP officers, the sheriff, and a group of veterans formed a procession along the route. Fire trucks and crowds assembled to honor Jason as the procession passed through small towns on the route, while road crews along the way took off their hats and saluted as he passed. Finally, hundreds of people assembled at Eversole's Mortuary to honor this fallen soldier. We are honored that this brave man called Ukiah home. (Courtesy of the Buzzard family.)

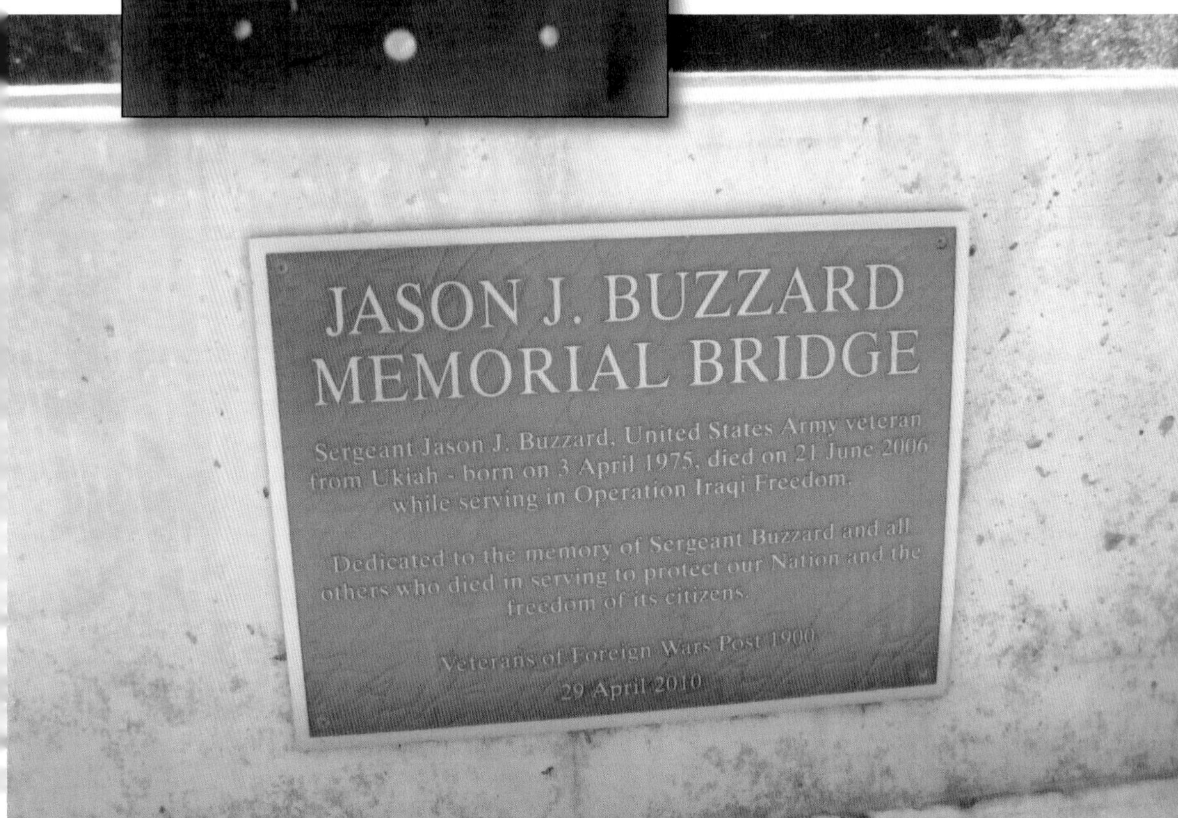

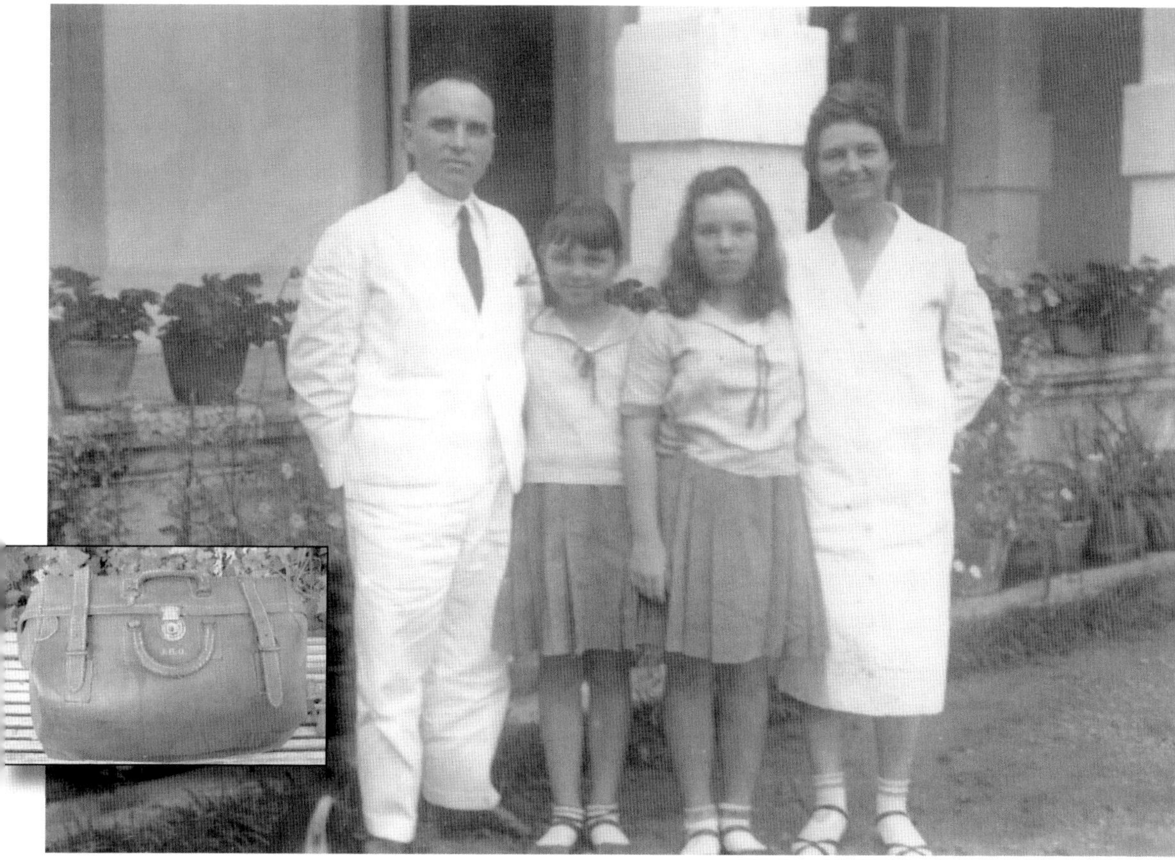

Dr. J. Earl Gardner

Dr. Earl Gardner and his wife, Ethel, finished their medical training at Loma Linda University in 1919 and moved to England for further study. Dr. Gardner obtained diplomas from the Royal College of Physicians (London) and the Royal College of Surgeons (Edinburgh). In 1914, he and his wife opened the first Seven-Day Adventist medical clinic in Georgetown, Penang, Malaya—then a British Colony. In 1931, they established a new hospital and worked there until 1937, returning to America to put their daughters, June and Earla, through high school.

They settled in Ukiah in 1939 and bought the practice of Dr. G.K. Abbott, including the building at 215 West Standley Street. It was a full-service practice with an X-ray machine and facilities for minor surgery, and Dr. Gardner even made house calls. He practiced, both alone and with partners, for over 40 years. Generations of young people grew up to stop the doctor on the street and proclaim that they were "Gardner babies." He was rarely seen without his customary suit and vest, even when gardening or walking on the beach. The City of Ukiah dedicated Gardner Park in his memory, located across the street from his office.

In 1974, the 90-year-old founder of the Hong Kong SCA Hospital retired, and a "younger man" (the 80-year-old Gardner) went to fill in until the new administrator arrived. This trip coincided with the 50th anniversary of Gardner's arrival in Penang, and one of the young men who Dr. Gardner helped through medical school escorted him back to the Malaysian hospital he had founded for the celebration—a high point in his life. His two daughters, Earle Aagaard and June Horsley, both became physicians; and his granddaughter, Candace Horsley, served as city manager of Ukiah for many years. (Courtesy of Nancy Biggins.)

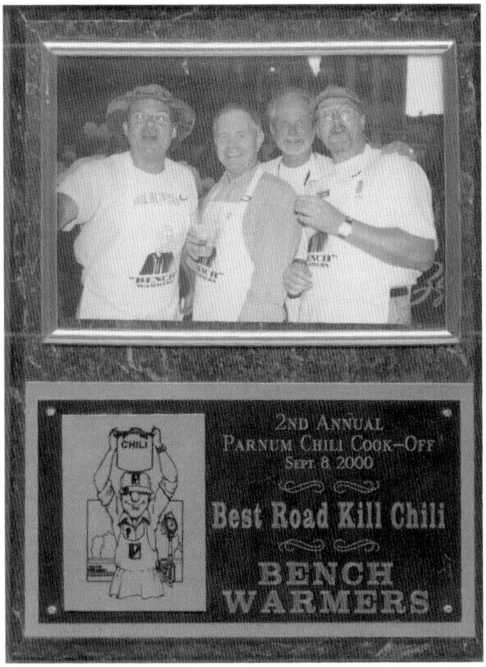

Judges' Chili Cook-Off

Pictured here on their plaque from the Parnum Chili Cook-off are, from left to right, Judge Jonathan Lehan, Judge Ronald Combest, Judge Henry Nelson, and Judge Ronald Brown. Ukiah holds this event every year, hosting teams formed by local businesses and organizations—including the Mendocino County Courthouse. Proceeds from the event support the Ukiah Boys and Girls Club. (Courtesy of Chili-Cook-Off Committee.)

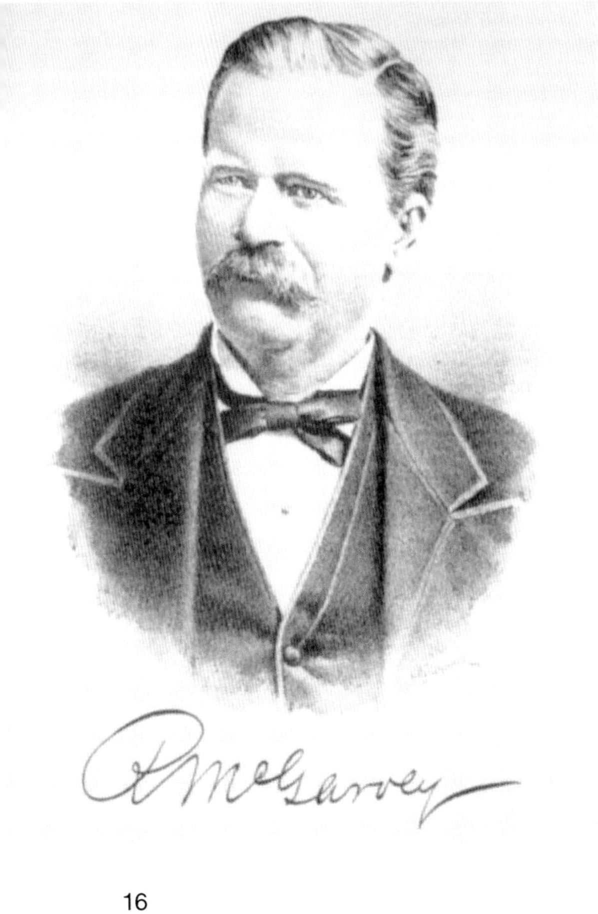

Judge Robert McGarvey

A native of Cincinnati, Ohio, Robert McGarvey gave up a teaching career in Indiana to study law. He had just begun his legal education when the Mexican War broke out, in which he fought and was wounded twice. When he was discharged, McGarvey returned to Indiana to continue studying to become a lawyer. In 1849, he wound his way to California and decided to make it his permanent home—arriving in Ukiah in 1861.

McGarvey started his law practice in Ukiah and became extremely successful. He went on to become district attorney and, in 1876, was elected to the state senate. In 1879, he was elected to the post of superior court judge.

McGarvey was also affiliated with the start of the Savings Bank. In 1891, he decided to plant a prune and pear orchard, which the locals thought a bad decision. McGarvey proved them wrong, however, and was very successful in his agricultural endeavors. The McGarvey's also gifted land to the city, including the site of the Saturday Afternoon Club and, in 1879, the site of a park. That land, McGarvey Park, is the oldest park in Ukiah and was recently the site of' Judge McGarvey's great-great-great-granddaughter's wedding. (Courtesy of Held-Poage Library.)

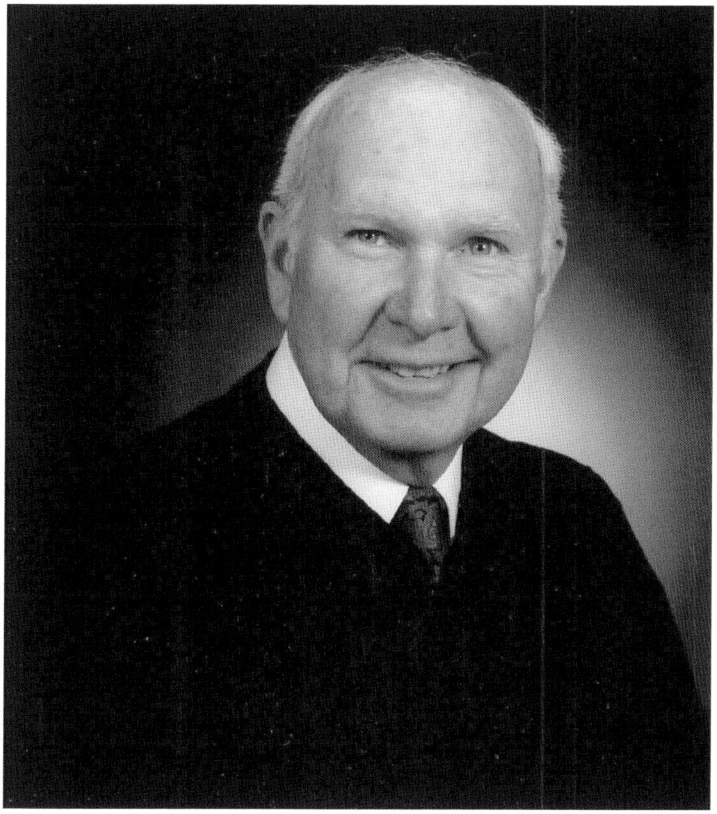

Judge John Joseph Golden

When John Joseph Golden passed, a newspaper headline read, "Golden remembered for brilliance, efficiency and work ethic on the superior court bench." The article went on to refer to the judge as a man of honor and ethics. He served in the US Navy in the Pacific theater during World War II. After his military service, Golden went to college and graduated from the University of Oklahoma, majoring in English with a minor in Spanish. Golden then enrolled in University of California's Boalt Hall and received his law degree in 1950. That same year, he was admitted to the California and federal courts and began to practice law with the Ukiah firm of Rawles, Nelson, and Golden. From 1967 to 1970, Golden served on the State Bar of California's Board of Governors, was state bar vice president from 1969 to 1970, and served on the California Board of Legal Specialization from 1970 to 1974.

In 1974, Gov. Ronald Reagan appointed Golden to the Lake County Superior Court. The court handled everything from felony and probate, to family law and everything in between. Golden thoroughly understood the law, and a colleague was once quoted as saying that he "held you to it. You couldn't slip anything past him. If you tried to, you did it at your own peril. He had a formidable intelligence, and the ability to look at a complex case and boil it down, without getting caught up in unnecessary details." Golden made all the old-timers in the legal profession adhere to the law, forcing some of them to learn their trade and not just go by what someone else had "gotten by with."

In 1997, Golden presided over the trial of Bar Lincoln, who was charged with killing a sheriff's deputy on the Round Valley Reservation in 1995. Lincoln was defended by well-known criminal defense attorney Tony Sierra, but Golden kept total control over a courtroom that many judges would have had a tough time of it.

Judge Golden was a true renaissance man, with a love of poetry, history, and music. He was a member of a quartet in the Ukiah area, singing old-time songs that warmed audience's heart. (Courtesy of Mary Golden.)

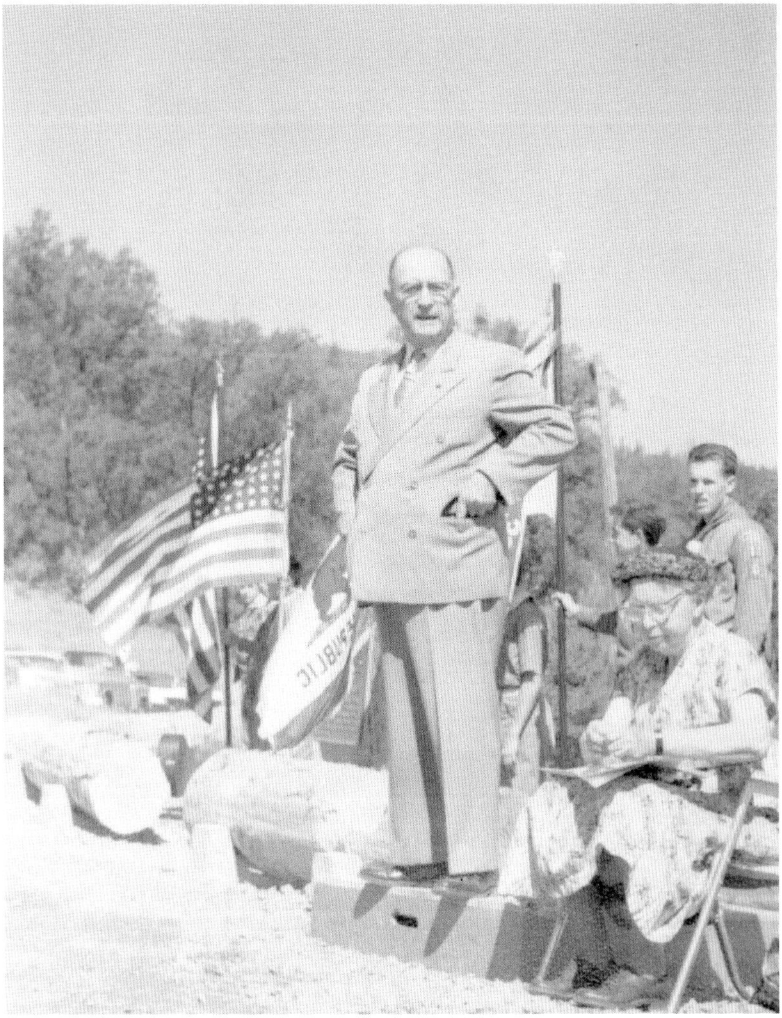

Judge Lilburn Gibson

From stacking hay to superior court judge—Judge Gibson was born in Ukiah in 1892 and spent his youth as a cowboy on his family's ranch. He had a pet mule that would take him to school every morning and come back to pick him up when the day was done. After his graduation from high school, he returned to the family ranch but his interest in learning 'continued. He found, as friends and neighbors said, that he had a natural talent for public speaking, and in his autobiography, *Some Reminiscences of My 74 Years in Mendocino County*, he wrote, "All the orators I have ever knew of became adept at public speaking by hard work and much practice."

A very colorful and well-liked man, Gibson would practice his speeches to his horse and the countryside as he went about his cowboy duties. After some time, he happened to meet Robert Duncan—then the district attorney for Mendocino County. Duncan asked Gibson if he would like to study for the bar, and after a little more than a year, Gibson passed the bar examination with flying colors and set up his own legal practice. In 1921, he received an appointment to fill the position of district attorney.

After 10 years of serving the county, Gibson resigned to enter private practice with Judge Hugh Preston. Then, the political bug bit him again and he ran for superior court judge. He ran unopposed and served through 1961. He also served as president of the Conference of California Judges and was president of the Fraternal Order of Eagles for over 40 years. (Courtesy of Held-Poage Library.)

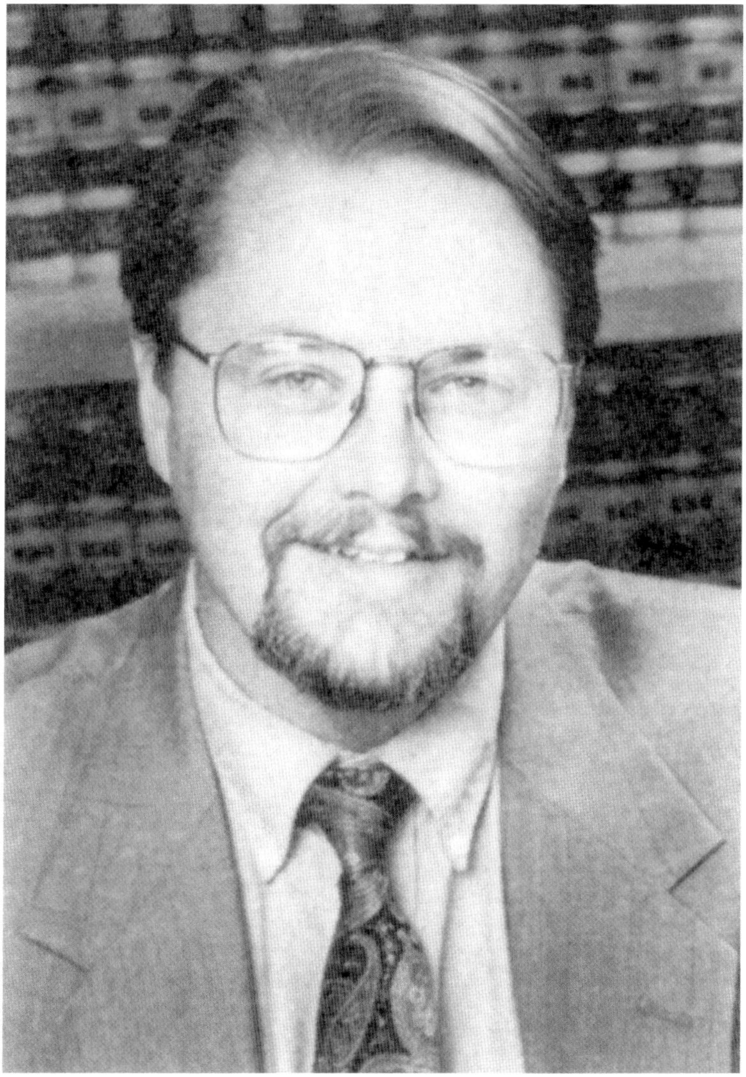

Judge Ronald Brown
According to Presiding Judge Richard Henderson, Judge Brown "exemplified all the best qualities of a jurist, committed to both the spirit and the principles of serving justice." He was a hero to both his family and the community.

Brown put himself through Sonoma State University and then went on to the Empire School of Law and earned his law degree. He worked as the school's law librarian and as a law clerk for the Sonoma County District Attorney's Office. Shortly after passing the bar, he accepted a position with the Mendocino County District Attorney's Office. After a few years, he was appointed Mendocino County Public Defender.

Judge Brown was elected to three terms as Superior Court Judge, the first of which began in 1996. He also donated countless hours to community service organizations that benefited the youth of Ukiah and Mendocino County, including Bowl for Kids, County Mock Trial, 4-H, Future Farmers of America, and the Chili Cook-Off that benefits the Boys and Girls Club. Judge Brown was truly a judge of the people and held great compassion and understanding for those who were in his courtroom. (Courtesy of the Held-Poage Library.)

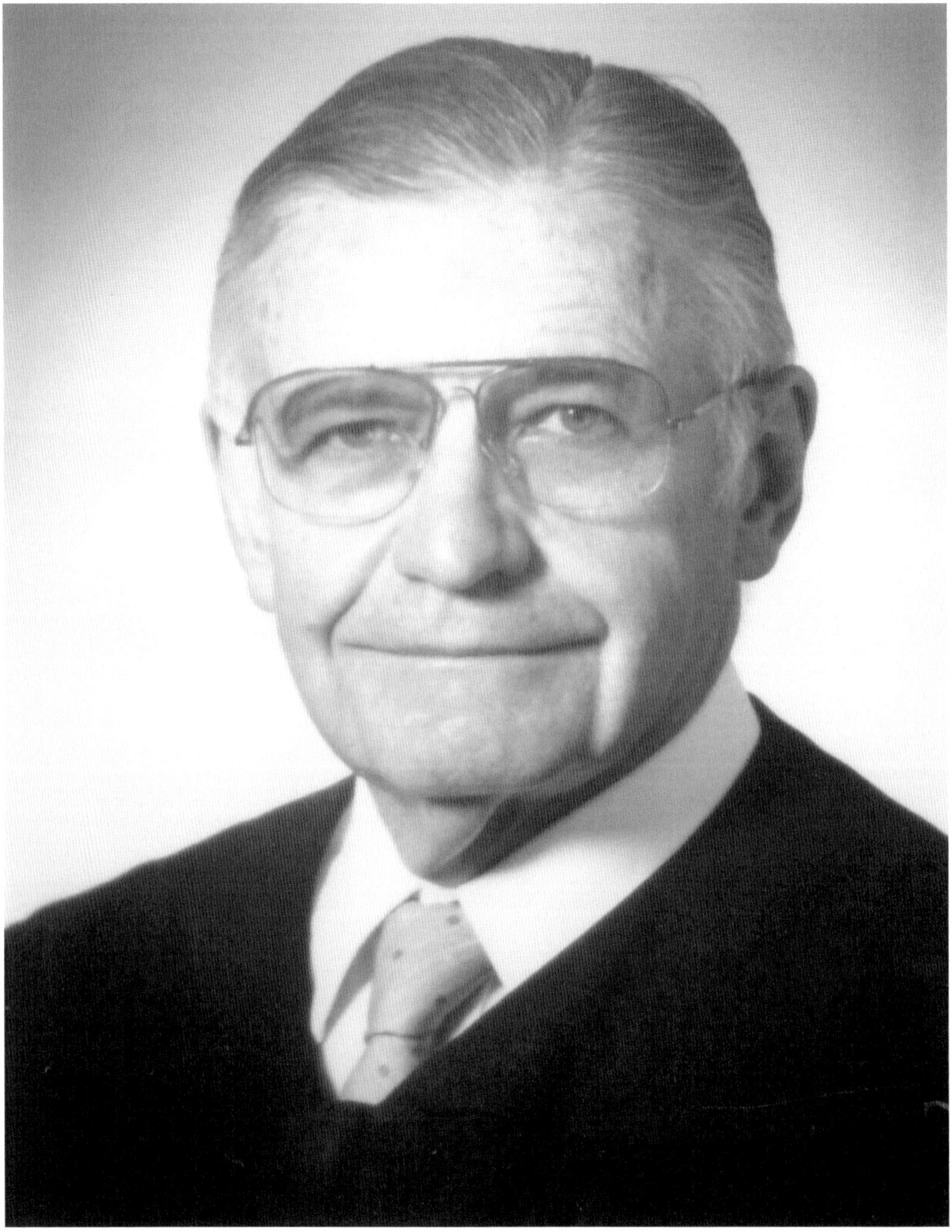

Judge Timothy O'Brien

Judge Timothy O'Brien's history in Mendocino County can be traced back to his great-grandfather, who came here from Ireland in 1856. Although the family lived in Stockton—where O'Brien graduated from high school—they kept a summer residence and ranch on the coast. His grandmother lived in Point Arena, and he spent his summers there riding and working on the family ranch.

During World War II, O'Brien served in the Pacific Overseas Air Service, with the 308th Bomb Wing. He entered law school after leaving the military and sped through in two years—passing the bar in 1'948. He was offered a job with the Attorney General's Office in Sacramento and the newly minted lawyer was quickly off to the state capital.

Returning to Mendocino County, he found that the local justice system was in the midst of some very interesting times. Nine local justice courts were being overseen by judges who were neither attorneys, nor law school graduates. Additionally, there were three distinct groups tasked with controlling the county's slot machine business. One wanted to control the slots outright, one wanted to bribe its way into the business, and the third did not want anything to do with the business. A grand jury was convened, accusations flew, and eventually several people who Judge O'Brien had worked with were indicted and eventually sent to San Quentin Prison.

In the aftermath, O'Brien was asked to become the first public defender for Mendocino County. He held that position for four years. In 1971, he was appointed by Governor Reagan to preside over the Superior Court, where he witnessed sweeping changes to the court system.

Today, Judge O'Brien is retired but remains an incredible font of knowledge regarding the history of Ukiah and Mendocino County. (Courtesy of Held-Poage Library.)

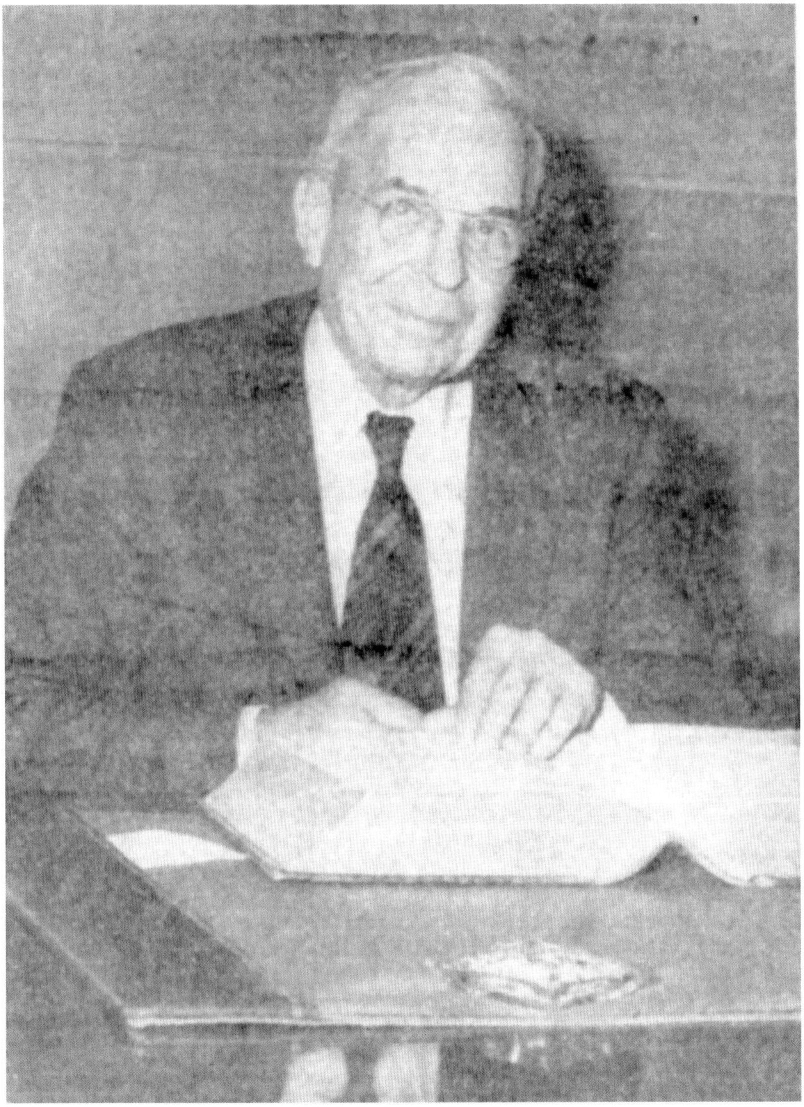

Judge Hale McCowan

A fourth-generation Mendocino County resident, Judge Hale McCowan came from a long line of civil servants. That line continues today with his son John, who currently serves as a Mendocino County Supervisor. John is heavily involved in environmental issues and has spent over 15 years personally helping to clean up creeks and parks in the area. John even still lives in the Clay Street home where his father was born, after his grandparents moved from Potter Valley.

Judge McCowan's great-grandparents came from Kansas and originally settled in Potter Valley. He graduated from Stanford, where he earned his law degree, before joining the Army and spending several years in the European Theatre. Leaving the service with the rank of first lieutenant, Hale returned home and joined his father's law practice—eventually taking control of the business when his father judge in 1952. He was later elected to serve as a judge himself, doing so from 1964 to 1976. Hale's son John was quoted as saying that, "He tried very hard to be fair," in his hearing cases that ranged from traffic violations and misdemeanors to the preliminary hearings of felony cases. (Courtesy of Held-Poage Library.)

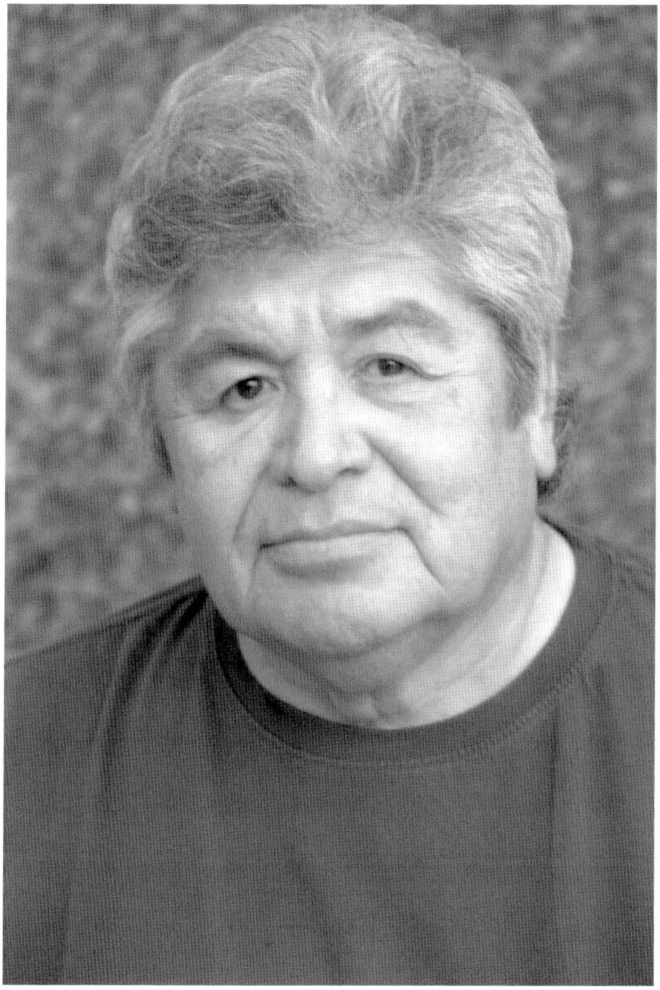

Joseph A. Myers
Designated a Distinguished Alumni from Ukiah High School, Joe Myers is someone from the Ukiah area who has gone on to make a big difference to the community and the country. In 2010, Mr. Myers, a Pomo Indian from Northern California, was given the Peter E. Haas Public Service Award. The honor is granted to University of California, Berkeley alumni whose personal efforts have made a significant public contribution to the United States, recognizing activities at the grassroots level and illustrating the impact that one individual can make through creative social change.

A graduate of UC Berkeley's, School of Law at Boalt Hall, Mr. Meyers is the executive director of the National Indian Justice Center (NJIC), which he founded in 1983. Mr. Myers also served as associate director of the American Indian Lawyer Training Program from 1976 to 1983, helping to create and manage the program's tribal court advocate training project. He is a founder and board member of the California Indian Museum and Cultural Center (CIMCC), which is a statewide, issues-based museum of California Indian history that emphasizes serving Native youths and their teachers.

Joe Myers also writes and lectures extensively on Native American issues. In addition to receiving the 2010 Peter E. Haas Public Service Award, he received national attention in 1993 when Attorney General Janet Reno recognized his work on behalf of victims of crime in Indian country. He is also the namesake of the Joseph A. Myers Center at UC Berkeley's Institute for the Study of Societal Issues, which opened in February 2011. (Courtesy of Joseph Myers.)

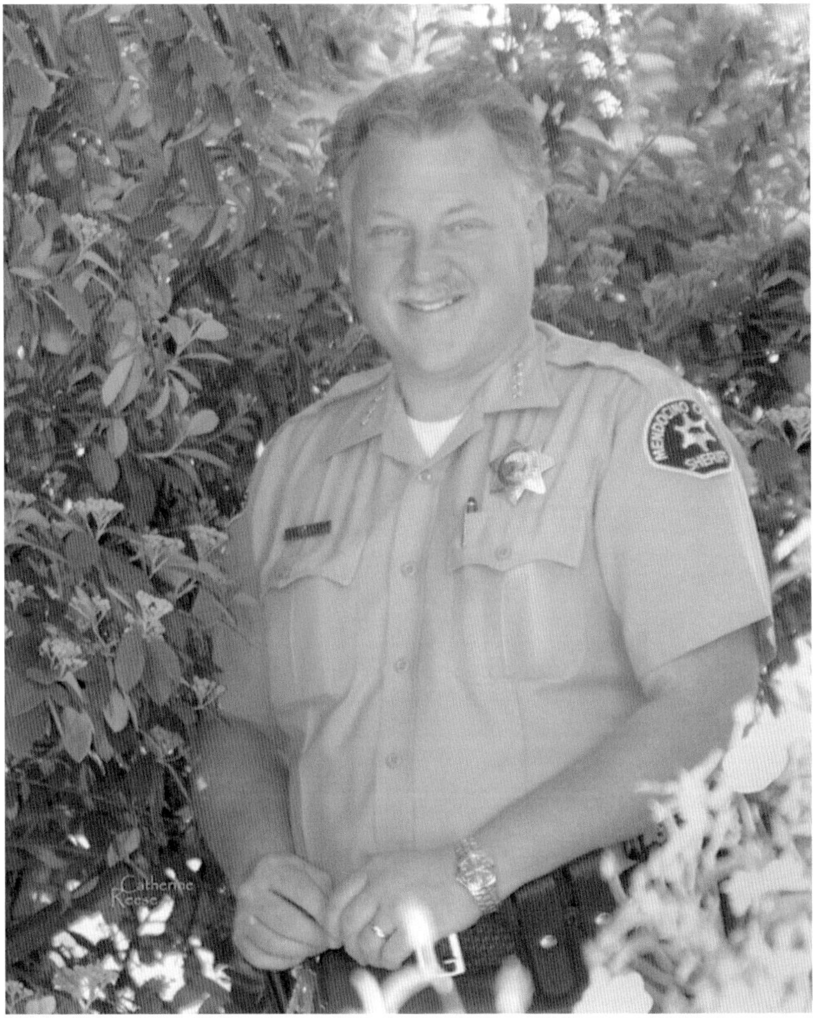

Sheriff Tom Allman (ABOVE AND OPPOSITE PAGE)

Being a sheriff in any area is difficult, but in a diverse agricultural area like Mendocino County, it can be particularly hard. As such, the area is fortunate to have a sheriff of Tom Allman's caliber. Tom was part of a group that trained an international police force in Kosovo in the late 1990s, and in the aftermath of Hurricane Katrina, he went to New Orleans to help. Elected sheriff in 2006, Tom was awarded the Governor's Medal of Valor by Gov. Arnold Schwarzenegger in 2008 after he pulled a woman from a burning car. When asked about the act, Tom said, "I was just doing what needed to be done."

Tom sees drug abuse and domestic violence as his top priorities. He says, "I have learned that the absolute primary responsibility of law enforcement has to be focused where the people are the victims; all other crimes come after that." In 2011, he led a 36-day manhunt across Mendocino County for a man who had murdered a conservationist and a city councilman who was a former mayor. Tom coauthored a book about the day-to-day search for the killer, *Out There in the Woods*.

This is a man who, when you see him on the street, always has time to say hello. If you're organizing a fundraiser and need someone to help cook or serve as auctioneer, Tom is your man. Amazingly, when one of the "bad guys" needs to turn themselves in, they say that he is the only one they trust to surrender to. Tom possesses a great sense of humor and doesn't take himself too seriously—he just wants to do his job and do it well. (Courtesy of Sheriff Tom Allman.)

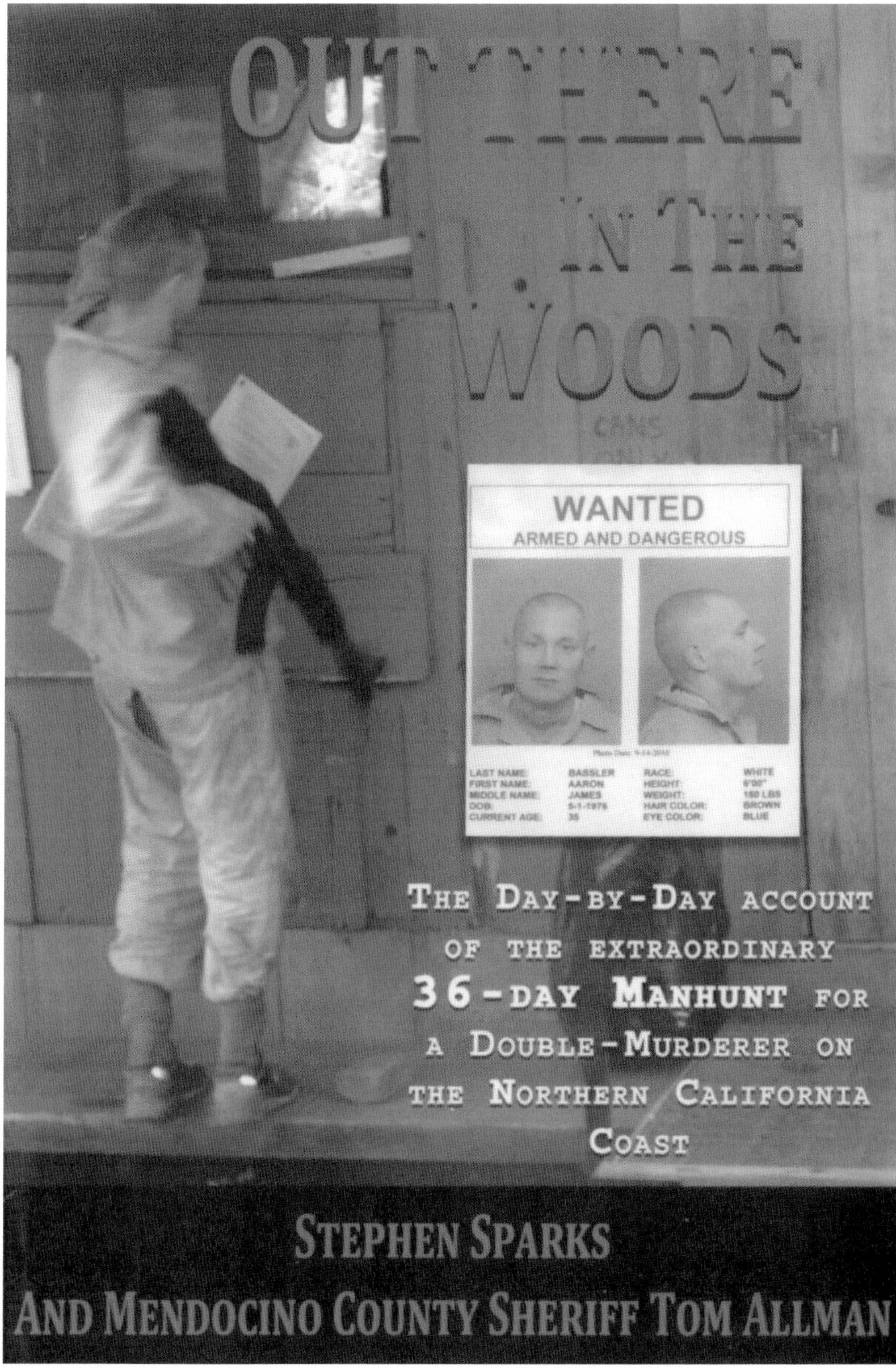
OUT THERE
IN THE
WOODS
WANTED
ARMED AND DANGEROUS
LAST NAME: BASSLER
FIRST NAME: AARON
MIDDLE NAME: JAMES
DOB: 5-1-1976
CURRENT AGE: 35
RACE: WHITE
HEIGHT: 6'00"
WEIGHT: 160 LBS
HAIR COLOR: BROWN
EYE COLOR: BLUE
THE DAY-BY-DAY ACCOUNT OF THE EXTRAORDINARY 36-DAY MANHUNT FOR A DOUBLE-MURDERER ON THE NORTHERN CALIFORNIA COAST
STEPHEN SPARKS
AND MENDOCINO COUNTY SHERIFF TOM ALLMAN

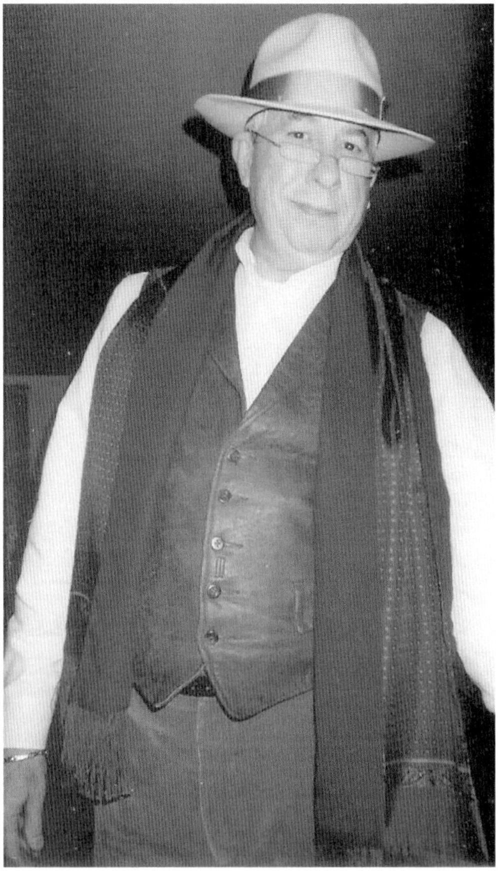

Duane Hill

When it comes to Duane Hill, Red Bluff's loss was Ukiah's gain. In the late 1990s, Duane took a position with the Lassen-ModocPumas-Tehama Community Action Agency. He established a welfare rights organization, created a housing authority, and was instrumental in establishing Tehama County's first senior center.

He graduated from Sonoma State and was named Distinguished Alumni of the Year. While he was attending college, he worked as a housing specialist for North Coast Opportunities in Ukiah. Working at NCO led to the formation of the Rural Communities Housing Development Corporation, a nonprofit organization established in 1975. In 1978, RCHDC opened the Walnut Village senior housing complex.

Duane worked nonstop to see that the need for affordable housing is met in rural areas like Ukiah and is recognized as a trailblazer for his efforts. As executive director of RCHDC, he led the organization to become Northern California's largest rural nonprofit housing development. The agency has built 19 developments, providing 528 affordable rental apartments. Duane Hill Apartments in Ukiah was named in his honor. (Courtesy of Duane Hill.)

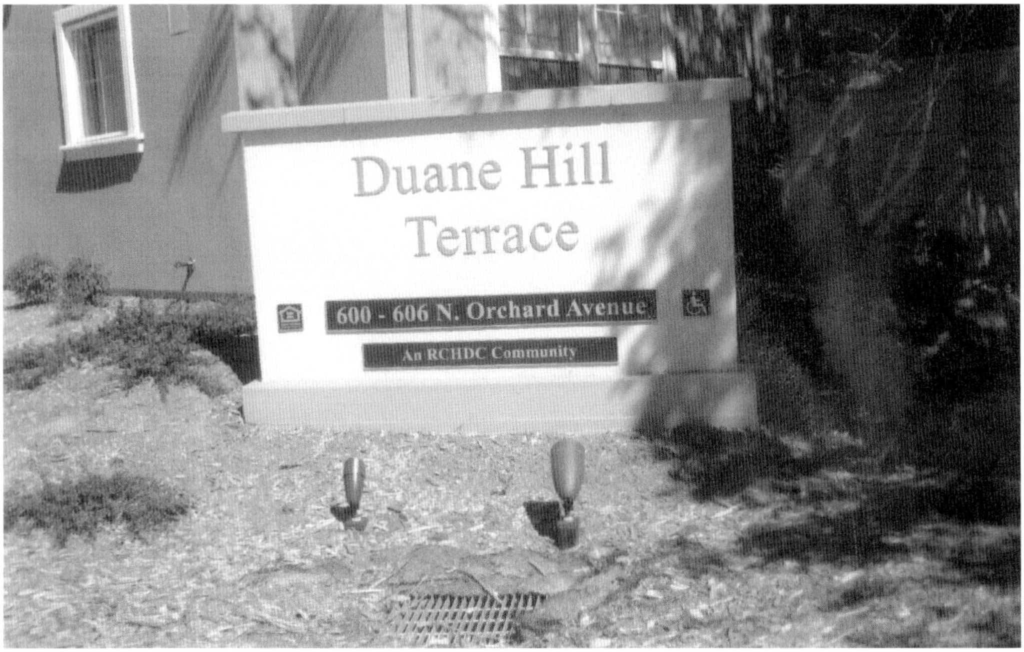

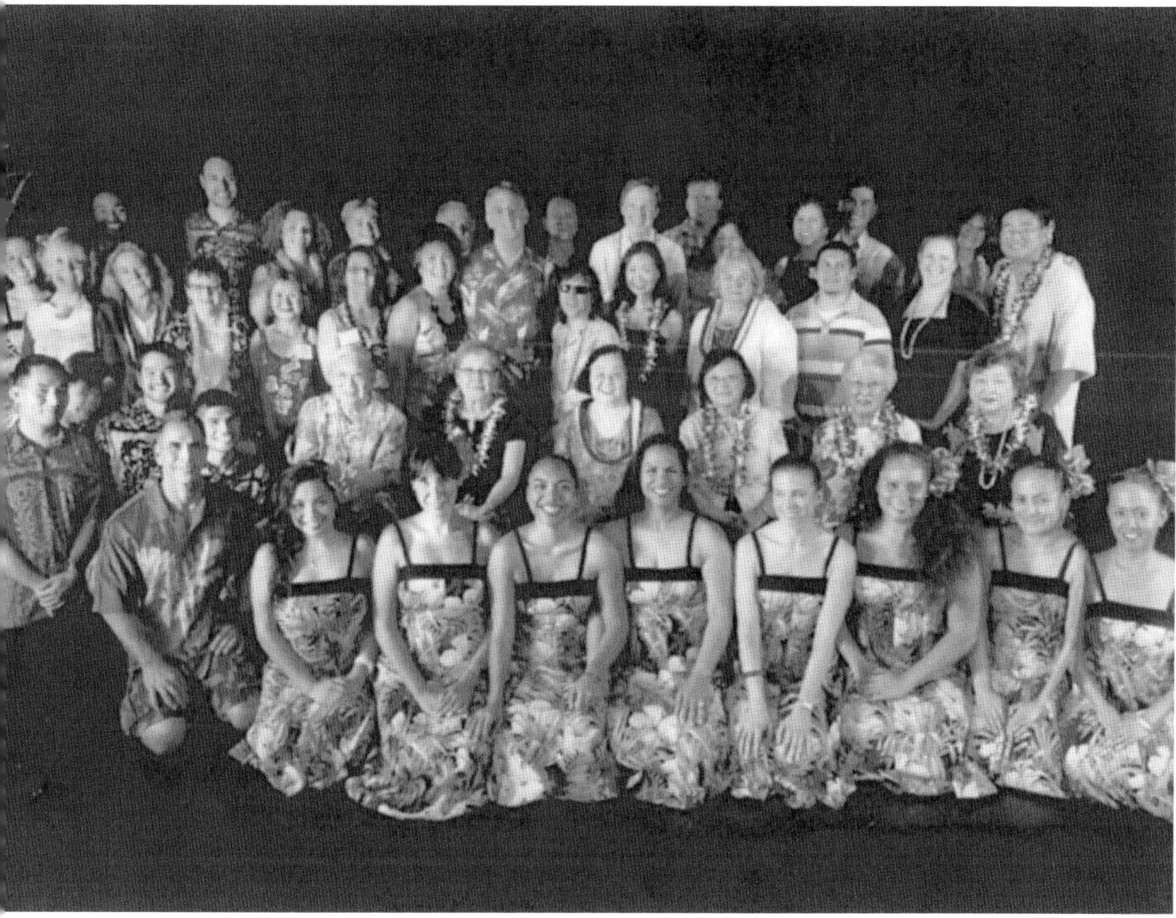

Seiji Sugawara

Seiji Sugawara was born in Hawaii but moved to Ukiah in 1977—providing the community with one of its great organizers. He taught business and real estate courses at Mendocino College until 1992 and served on the Millview Water Board, Ukiah Unified School Board, and with many nonprofits as a volunteer. Seiji was also a board member for the School of Performing Arts and Cultural Education (SPACE), and a member of the Community Care Board and the Inland Mendocino Land Trust Board. If you were lucky enough to have Seiji on your board, you were guaranteed to have whatever job he took on accomplished.

He was also active in Democratic politics and served on both the Mendocino County Democratic Central Committee and the Ukiah Democratic Club. Additionally, Seiji served as the First District supervisor and was admired for his efforts to help avert financial problems with the county budget.

Seiji worked with the Rural Communities Housing Development Corporation for over two decades, serving as the president of the board. A new RCHDC location was even named in his honor. Duane Hill, the executive director of RCHDC said, "Seiji was humble. He didn't like to be thanked a lot." After Seiji died in 2003, an annual memorial luau was held for several years at SPACE. Seiji's lifetime motto was, "Give more than you take," and he was certainly a shining example of that mantra. (Courtesy of SPACE.)

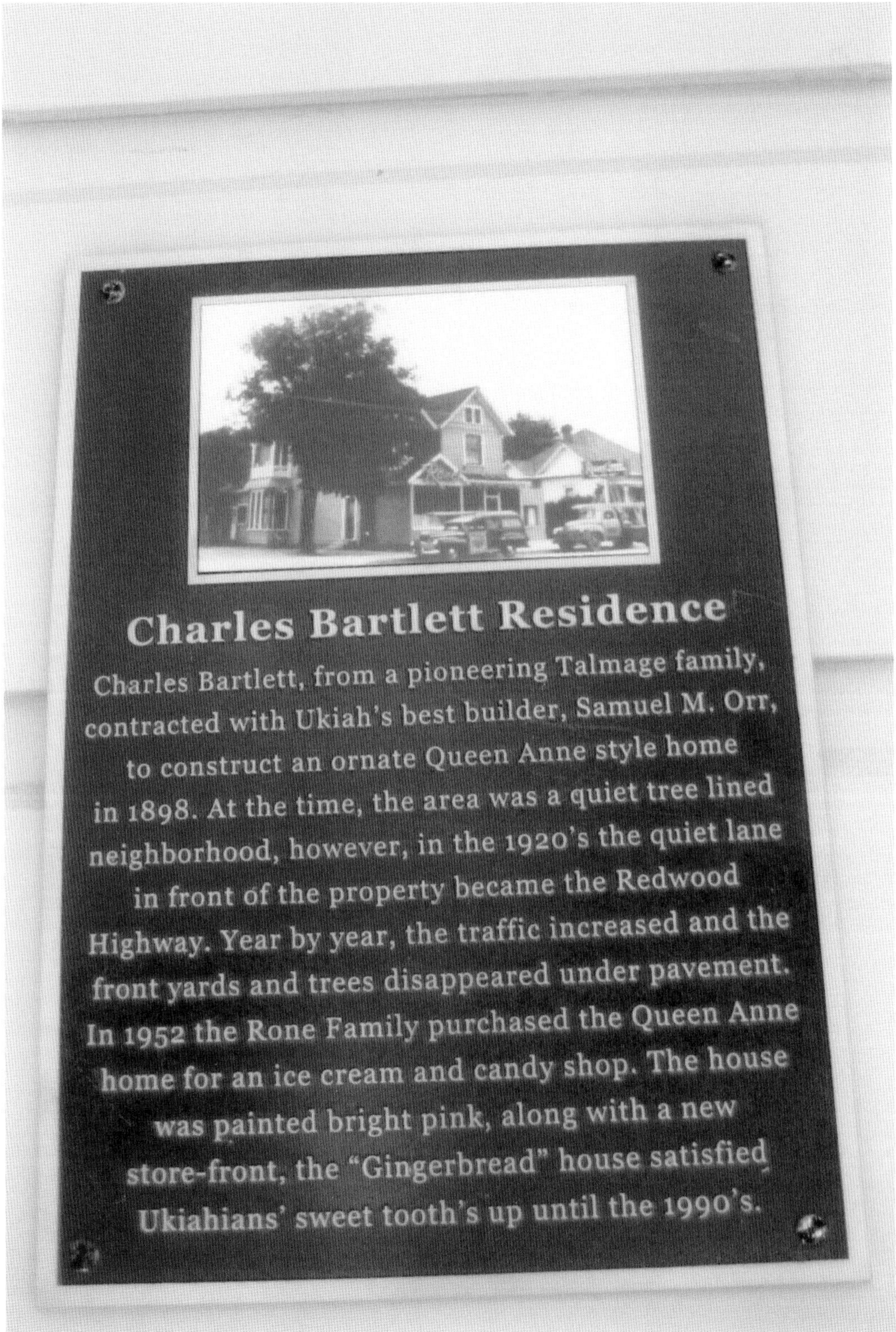
Charles Bartlett Residence
Charles Bartlett, from a pioneering Talmage family, contracted with Ukiah's best builder, Samuel M. Orr, to construct an ornate Queen Anne style home in 1898. At the time, the area was a quiet tree lined neighborhood, however, in the 1920's the quiet lane in front of the property became the Redwood Highway. Year by year, the traffic increased and the front yards and trees disappeared under pavement. In 1952 the Rone Family purchased the Queen Anne home for an ice cream and candy shop. The house was painted bright pink, along with a new store-front, the "Gingerbread" house satisfied Ukiahians' sweet tooth's up until the 1990's.

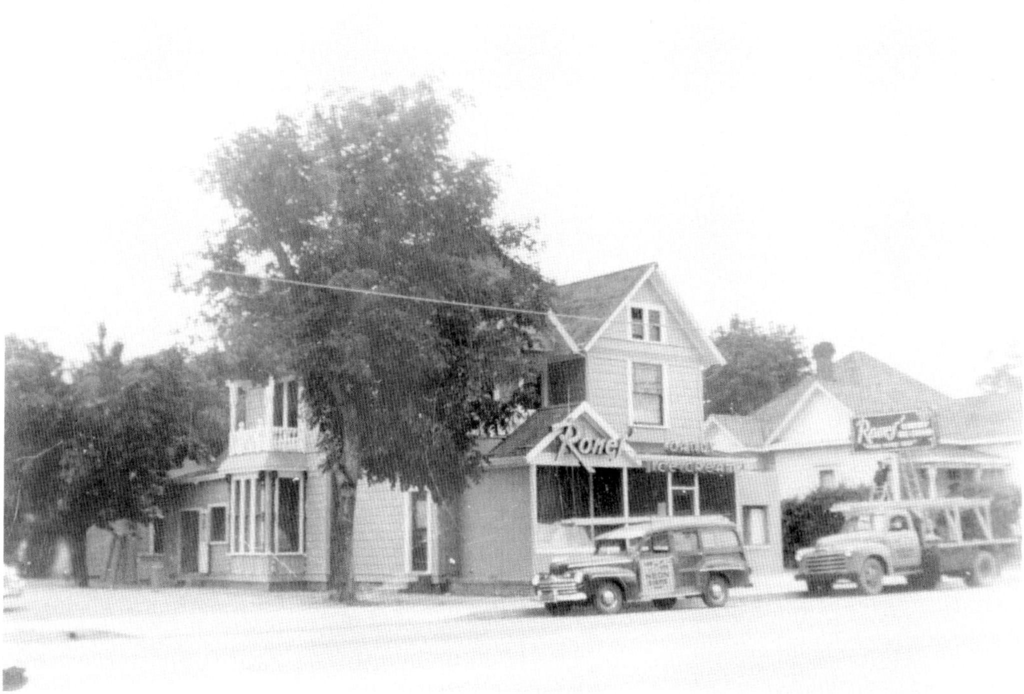

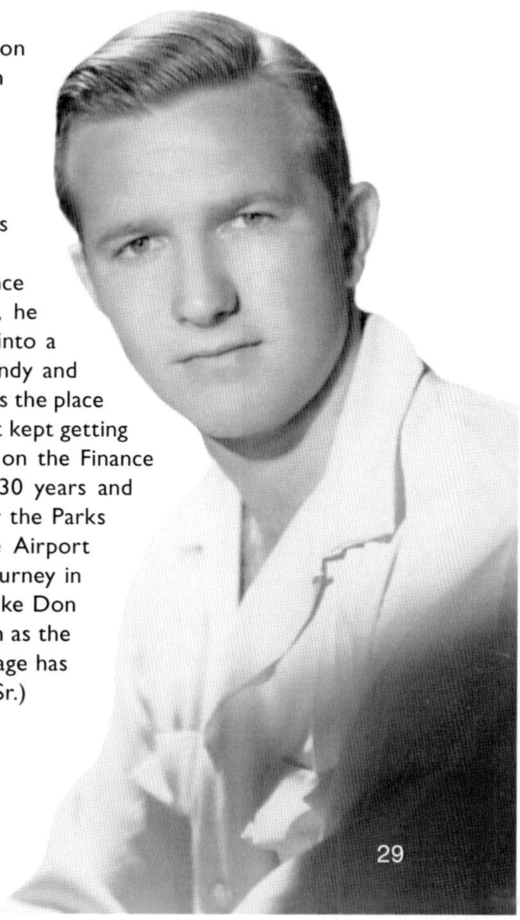

Don Rones Sr. (ABOVE, RIGHT, AND OPPOSITE PAGE)
From being an eyewitness to the bombing of Pearl Harbor on December 7, 1941, to serving as the mayor of Ukiah—Don Rones has done it all over his 98 years. Rones served for four years on the city council before taking the position of mayor of Ukiah from 1957–1958. Whether he was serving as president of the local Rotary Club or acting as president of the Ukiah Chamber of Commerce, people could find Rones rolling up his sleeves and helping wherever he was needed.

Rones's professional career was diverse and included once serving as the CEO of a gas company. In December 1951, he purchased a local candy and ice cream store and turned it into a successful business. Everyone in town knew that Rones' Candy and Ice Cream Store, in the pink house on North State Street, was the place to go. Don sold the business in 1962, with plans to retire, but kept getting involved in community activities. Since then, he has served on the Finance Committee for the Ukiah Valley Medical Center for over 30 years and been president of the Men's Golf Club, a board member for the Parks and Recreation Commission, and a board member for the Airport Commission. He helped to establish the Invitational Golf Tourney in 1960 and can still be found playing golf every week. People like Don Rones, with their energy and dedication, are what keep Ukiah as the great town that it is. Note that the plaque on the opposite page has the Rones name misspelled slightly. (Courtesy of Don Rones Sr.)

John Mayfield Jr.

From a one-room schoolhouse on Orr Springs Road and working in the family lumber business, to serving the president of the United States, John Mayfield is not just a businessman and entrepreneur but someone who is genuinely involved with the community at the local, county, and state levels. John and his wife, Sandy, both graduated from Humboldt State University and then returned home to Mendocino County. There, he ran for a position with the board of supervisors and won—becoming the youngest supervisor in the state at the age of 27. He was subsequently reelected and became chairman in 1965. John tells a story that, just after the election, a man came to the house to speak to John's father, assuming—because of John's age—that it was his father who had been elected.

John has a long history of service in the public and private sectors. He was manager of International Wood Products in Humboldt County and then manager of Mendo Hill and Lumber from 1960–1966. From 1968–1970, he was deputy director of the Department of Conservation for the State of California, appointed by Gov. Ronald Reagan. Then, in 1986, now-president Reagan appointed John to the National Advisory Committee on Oceans and Atmosphere and the Department of Conservation. Since 1971, he has worked with Microphor—a manufacturing company in Willits—and served as the owner. Over the years, John Mayfield was appointed by three different California governors to assist in programs.

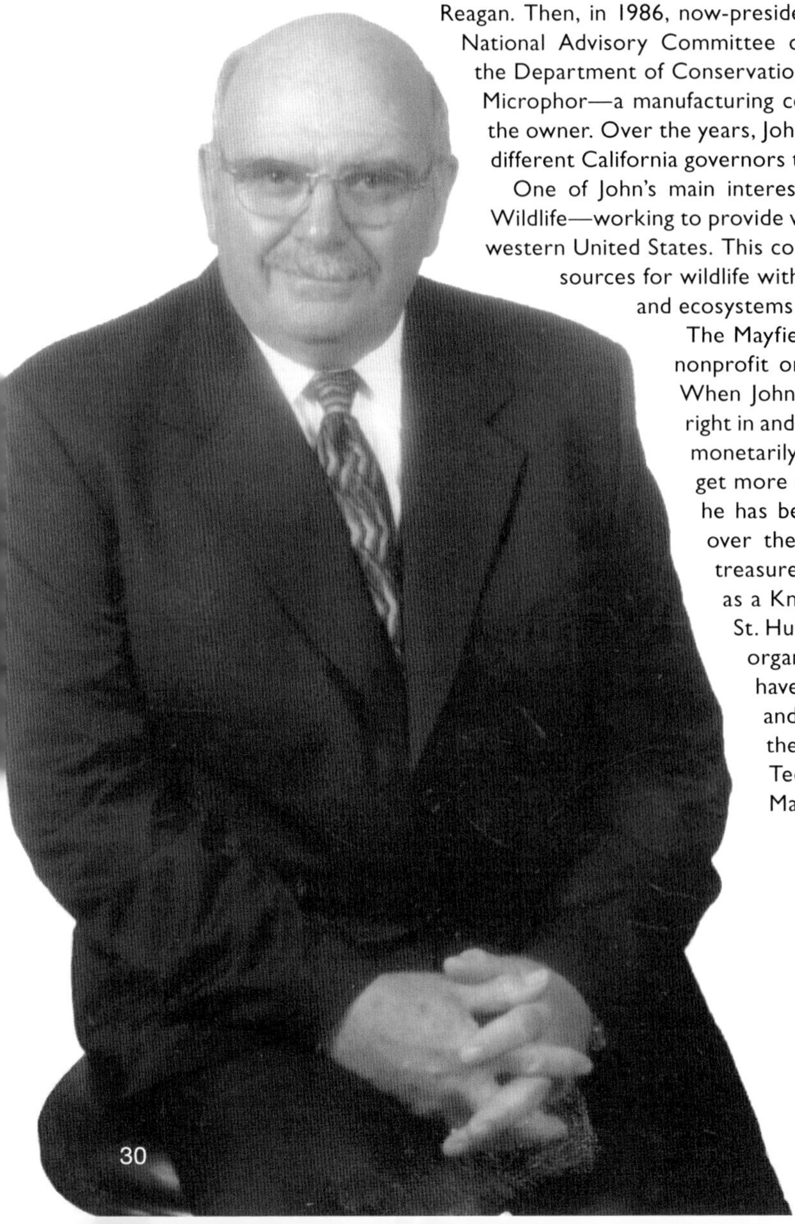

One of John's main interests is the organization Water for Wildlife—working to provide windmills and water guzzlers in the western United States. This conservation project provides water sources for wildlife with the goal of sustaining the wildlife and ecosystems of arid regions of the West.

The Mayfields are heavily involved in helping nonprofit organizations throughout the area. When John sees a need, he and Sandy jump right in and help in any way they can—not just monetarily but by networking with others to get more of the community involved. While he has been the recipient of many awards over the years, one of recognitions John treasures most highly was his appointment as a Knight of the International Order of St. Hubereus. This Austrian international organization recognizes those who have done much to protect animals and wildlife. John and Sandy are the parents of three children: Jim, Ted, and Susan. (Courtesy of John Mayfield Jr.)

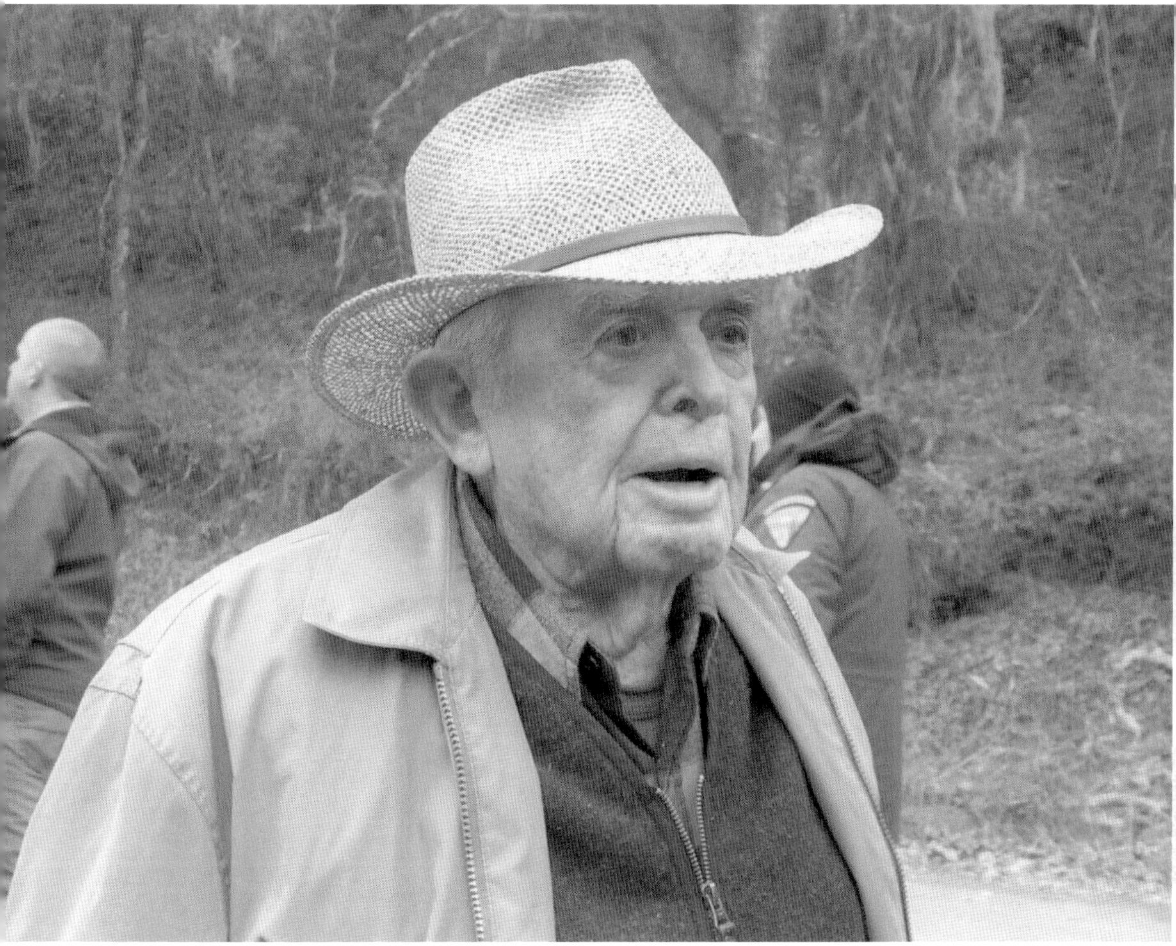

Bill Townsend
The fish have a friend in Bill Townsend. Still an active volunteer at 97 years of age, Bill was recently honored by the Department of Fish and Game, which renamed the Coyote Valley Fish Facility as the Bill Townsend Conservation Fish Hatchery.

In the late 1940s, Bill came to Ukiah and started a program to help rescue the fish in the creeks. He has been working with the Fish and Game Program since 1950, brokering a deal with the City of Ukiah to lease the Rod and Gun Club's hatchery facility to the Fish and Game Program for $1 a year. That lease remains in place to this day.

Townsend is pleased that, thanks to his efforts many years ago, there is a place that children can go and learn how to fish. There are also trout derbies held every year for the kids. Townsend says, "We owe it to our kids to teach them a different way of life than in the big city." (Courtesy of Held-Poage Library.)

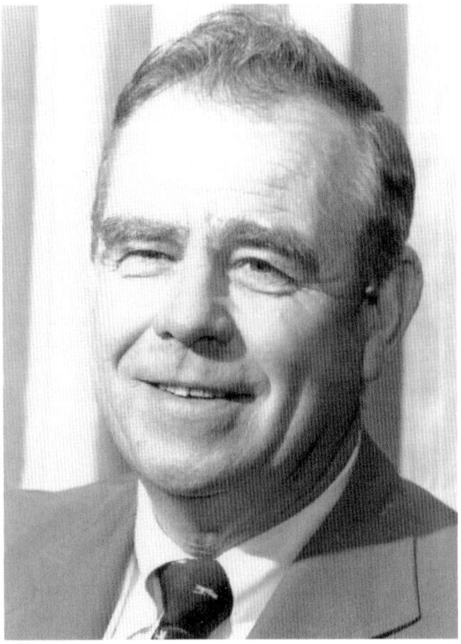

Alex Thomas

The lovely public plaza in downtown Ukiah is named after Mr. Thomas. Alex's father was Ukiah's postmaster before going to work in the valley's pear growing and packing industry with his brother-in-law, Lou Cunningham. This family business goes back over 75 years and, at one time, the Thomas family operated the largest pear packing facility in California.

Alex Thomas was one of the founders of the Russian River Flood Control District and fought hard to not sell water rights to Sonoma County. He served as a member of the advisory committee for the Ukiah General Plan and was chairman of the St. Mary's School building drive. He was also director and chairman of the board for the North Coast Federal Land Bank. (Courtesy of Held-Poage Library.)

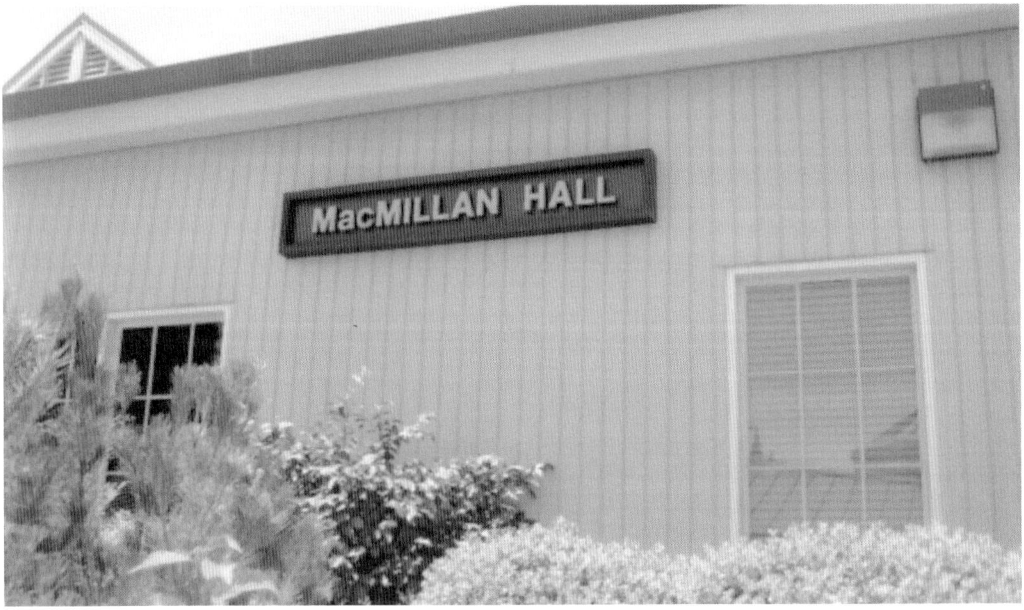

Dr. Tom MacMillan

Dr. MacMillan came to Ukiah in 1973 to work as the new dean of student personnel services at Mendocino College. While there, he also taught philosophy, English, and religion. Dr. MacMillan last his battle with cancer in 2002. MacMillan Hall at the college is named in his honor.

The local newspaper described Dr. MacMillan as "a man for all seasons." He held degrees from the University of California at Berkeley, with a doctorate in education and counseling. He was also the recipient of an honorary doctorate from Dharma Realm Buddhist University on Talmage Road and graduated from Moody.

After the terrorist attacks of September 11, 2001, Dr. MacMillan organized a group to educate young people about the Islamic faith so they would understand that the tragedy was the action of a small group of radical individuals. (Courtesy of Mendocino Community College.)

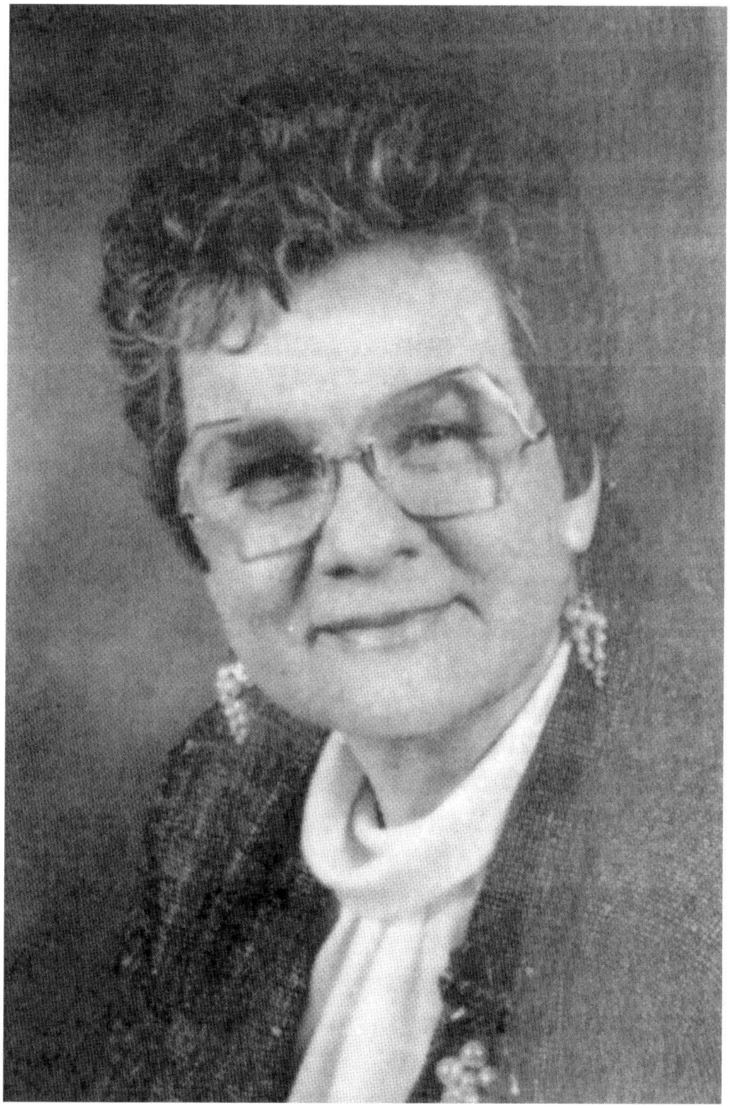

Marilyn Butcher
From growing up in the country and playing in her cowgirl outfit to traveling the world as a TWA airline hostess, Marilyn did it all. She worked on the second commercial transcontinental jet flight ever flown. After she married, Marilyn returned to Ukiah to raise a family.

In her later years, Marilyn became involved in local politics and was nominated to fill the vacated first district supervisor's seat. Governor Deukmejian selected Marilyn for the position, making her the first female supervisor in Mendocino County. She was later reelected for two more terms. She was also an avid volunteer—serving as president for the local chapter of the American Cancer Society, the Republican Women's Organization, and the Soroptimists. Marilyn also served as the Mendocino County representative to the Golden Gate Bridge Centennial and the Sister Bridge Celebration in Tokyo.

In 2010, the Ukiah Dolphins Club honored Marilyn for her 40 years of dedicated support and involvement. That year's meet was dedicated to Marilyn in honor of her lifetime promotion of the Ukiah Dolphin Swimming Organization, and the well-being of the children who have been members of that organization. (Courtesy of Held-Poage Library.)

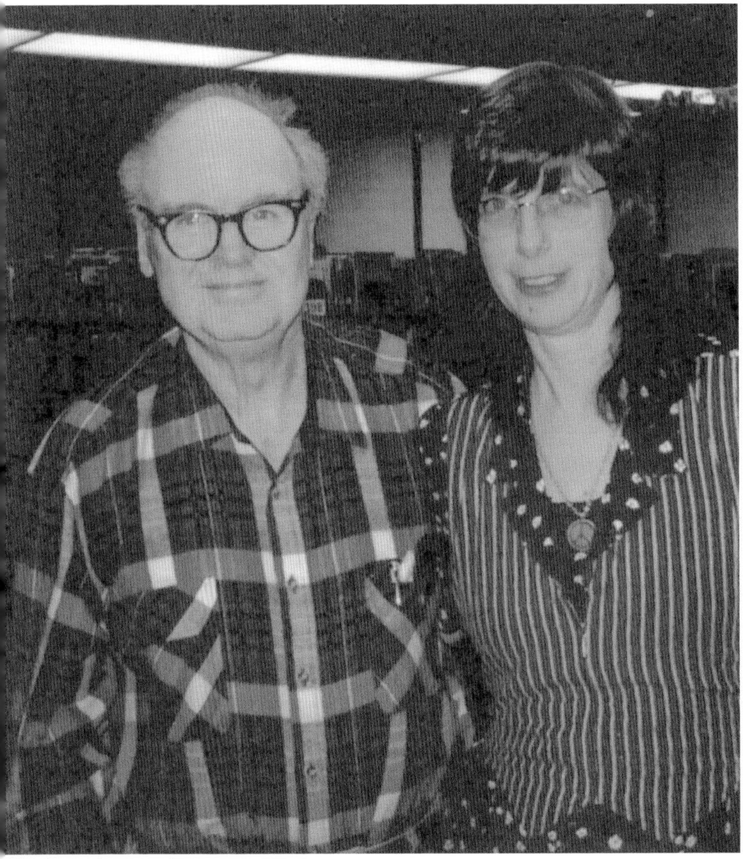

Darryl "Mac" McKibbin

Darryl and his wife, Polly, have spent countless hours as volunteers at the county library, working with the Friends of the Library program. Whether serving on the board of directors, or in the basement sorting and pricing books, this couple could always be counted on to do whatever was needed. The two of them can still be found at the library these days, helping with the monthly book sales.

Darryl began his distinguished career as a missile scientist for the Lockheed Corporation in the 1950s. He then spent 30 years working for NASA as a space scientist. In this position, he was responsible for much of the instrumentation found on numerous satellites and space vehicles. McKibbin credits his many childhood hours at the library with instilling in him the thirst for learning that eventually led to a career as a scientist. (Courtesy of Polly McKibbin.)

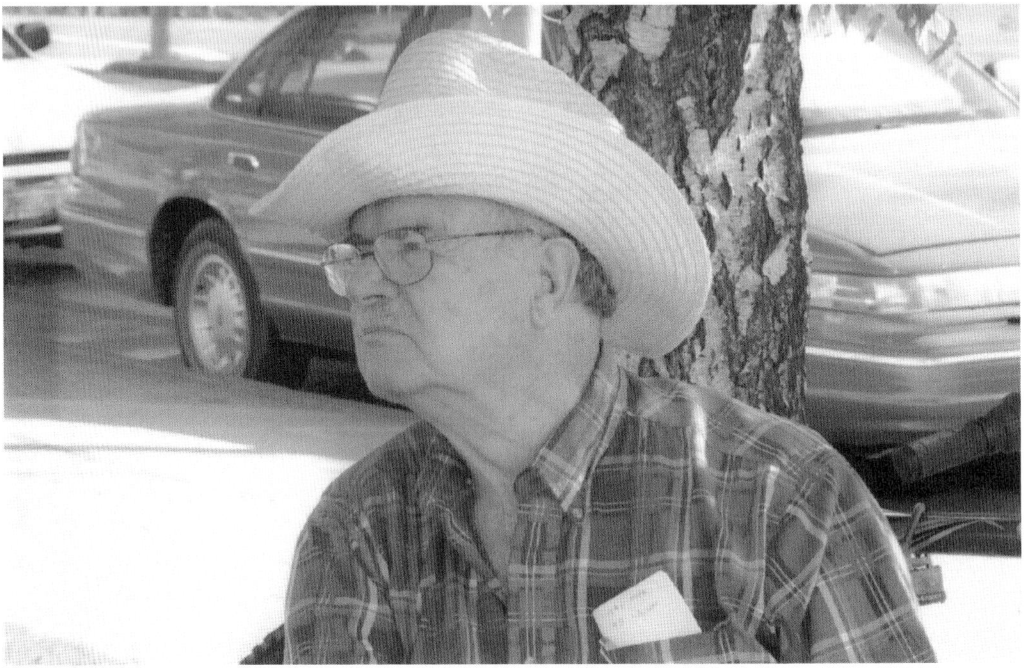

Rod Shippey

Roderick "Rod" Shippey was a maverick farm adviser who dedicated himself to furthering agriculture in Mendocino County and the world. Born in Long Beach, California, he attended UC Davis, where he earned a degree in animal husbandry. He moved to Ukiah and started his career in farming by tending pigs for Alex Thomas. Shippey began working for the University of California as a livestock advisor in 1956 and, during that time, he established the 4-H Junior Livestock Auction. Carre Brown was quoted as saying that Rod "created some amazing programs." Rod helped timber companies turn ash to fertilizer and taught ranchers how to better manage their rangeland. Cattle rancher Mac Magruder said of Rod, "It was his mission to make agriculture viable."

Shippey eventually retired but that didn't stop him from working. He signed up to work for the Volunteer Over-Seas Cooperative Assistance. With this group, Rod went to Barbados to work on a grading system for sheep, and visited Egypt to introduce new methods of harvesting and packing grapes. He also worked extensively in Bolivia, Russia, Nicaragua, Slovakia, and Azerbaijan, where he lived with farm families. At one point Rod was even under contract with George Lucas, advising the director on cattle and fencing at his Marin ranch properties.

Rod served on the Ukiah Community Concert Board, and was a member of Leadership Mendocino, Kiwanis, the Farm Bureau, and the Mendocino County Wood Growers. Rod will always be remembered for his enthusiasm, welcoming spirit, and generous support. Thoughtful, incisive, and a friend to all, Rod's sense of humor was second to none. Today, the University of California's Hopland Research and Extension Center is home to Rod Shippey Hall—named in his honor. (Courtesy of Arlene Shippey.)

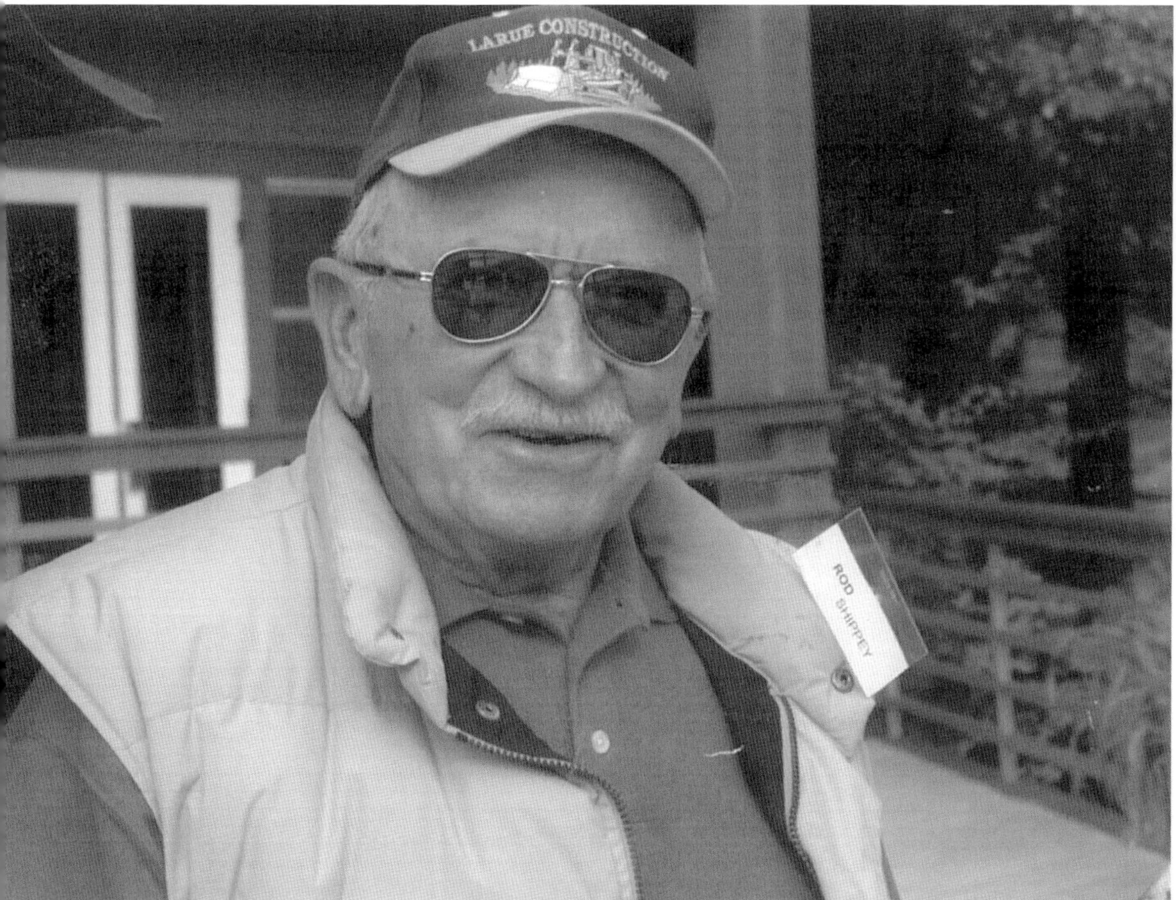

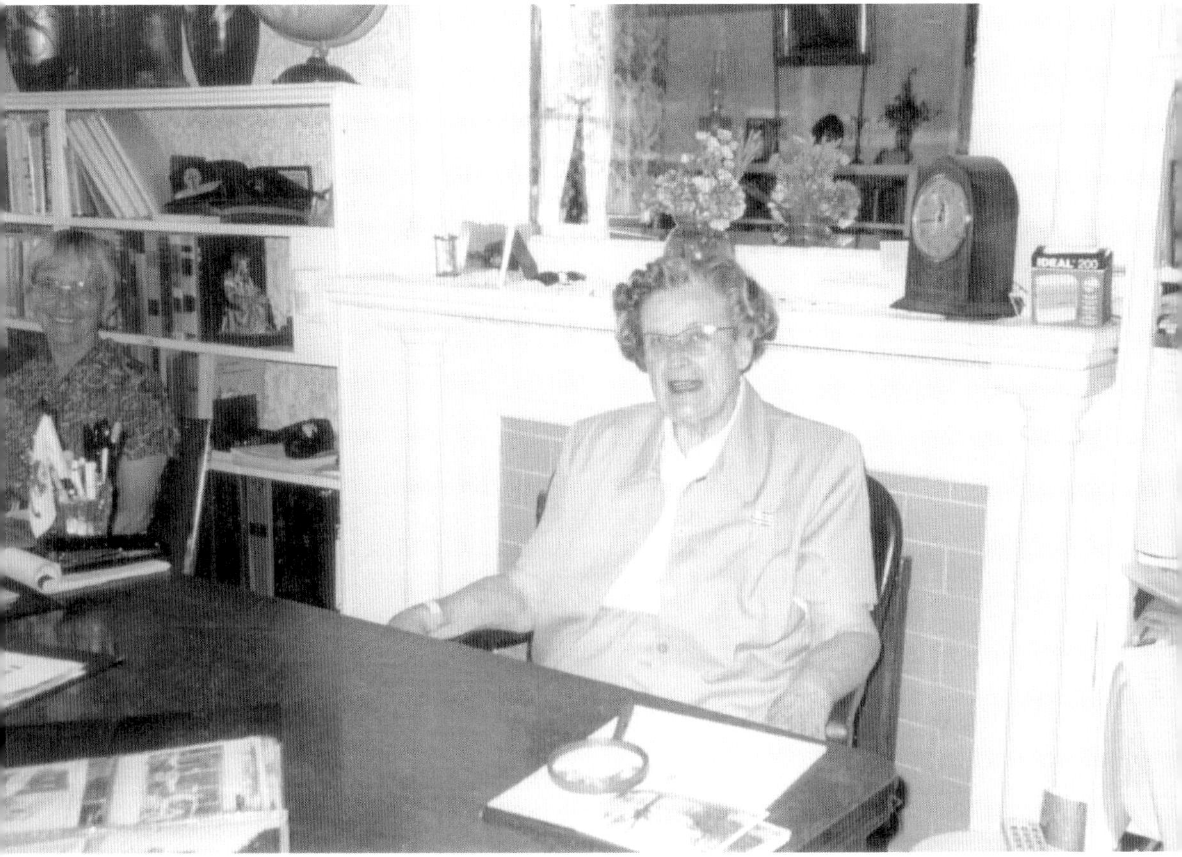

Lila Lee

For more than three decades, Lila Lee was a mainstay at the Held-Poage Library. Working at the Held-Poage was Lila's idea of "play," and she donated almost 200 hours a month to that institution. She was also a respected authority on history and was recognized by the California Historical Society with an award for her long service. In 1994, Lila was voted Citizen of the Year by the Ukiah Chamber of Commerce. Meanwhile, her husband, Robert, maintained a collection of photographs numbering in the thousands, which has been donated to the Grace Hudson Museum for use by scholars and researchers. (Courtesy of Held-Poage Library.)

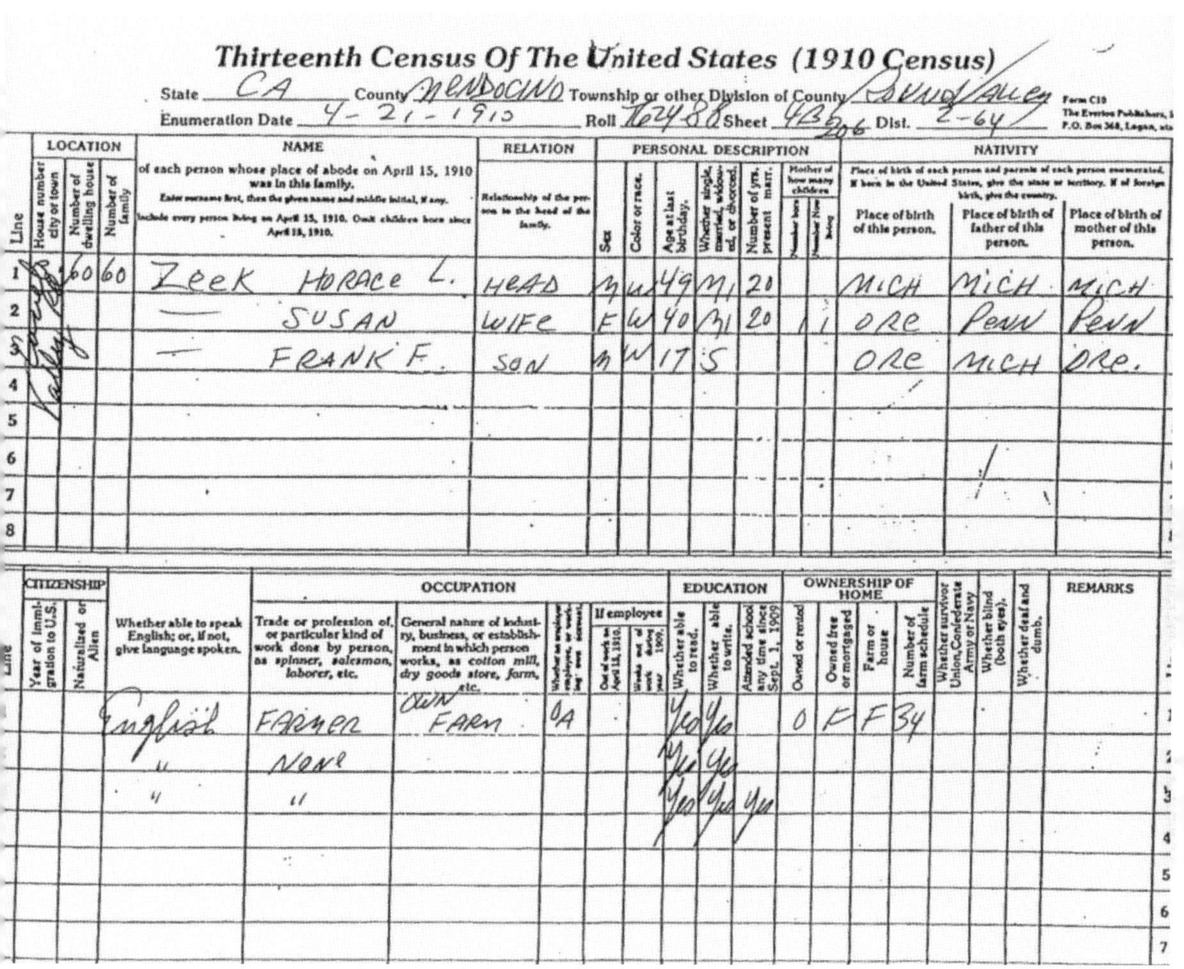

Thirteenth Census Of The United States (1910 Census)

State CA County Mendocino Township or other Division of County Round Valley Form C10 The Everton Publishers, Inc. P.O. Box 368, Logan, Utah
Enumeration Date 4-21-1910 Roll T624 88 Sheet 4B 206 Dist. E-64

Line	House number	Dwelling number	Family number	Name	Relation	Sex	Color or race	Age at last birthday	Single, married, widowed, or divorced	Number of yrs. present marr.	Mother of how many children: Number born	Number now living	Place of birth of this person	Place of birth of father of this person	Place of birth of mother of this person
1		60	60	Zeek Horace L.	Head	M	W	49	M1	20			Mich	Mich	Mich
2				— Susan	Wife	F	W	40	M1	20	1	1	Ore	Penn	Penn
3				— Frank F.	Son	M	W	17	S				Ore	Mich	Ore.
4															
5															
6															
7															
8															

Line	Year of immigration to U.S.	Naturalized or Alien	Whether able to speak English; or, if not, give language spoken	Trade or profession	General nature of industry	Employer, employee, or own account	Out of work on April 15, 1910	Weeks out of work during year 1909	Whether able to read	Whether able to write	Attended school any time since Sept. 1, 1909	Owned or rented	Owned free or mortgaged	Farm or house	Number of farm schedule	Whether survivor Union/Confederate Army or Navy	Whether blind (both eyes)	Whether deaf and dumb	Remarks
1			English	Farmer	Own Farm	OA			Yes	Yes		O	F	F	34				
2			"	None					Yes	Yes									
3			"	"					Yes	Yes	Yes								
4																			
5																			
6																			
7																			

Frank Zeek

Frank Zeek was born in Oregon. When his family moved to Mendocino County, he attended schools in Fort Bragg and Westport before finally graduating from Covelo High School. From there, Frank moved on to continue his education at San Francisco State Teachers College. He began teaching in 1915, working at elementary schools in Covelo, then Redwood Valley, and finally, Ukiah.

Frank spent almost 40 years as educator—most of them in the Ukiah area—eventually becoming superintendent of the old Ukiah Union Elementary District and the principal of Northside Elementary. He was also very active in the community, serving as a member of the planning commission, a VISTA volunteer, with the Juvenile Justice Commission, and as the chairman of the Ukiah Salvage-for-Victory campaign—a World War II–era rationing effort that oversaw the collection of papers and tin cans.

The community was all the better for Frank's organizational skills, which resulted in the development of the school building program. During his tenure, the Pomolita, Northside, and Nokomis schools were constructed to address the increasing population of Ukiah. In 1955, Northside Elementary was renamed Frank Zeek Elementary, in his honor. (Courtesy of Held-Poage Library.)

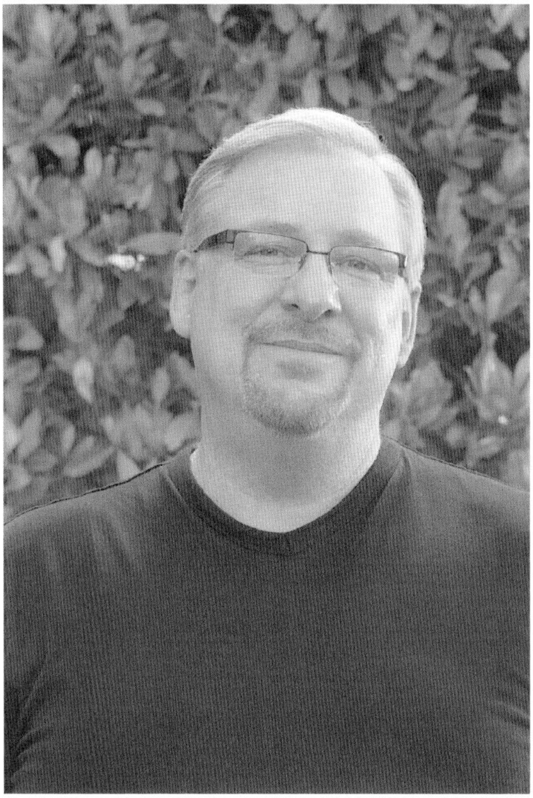

Rick Warren

Rick Warren—who *Time* magazine named as one of the 100 Most Influential People in the World in 2005—was a 1972 graduate of Ukiah High. He is one of the most recognized and influential pastors in the world and is the founder of Saddleback Church, the eighth largest church in the United States.

A pastor, philanthropist, theologian, global strategist, and author, Rick has spoken around the world on the issues of poverty and the lack of education and employment opportunities. His 2002 book *The Purpose Driven Life* was a *New York Times* bestseller and has sold over 30 million copies. After the huge success of this book, Rick returned the previous 25 years of his salary to Saddleback Church, using the sales proceeds. In 2006, his church hosted the Global Summit on AIDS, which was attended by Barack Obama. (Courtesy of Rick Warren family.)

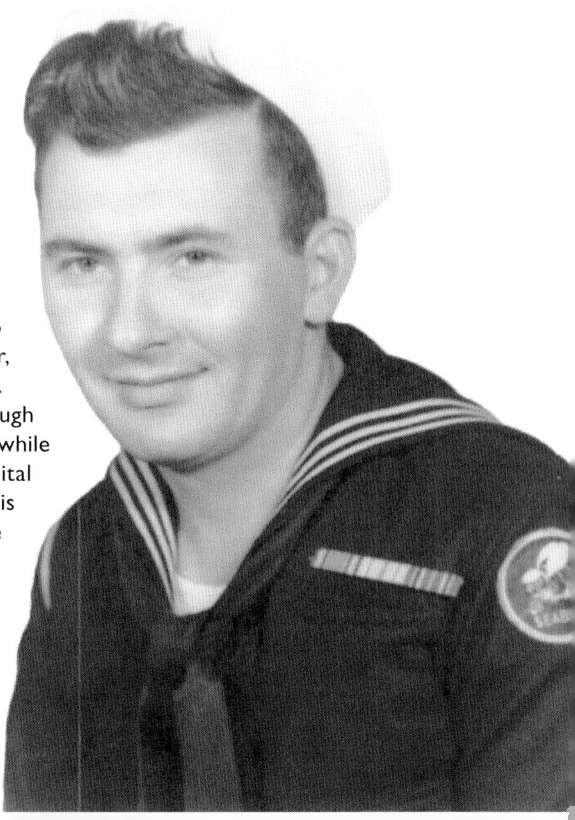

Alex Rorabaugh

Alex Rorabaugh was a man who cared about his community. After serving with the Navy Seabees, Alex moved to Hopland in 1956 and then to Ukiah shortly thereafter. He worked in the timber, lumber, and mining industries until his retirement.

Along the way, Alex helped fund the Alex Rorabaugh Cultural Center and the Hopland firehouse while making donations to the Ukiah Adventist Hospital and other community organizations. It was his feeling that you should share your good fortune with the area in which you lived. (Courtesy of Rorabaugh family.)

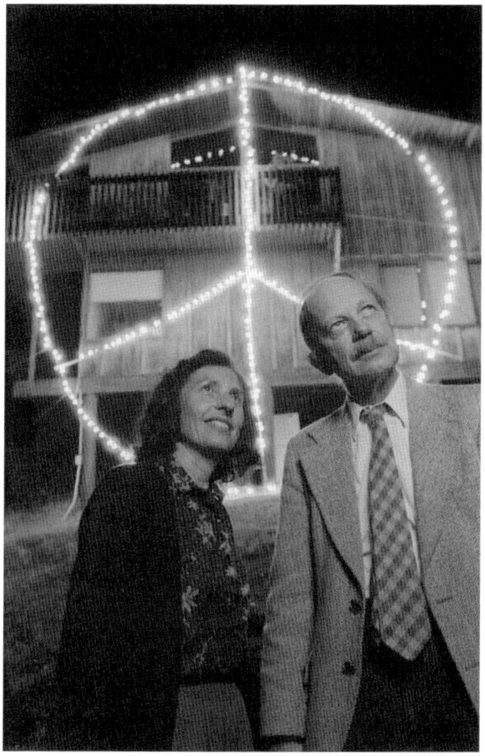

Dr. Robert Werra
In 2005, the California Academy of Family Physicians presented Dr. Robert Werra with the Family Physician of the Year award. For more than four decades, Dr. Werra has practiced in the Ukiah area—dedicating his life to the health and wellbeing of his patients. Even today, in his 80s, the doctor keeps busy by volunteering or counseling with the Children and Family Services Program. In the 1970s, he helped found Hospices of Ukiah and has been its medical director since 1982. In the early 1970s, Robert and his wife, Marlene, with the help of their children, created the large peace symbol seen here in the western hills. (Courtesy of Evan Johnson.)

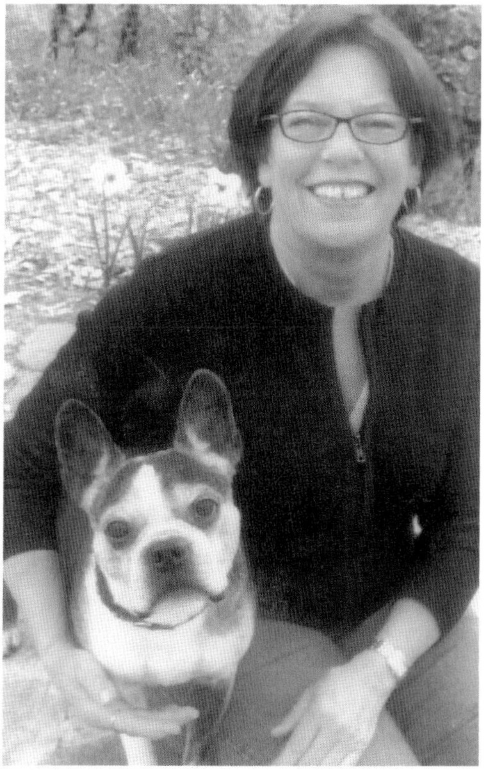

Dr. Sara Rice
Down at the Mendocino Animal Hospital, Dr. Sara Rice gives animal owners the impression that their pets—be they dog, cat, or rat—are not just members of their family, but hers as well. After getting her BA in European history, Dr. Rice went on to receive her VMD from the University of Pennsylvania. After graduation, she moved to Northern California and started working with Dr. Tom Broaddus at the Mendocino Animal Hospital—eventually taking ownership of the clinic in 1982. Dr. Rice always has time to talk and address a patient's concerns. After hours, Dr. Rice and her staff can be found contributing to the community in many ways. (Courtesy of Dr. Sara Rice.)

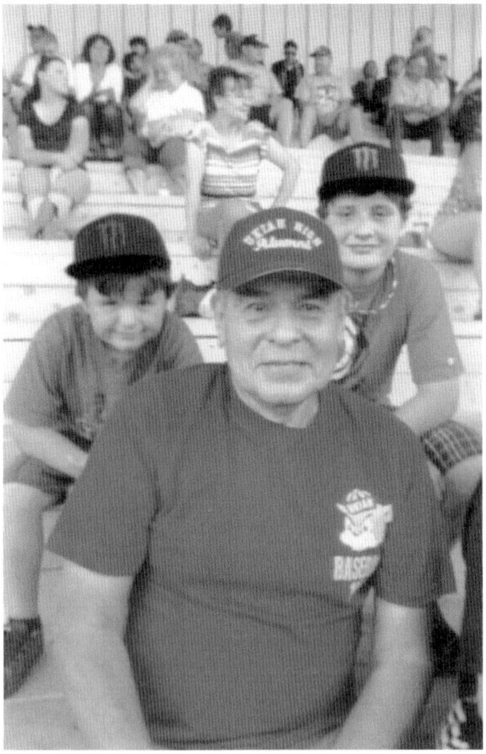

Ralph Maize

One of the greatest baseball players to come out of Ukiah High School, Ralph Maize threw consecutive no-hitters for the Wildcats in 1958. Ralph first beat Novato High 8-0, allowing no hits through nine innings. A few days later, in early May, Ralph blanked the opposition once again—ending a game against an exceptionally strong Petaluma team with a 1-0 score.

After he was drafted into the US Army in 1963, Ralph served as a military police officer at the United States Military Academy at West Point. He played on the baseball team there for two years. Upon his return to Ukiah, Ralph put his military experience to good use in the Mendocino County Sheriff's Office. The first Native American ever hired by that office, he eventually retired after 20 years as the assistant sheriff.

Ralph was also once employed by the Bureau of Indian Affairs in Arizona, where he served as a supervisor of criminal investigations. His duties took him to five western states and put him in charge of law enforcement on several large reservations. Around 1991, he transferred to the Bureau of Land Management as a special agent. He remained with the bureau until his retirement in 2003. In all, Ralph spent over 40 years in law enforcement. One of the cases he worked on—a murder that took place across the street from the Philo Post Office—was featured on Bill Kurtis's A&E television program *Cold Case Files*. Ralph was interviewed and taped for the show.

Ralph has also served on the Sherwood Valley Tribal Council, working for the tribe's nearly 400 members. He was also appointed trustee to the Pinoleville Trust Property, making him responsible for over 840 members

In the late 1990s, Ralph and his sister Verle Anderson started the Native American History Project, Inc. The organization researches and preserves information about the Native Americans in the Mendocino County area and beyond. He and his wife, Susan, volunteer with the Mendocino County Animal Spay and Neuter van. Together, they travel to *rancherias* and reservations and encourage residents to spay and neuter their dogs and cats. His presence has made many of the older people visited much more willing to participate in the program. (Courtesy of Ralph Maize.)

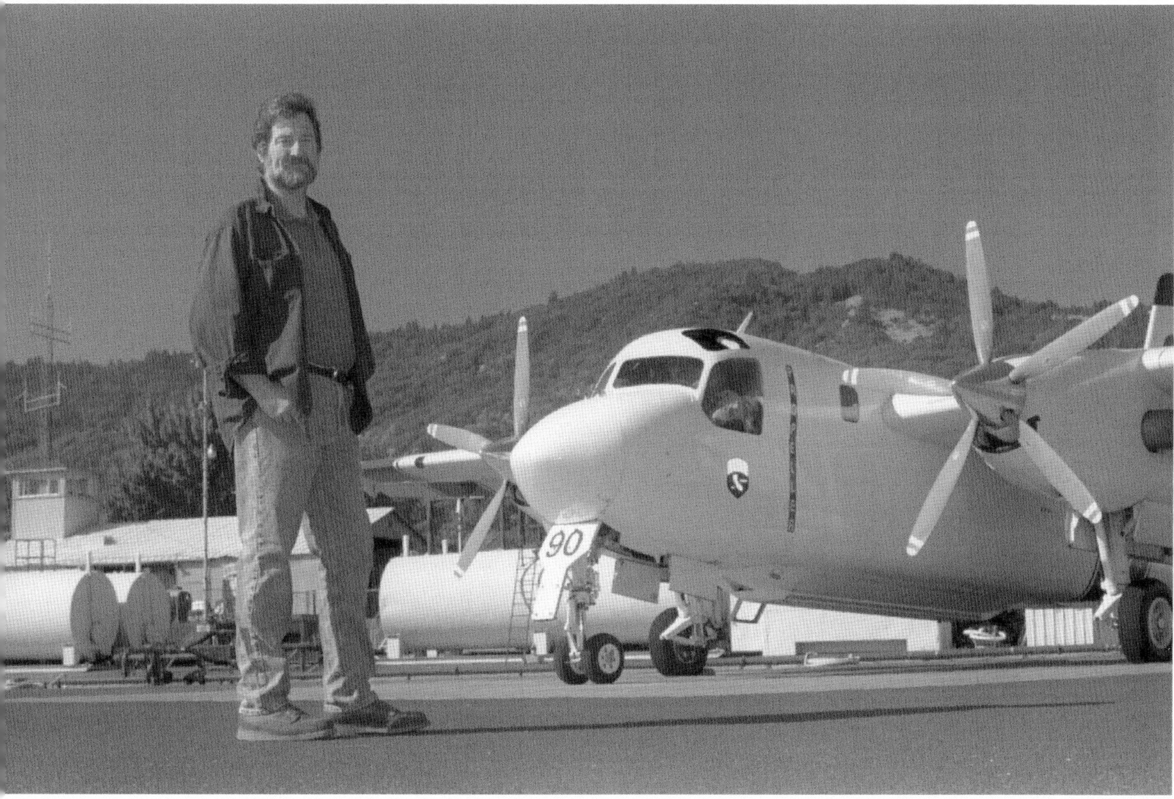

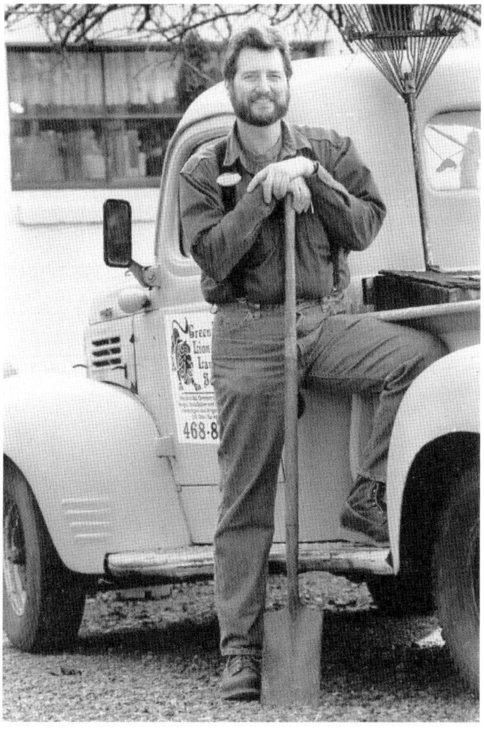

Richard Shoemaker

Four generations of Shoemakers have lived in Ukiah Valley. Richard started his first business at the age of 10, doing yard work, holding yard sales, and publishing a neighborhood kid's newspaper. Even as a kid, he was destined to be an entrepreneur.

As an adult, Richard was the founder and owner of Green Lion Landscape Services, which at one time put over $6 million into the local economy. As time passed, he became interested in city government. He became a Parks and Recreation Commissioner, then a city planning commissioner, and in 1992, a city council member—a position that he held for 10 years.

After several years of working as a consultant and project manager, Richard ran for and was elected to the position of county supervisor. Today, Richard serves as executive director of the Alex Rorabaugh Ukiah Valley Cultural and Recreation Center, which features a library, children's room, outdoor play area, and offices for community organizations. (Courtesy of Richard Shoemaker.)

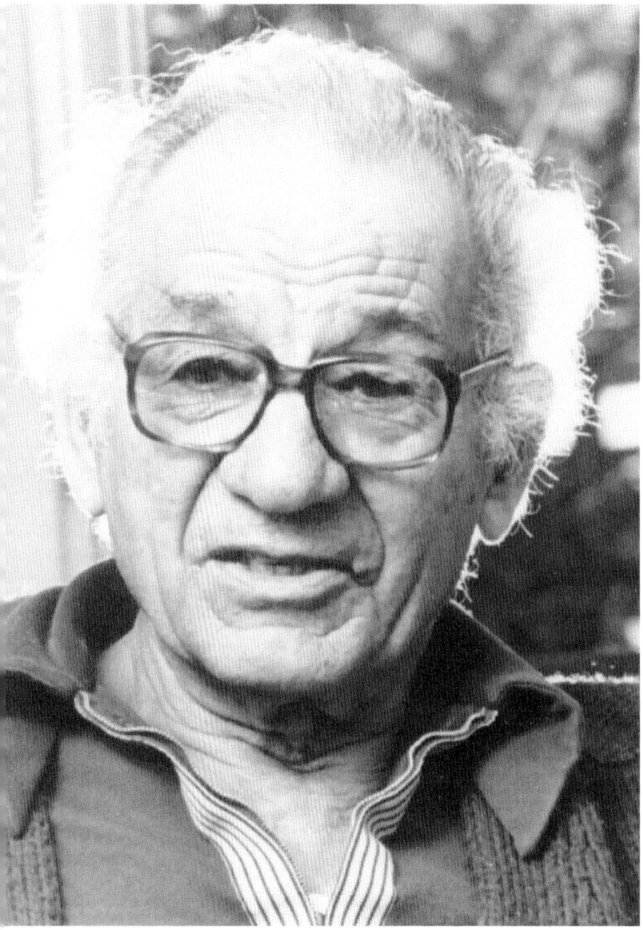

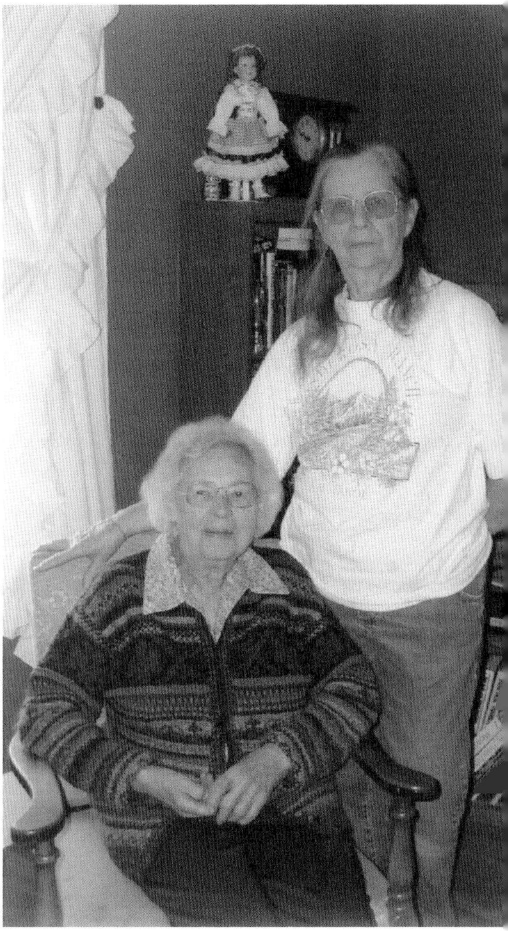

Ted Feibusch (ABOVE AND OPPOSITE PAGE)
Ted Feibusch arrived in San Francisco a penniless Russian immigrant. He worked odd jobs, doing whatever he could to make a living for himself and his bride. They lived frugally so they could save money and invest in their future. Eventually, the Feibuschs made their way to Ukiah, and Ted, a trained engineer, took their savings and invested in local buildings that were in disrepair—working day and night to renovate them. Some buildings in Ukiah still fly the Feibusch banner.

As an engineer, Ted developed many ideas and plans that he presented to the City of Ukiah. As is often the case, it was an uphill battle for Ted to convince local politicians of the value of what he proposed. In 1982, he proposed Measure D, which provided that the mayor should be elected by voters. He was quoted as saying, "Candidates for mayor would be forced to campaign on the issues. Ukiah would be able to make a choice based on the issues."

Possessed of a wry sense of humor, Feibusch once commissioned a large monument to be erected on the entrance to one of his buildings—dedicated "to the ladies of the night who plied their trade upon this spot." Feibusch was known as a tight-fisted businessman but still sent his employee's children—as well as their children—to college and enabled them to obtain their master's degrees. Pictured above in the second image are Else Feibusch (seated) and Dorothy Tracy (right). (Courtesy of Feibusch family.)

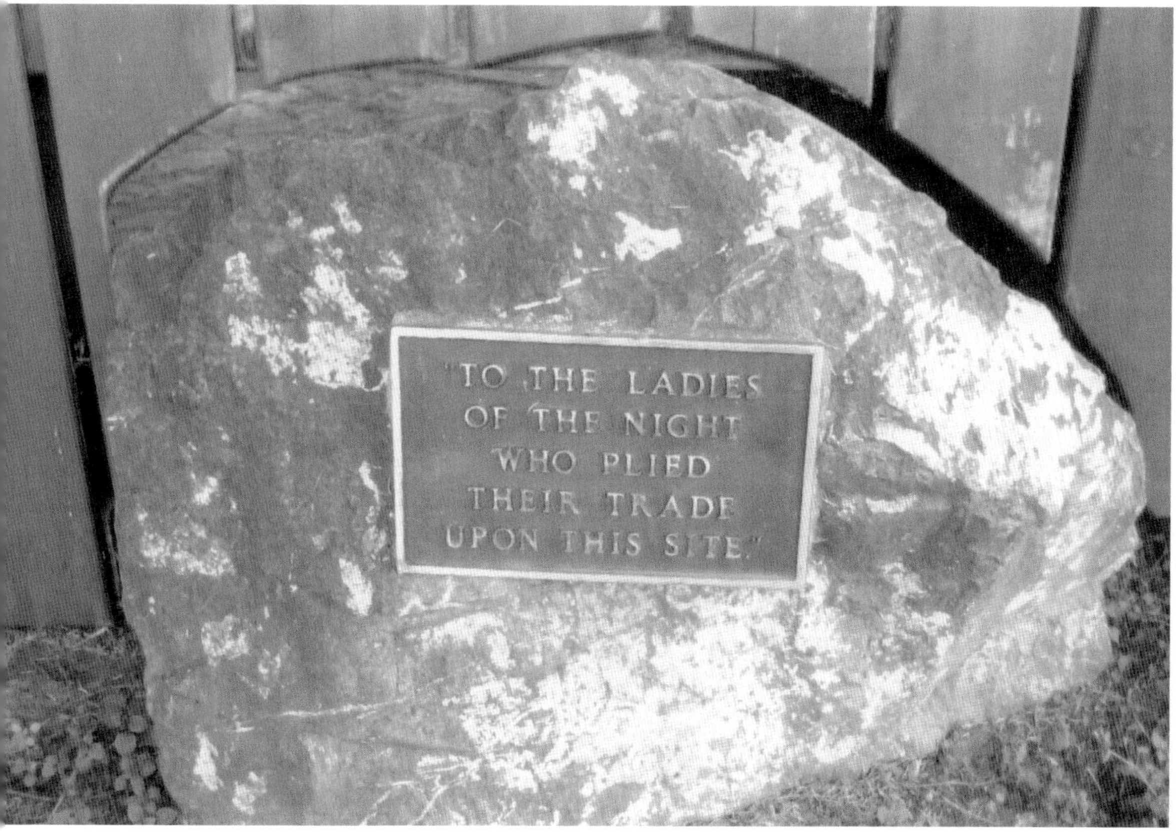
"TO THE LADIES
OF THE NIGHT
WHO PLIED
THEIR TRADE
UPON THIS SITE."

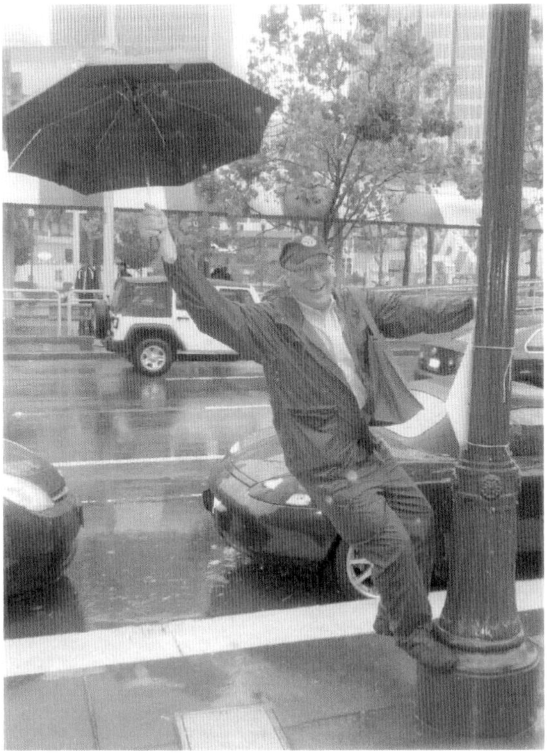

John Bogner (ABOVE AND OPPOSITE PAGE)
After growing up on his grandfather's dairy farm business and working in the family moving business, John Bogner finally found his calling in the real estate business. For over two decades, John was the agent with the most closed sales in the industry. Everyone knew John and went to him for his expertise in selling their home or buying a new one.

The list of the nonprofits and civic organizations that John volunteered with could be a book in itself. The one-time president of the Ukiah Chamber of Commerce was also once the recipient of the Chamber's Outstanding Citizen of the Year award and the director of the annual Mardi Gras fundraiser at his alma mater—St. Mary's School.

Whether it was acting as auctioneer at a fundraiser or working as a director of the Mendocino College Foundation, John was always front and center to help his community. For St. Patrick's Day he always hosted a huge party, visiting with old friends while introducing new people to Ukiah. He would also don stilts and an Uncle Sam costume for Ukiah's annual Fourth of July Parade.

John loved his hometown, letting everyone far and wide know what a terrific place it was to live. He had a knack for getting the locals to volunteer wherever they were needed. John was such a joy to work with that no one minded when they answered the phone and heard, "Can you help me out here; just a little of your time is all I need." John always let someone that they were appreciated and made volunteering a fun way to help the community.

When John passed away at the age of 60, Mayor Mari Rodin described him as a "warm, jovial man [for] whom love of and commitment to community was a religion," and community leader Martha Barra said, "I don't know of anyone who was more generous to local nonprofits really needing help."

John will always be remembered and missed in his beloved Ukiah. After his death in 2011,the South Ukiah Rotary paid tribute to John by refurbishing a gazebo that had stood on the west side of the Old Mendocino County Courthouse. John had located the gazebo several years earlier and intended to restore it to its former grandeur, but he did not get around to it. His longtime friend Gary Nix also spearheaded the creation of the John Bogner Scholarship for Fine Arts. (Courtesy of Gary Nix.)

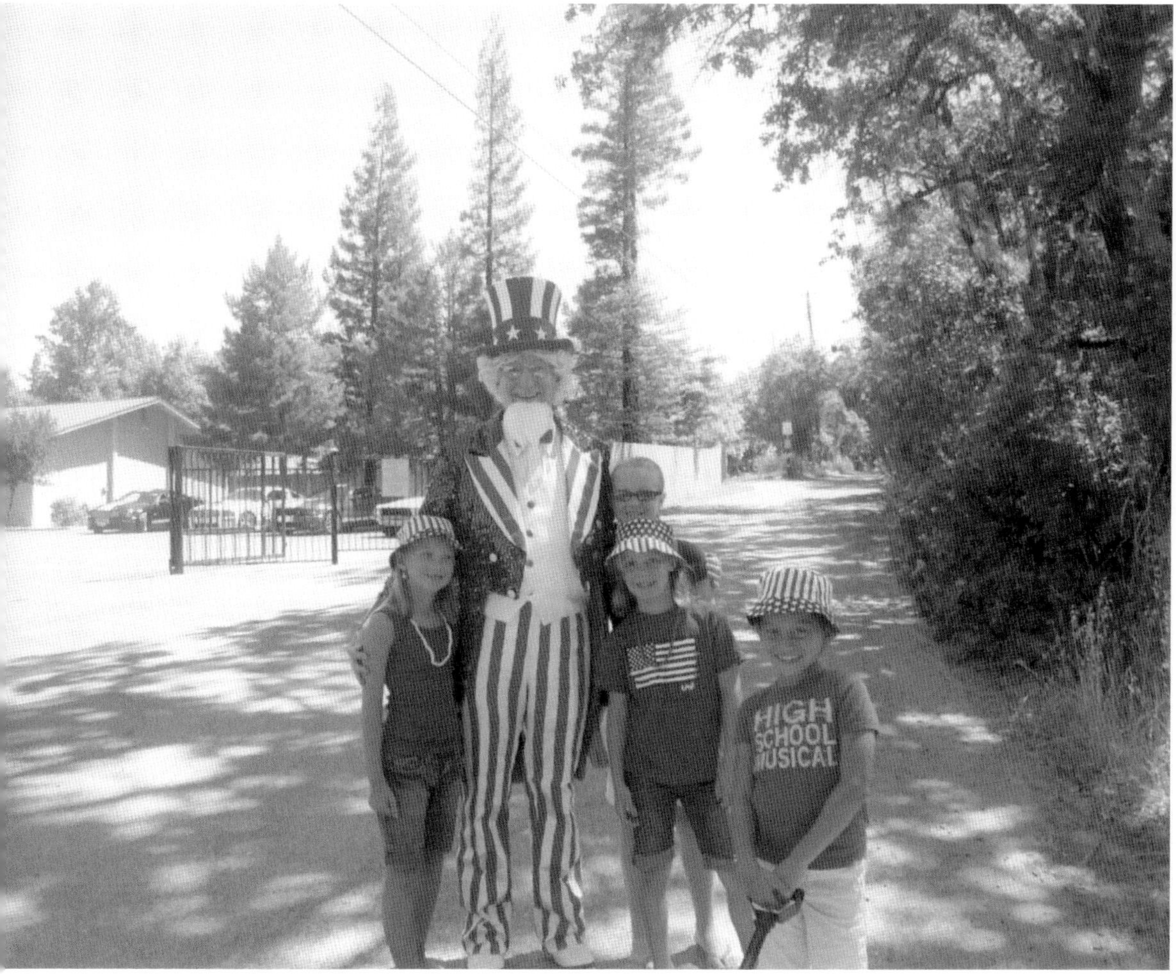
HIGH
SCHOOL
MUSICAL

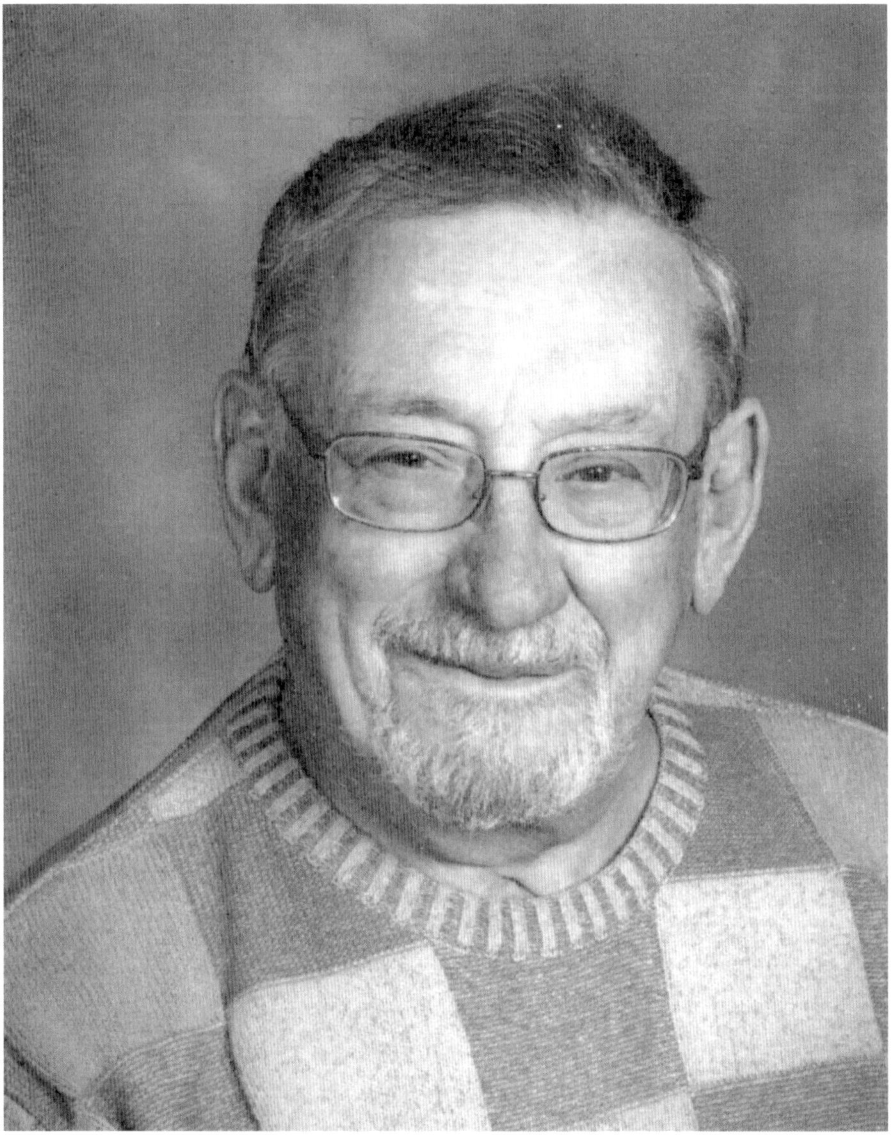

Al Beltrami

The son of Italian immigrants, Al Beltrami was born and raised in nearby Modesto. He attended a junior college before moving on to UC Berkeley, where he received his degree in public administration. When his tour in the US Navy was up, Al made use of that degree—heading into a career managing local governments. He had been working for just two years when he was offered a job as Mendocino County's administrator.

He and his bride, Patricia, fell in love with Mendocino County and put down roots in Ukiah. He served as county administrator for almost 30 years before retiring. John Mayfield, a close friend and coworker, described him as "one of the most competent people I ever worked with."

After his retirement, Al served on the North Coast Water Quality Control Board and was cofounder of the Employers Council of Mendocino. He also donated money to the local community college and more than $250,000 toward a new emergency waiting room at the Ukiah Valley Medical Center. (Courtesy of Held-Poage Library.)

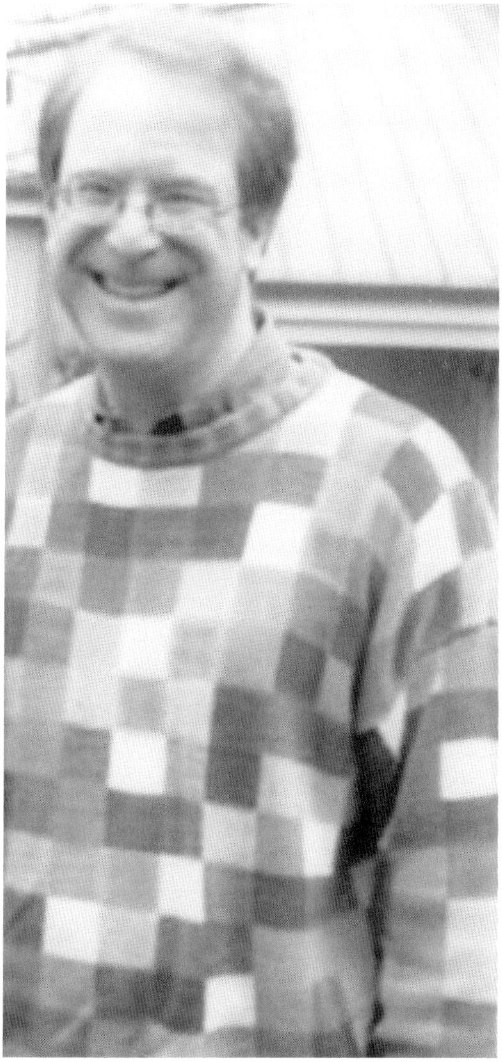

Reid Edelman

In 2000, Ukiah's Mendocino College was fortunate enough to convince Reid Edelman to move to town and head up the theatre department. A student of the American Conservatory Theatre, Reid became the recipient of such awards as the Louis Sudler Prize for Excellence in the Creative Arts and the Robert Golden Medal for Achievement in the Humanities while earning a degree from Stanford University. He then participated in a professional actors program at Rutgers University's Mason Gross School of the Arts and underwent graduate work at Harvard University, where he helped initiate a program in Arts Education.

After completing his education, Reid went on to serve as director and educator for Boston's Huntington Theatre Company. He then spent time with the Harvest Theatre Company in San Francisco, where he founded a professional theatre company that produced work from playwrights such as Tennessee Williams to Shakespeare.

Since coming to Ukiah, Reid has produced an amazing track record of theatre productions—helming musicals, dramas, and Shakespearean productions, as well as auditioning and presenting new works written by students and local residents. Ukiah is home to outstanding theatre work thanks to Reid Edelman. (Courtesy of Gary Nix.)

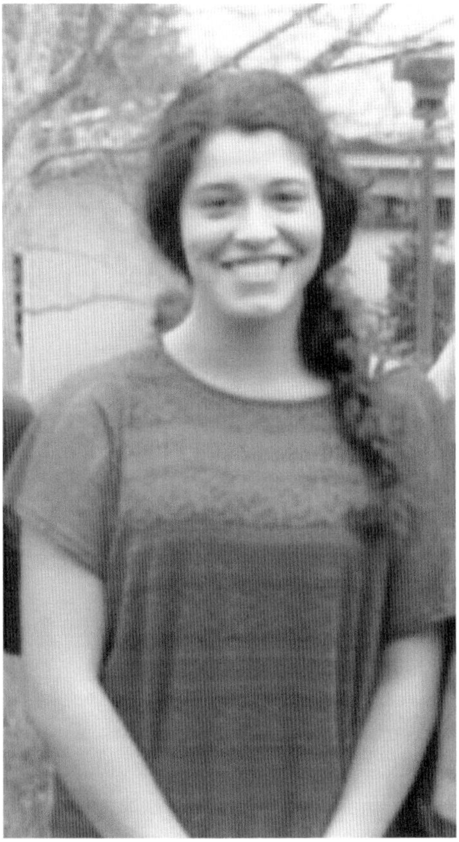

Monique Marmon

Monique Marmon is the first recipient of the John Bogner Scholarship for Fine Arts, which she was awarded for her study of theater. Her love of acting and singing began with her involvement at SPACE, when she was in elementary school. That passion has persisted through high school—where she served as president of the drama department for two years—and college. Monique's dream is to use her education to teach theatre to children who may not otherwise have access to programs that allow them to express themselves. (Courtesy of Gary Nix.)

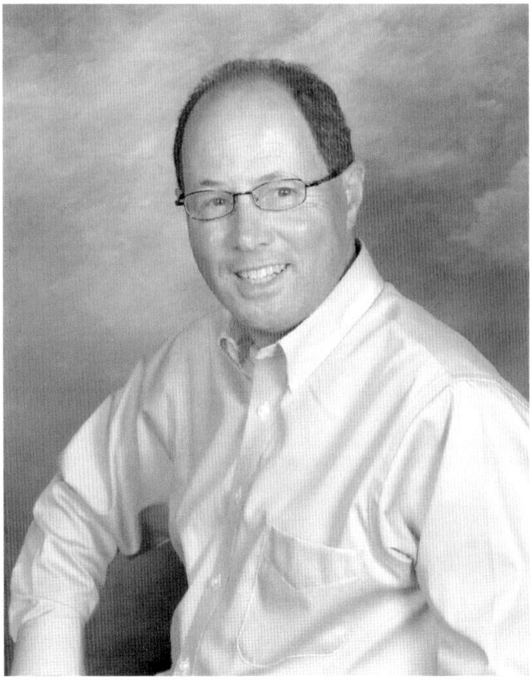

Gary Nix

Gary Nix was instrumental in establishing the John Bogner Scholarship for Fine Arts. Over the years, Gary has devoted his life to volunteering with local nonprofits and serving on the boards of many nonprofit and professional organizations. He has also been the chairman of the Cultural Arts Advisory Board for the City of Ukiah, a member of the steering committee that generated the current General Plan for the City of Ukiah, and a member of the board of directors of the California Association of Realtors. Not simply a booster for Ukiah, Nix gives back to the community through his involvement in many areas. He currently serves as the director of the Mendocino College Foundation Board. (Courtesy of Gary Nix.)

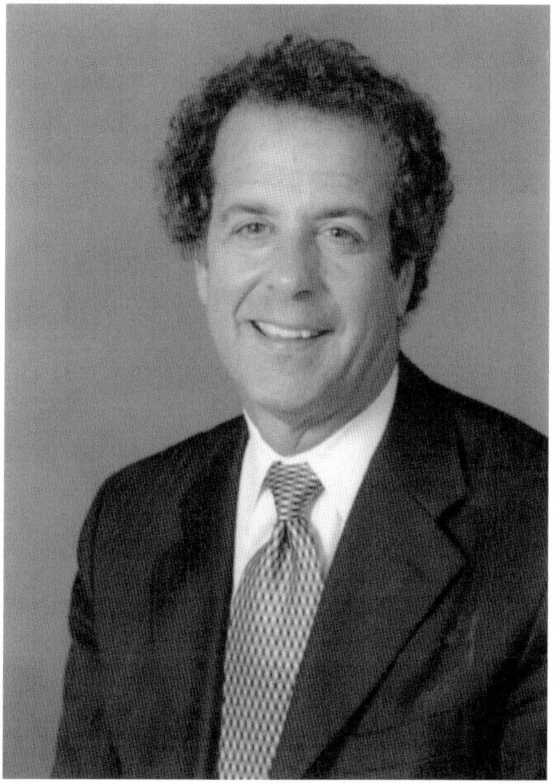

Marty Lombardi
In his decades with the Savings Bank of Mendocino County, Marty Lombardi has embodied every aspect of the "banker for the people." When you talked to Marty at the bank or on the street, he gave you the feeling that you were the most important person in town.

Marty could also be found serving on just about every nonprofit board in the valley. He spent years on the hospital finance committee and as a volunteer at the middle school, the high school, the Boys & Girls Clubs, and with MESA (Mathematics, Engineering, Science Achievement). Together with Paul Dolan and Tim Buckner, Marty founded the Mendocino Agricultural Families Scholarship Fund, which ensures that the children of farmworkers have an equal opportunity to get a college education.

Always a gentleman and always impeccably dressed, Marty often asked, "In the long run, the only thing that matters is, were we honorable people?" (Courtesy of Marty Lombardi.)

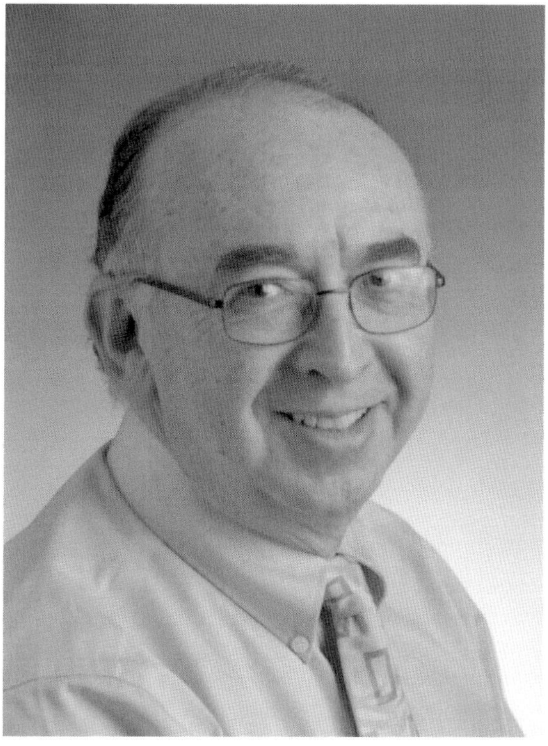

Dr. Guy Teran
Think there's no such thing as an old-fashioned country doctor? Then you haven't met Dr. Guy Teran—a man whose bedside manner and compassion makes all the difference to his patients.

Fluent in Spanish, Guy makes sure that his Hispanic patients know that there is someone who understands them. He also has a special appreciation for the elderly and can always be seen in his visiting people in the local nursing and care facilities during his off hours.

Several years ago, a local surgeon talked to Guy about going to Guatemala as a volunteer. He went and immediately made such a connection with the Guatemalan people that he now makes the trip annually—helping those who don't enjoy the availability and quality of health care that we have in Ukiah. And yes, on occasion, he has been known to make house calls. (Courtesy of Dr. Guy Teran.)

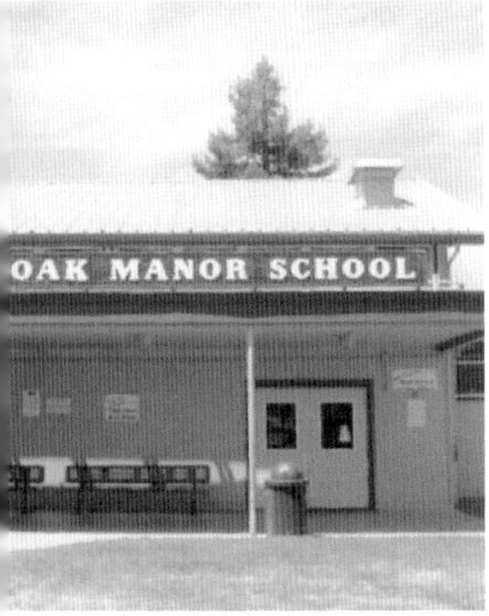

Aaron Rodgers

From Oak Manor Elementary School to 2008, Green Bay Packers starting quarterback Aaron Rodgers has certainly gone far. Rodgers led the Packers to victory at Super Bowl XLV in 2011, earning the title of MVP, and went on to be named Athlete of the Year by the Associated Press. Aaron is currently the only quarterback to have a career passing rate of over 100 in a regular season and has the highest touchdown to interception ratio in NFL history.

At the age of 10, Aaron was featured the front page of the *Ukiah Daily Journal* after he won a local free throw competition. He attended Butte Community College and, while there, received an athletic scholarship to the University of California at Berkeley. He then played for UCB's Golden Bears from 2003 to 2004. Aaron's father was a football player as well—an offensive lineman at the California State University at Chico from 1973 to 1976. (Courtesy of Oak Manor School.)

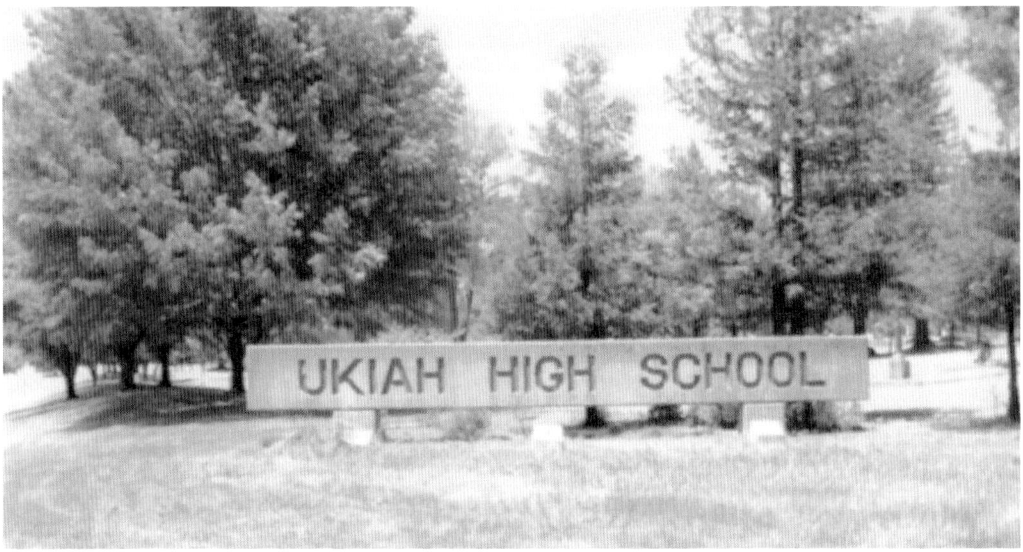

Hal Perry

After starting his athletic career at Ukiah High School, Hal Perry first won fame as a starter at the University of San Francisco NCAA championship games in 1955 and 1956. Together with future Hall of Fame players K.C. Jones and Bill Russell, Hal provided the San Francisco Dons with their first African American starting roster.

Teammates remember Hal as an outstanding player who was always a gentleman on the court. One player for the Dons, Mike Farmer, is quoted as saying, "When I got to USF, I had never talked to anybody like Hal. Every night, he would study to learn new words. He played several musical instruments; I will always remember his energy and his enthusiasm."

Hal played briefly with the Harlem Globetrotters, but the team's owner, Abe Saperstein, told him that he was too smart to spend his life traversing the country playing for entertainment rather than competition. Saperstein offered to pay Hal's way through law school, and he took the offer—enrolling in Lincoln Law School. After graduating, Hal worked for the district attorney's office in Oakland before opening a successful private practice.

Hal was very active in the Oakland community, working with young people and with his church—where he sang in the choir. He was inducted into the USF Hall of Fame, and in 2008, he was inducted into the Multi-Ethnic Sports Hall of Fame. (Courtesy of Ukiah High School.)

CHAPTER TWO

Business Community

While big-box stores seem to be taking over the country, Ukiah is fortunate to still have local businesses that have been in the community for—in some cases—generations. From the bakery to the construction company, these local businesses value their customers, and if you need something special, they will go out of their way to accommodate you. Ukiah's bookstore, will still call you when the book that you ordered comes in, and the shoe store has collected several thousand pairs of shoes to distribute to the community over the years. There is even a major construction company that has given tens of thousands of dollars to local nonprofits.

These businesses give back to the area in a myriad of ways. For them, it's not just about business and the bottom line—it's about community.

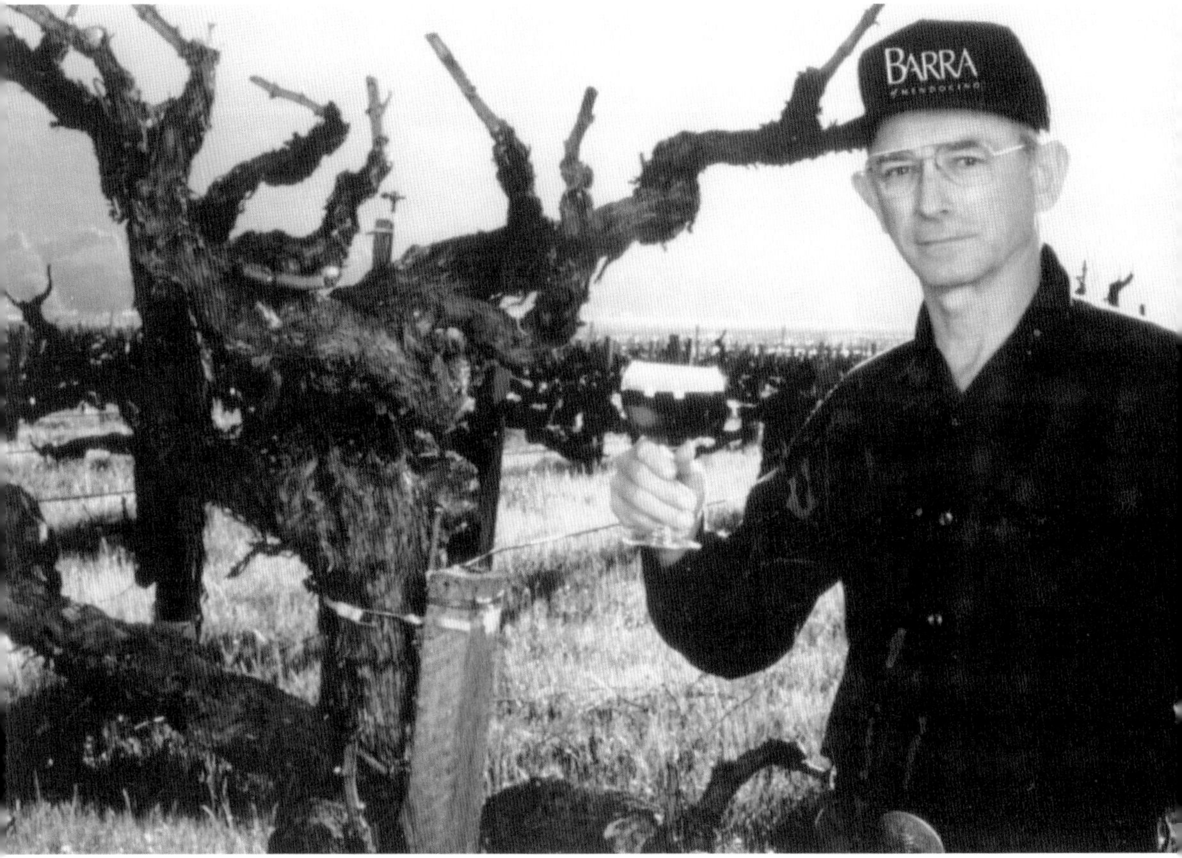

Charlie Barra

Charlie grew up in Redwood Valley with his two brothers. As soon as he was old enough, he worked alongside his family on their farm and, as a young teenager, took jobs with neighboring vineyards. At the age of 19, he leased land from a neighbor and proceeded to farm on his own.

Farming his own land appealed to Charlie more than finishing school, but his school's principal made a deal with him: He was so close to graduation that, if he attended school a half day and worked at farming a half day and on weekends, he could graduate and farm, too. Charlie had no money of his own to pay for leasing the land, so he stuck a deal with the neighbor who would provide the land, too. Charlie would do the grunt work, and at the end of the season, they would split the profits. This plan worked well. For several years, Charlie and his neighbor were business partners. In 1955, Charlie purchased 110 acres in Redwood Valley, where, in the late 1950s, he designed a moving gondola that enabled pickers to fill a bucket with grapes, dump it on the gondola, and move on.

In 1963, Charlie founded the California Grape Growers Association, which allowed all of the local growers to have access to information from their peers. A few years later, he established Redwood Valley Cellars. With the help of his wife, Martha, Charlie has built Redwood Valley Cellars into a premier tasting room and a venue for art and music. Every year, nonprofits hold fundraisers at the Cellars, while the Barras support the Grace Hudson Museum and a multitude of other civic groups in Ukiah and Mendocino County. Together, they founded and direct the St. Mary's School Mardi Gras, which, over the years, has donated more than $2 million to St. Mary's School. (Courtesy of Martha Barra.)

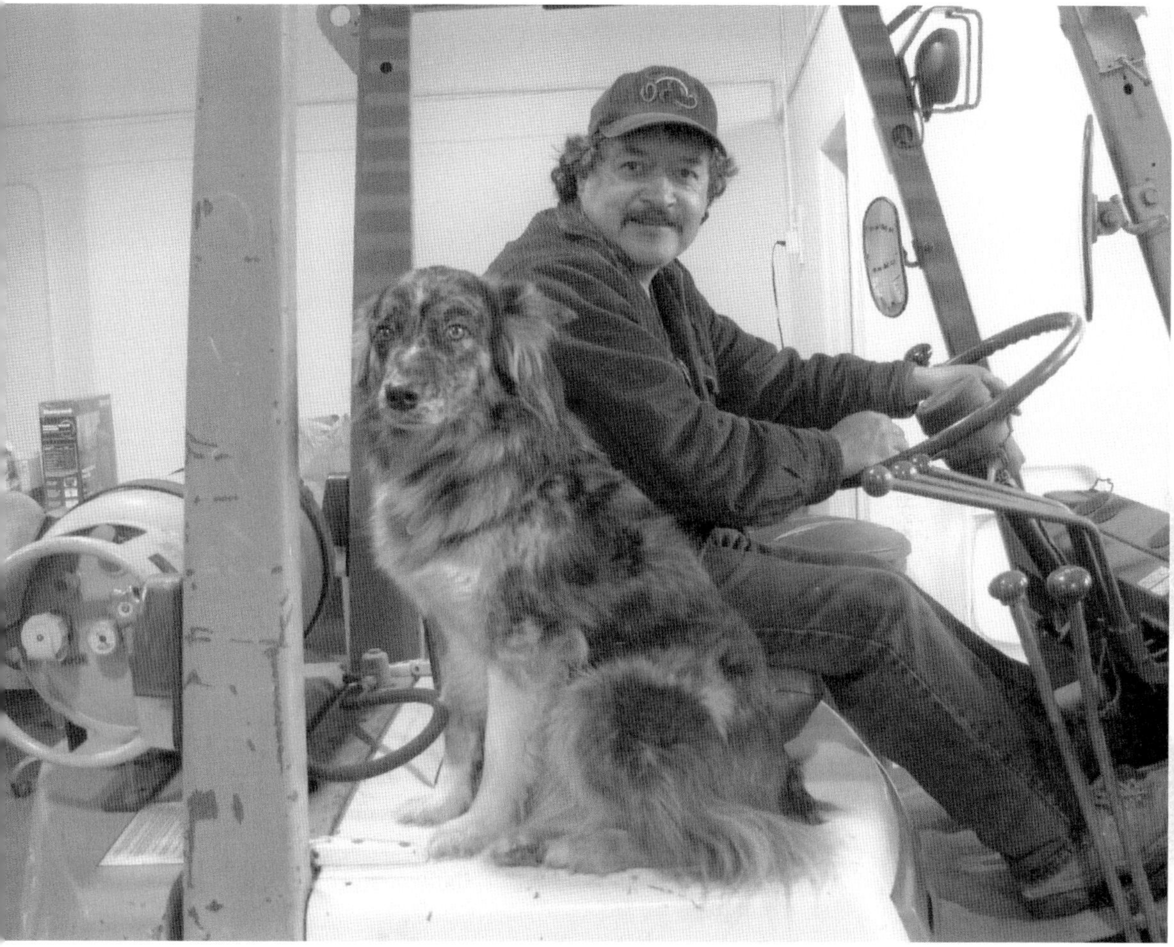

Victor Simon

A native of Michocan, Mexico, Victor Simon moved to Ukiah in the 1980s. There, he fine-tuned his natural talent as a wine grower and maker, learning the art of the soil reaping the rewards produced by it.

Today, Victor operates Simaine Cellars with his wife, Brenda. Simaine is a small, family-owned—and award winning—producer of fine wines. Victor serves as the winemaker and runs the tasting room, while Brenda is the driving force that keeps him on track. Brenda has successfully blended together her knowledge of the business and her love of wine, which has helped Simaine to thrive. Simaine has also recently begun holding monthly cabaret evenings, with the likes of Paula Samonte, Paul McCandless, and Dawn Senfren appearing regularly.

Victor always has the time to answer questions about the wine and share a joke. Always smiling, he is a man with a terrific sense of humor. (Courtesy of Victor and Brenda Simon.)

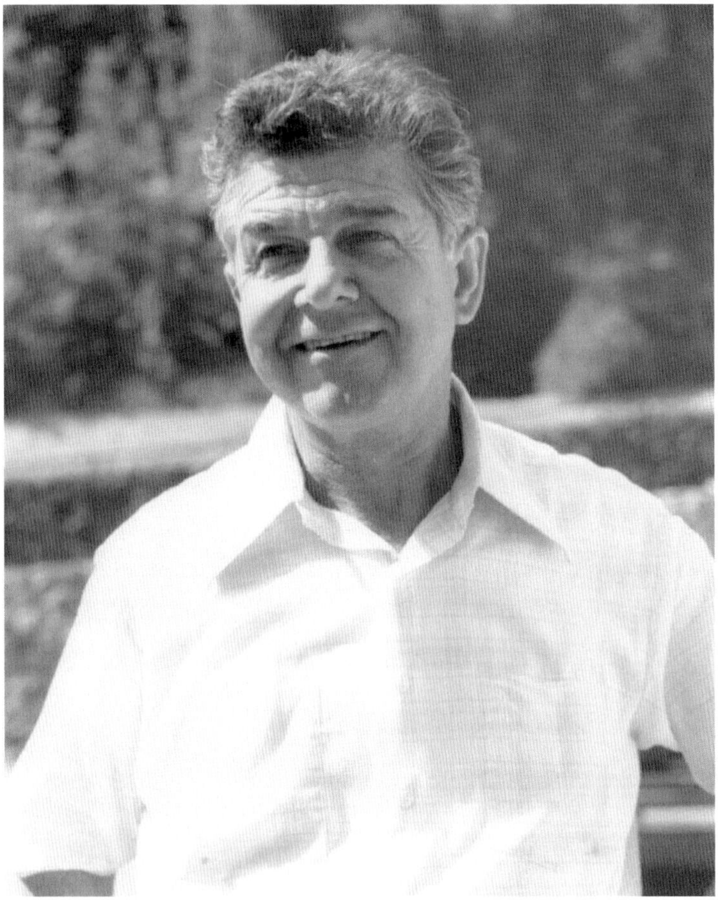

John Parducci

Remembered today as "Mr. Mendocino," John Parducci moved with his family to Ukiah in the 1920s. John and his brothers worked with their father to build Parducci Wine Cellars in the early 1930s. After attending college in nearby Santa Rosa, John returned to the valley and took over as winemaker in 1940.

John's goal was to produce an affordable, quality wine that everyone could enjoy. John was active in the wine business for over 70 years. He was the first Mendocino County winemaker to put a varietal on the label, and during his later years, he worked with his grandson at the McNab Ridge Winery—carrying on the family tradition.

John was honored many times, including being named Winemaker of the Year at the Los Angeles County Fair, being inducted into the Vintners Hall of Fame, earning a lifetime achievement award at the California State Fair, and being named Mendocino County Agricultural Man of the Year by the Mendocino County Agricultural Association. He was also president of the Ukiah Rotary Club for a time, as well as the Pomo Shrine Club.

Mike Genilla once said of John, "He was a contrary and crusty character, and he could be the kindest, sweetest, loving man you ever met." Genilla also recalled one of his favorite Parducci stories, when John was asked to speak before a large group in Texas. John started out by talking about pink zinfandel being nothing more than soda pop. Everyone got quiet, and it was then that John realized that they were all drinking pink zin. Explaining himself to the public relations people later, John said, "Well, I was just telling them what I thought." That was John—down to earth, real, and honest in his opinions. (Courtesy of *Ukiah Daily Journal.*)

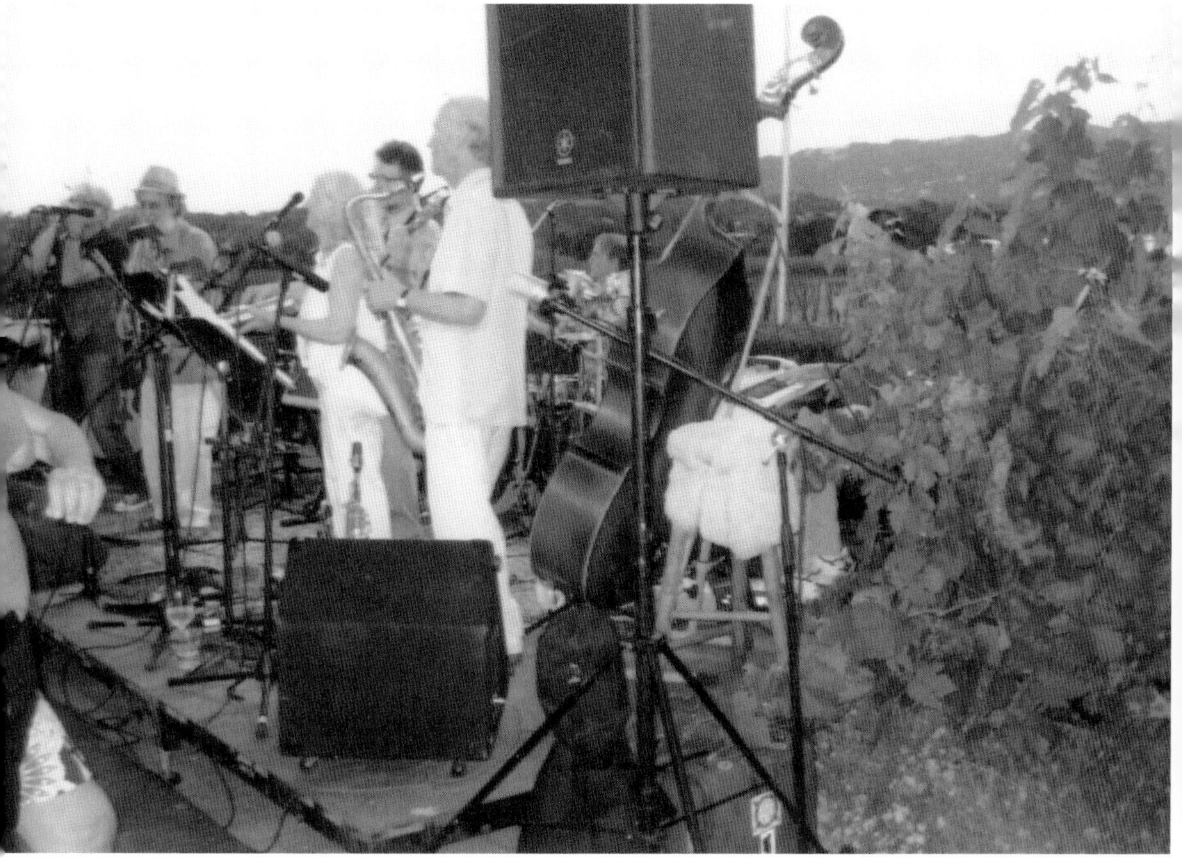

Concert at Parducci Wine Cellars
This Will Siegel & Friends concert was produced in July 2014 by Spencer Brewer for the Acoustic Cafe at Parducci Wine Cellars.

The Nelson Family (BELOW AND OPPOSITE PAGE)
Greg Nelson and his sons Chris and Tyler have made the Nelson Family Winery into one of the leading wineries in Mendocino County. Greg's father and mother moved from what is now Silicon Valley in 1952 and bought the land that they would turn into a winery. At one time, the property was part of a Mexican land grant and was owned by a family of homesteaders. Now it is an award-winning wine enterprise.

Chris, the winemaker, lives above the winery—behind their grandmother's house and the tasting room—while Tyler coordinates projects at the organically certified facility. A portion of the farm is leased to a family who use it to raise the best strawberries in the county, and at Christmas, people flock to the Nelson Family Winery to cut their own Christmas tree. Summers bring several weeks of concerts to a redwood grove on the property, with performers ranging from the Ukiah Symphony, to a bluegrass band, to a medley of Broadway show tunes. Many of the area nonprofits hold their fundraisers at the winery, with assistance from the family. (Below, courtesy of the Nelson family; opposite, courtesy of Erica Olsson.)

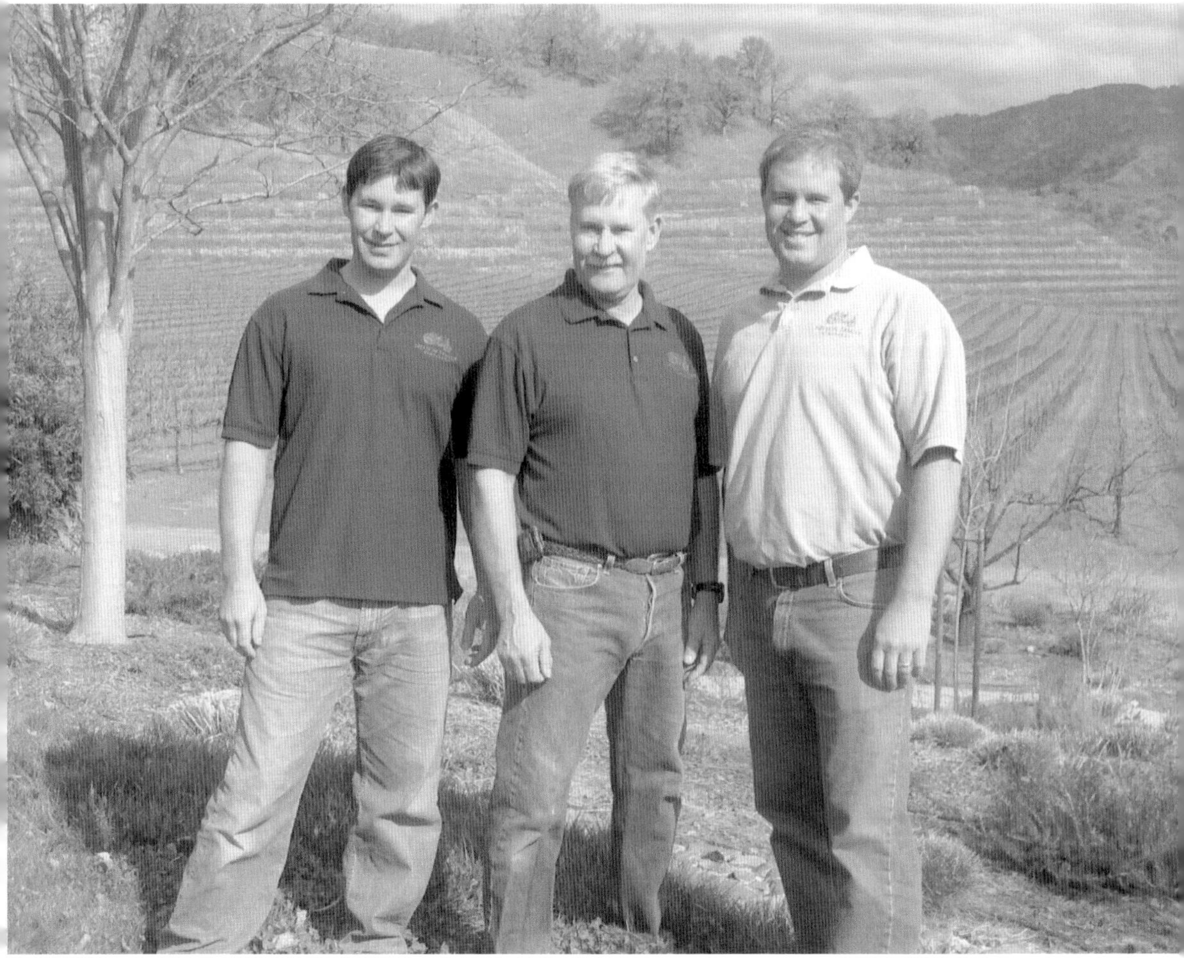

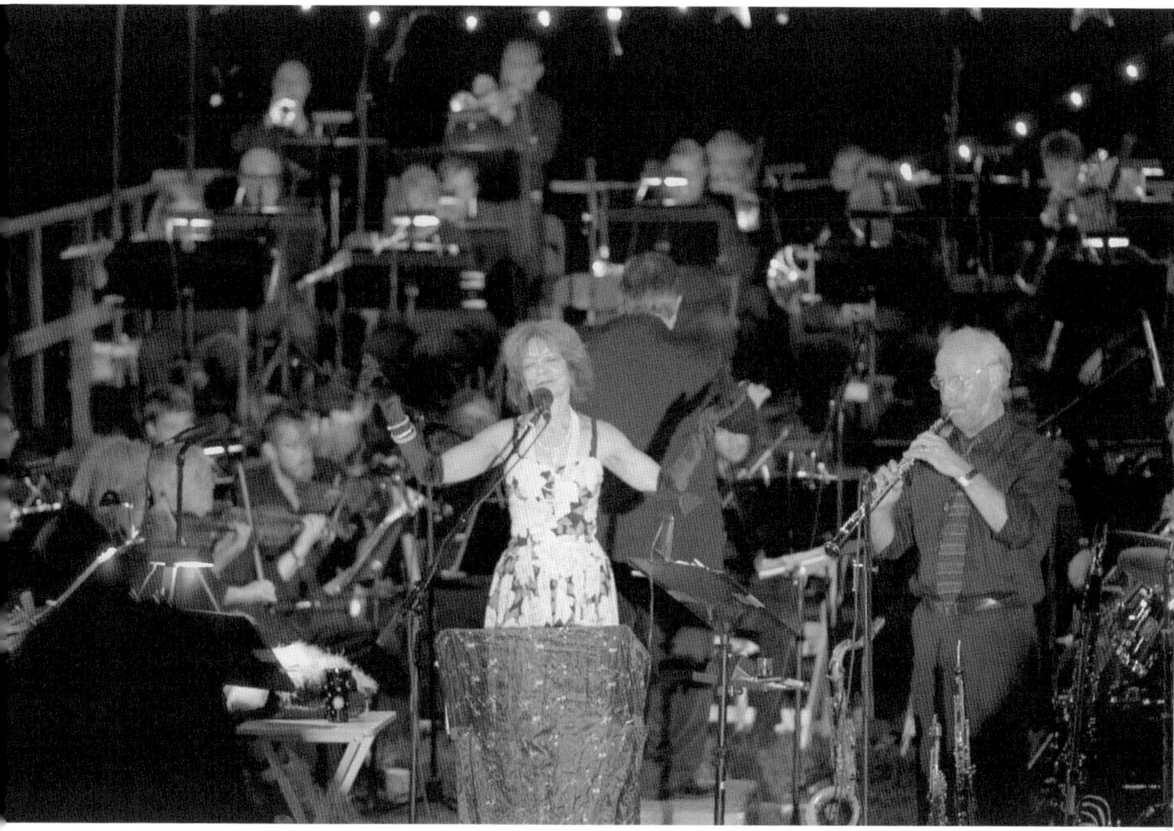

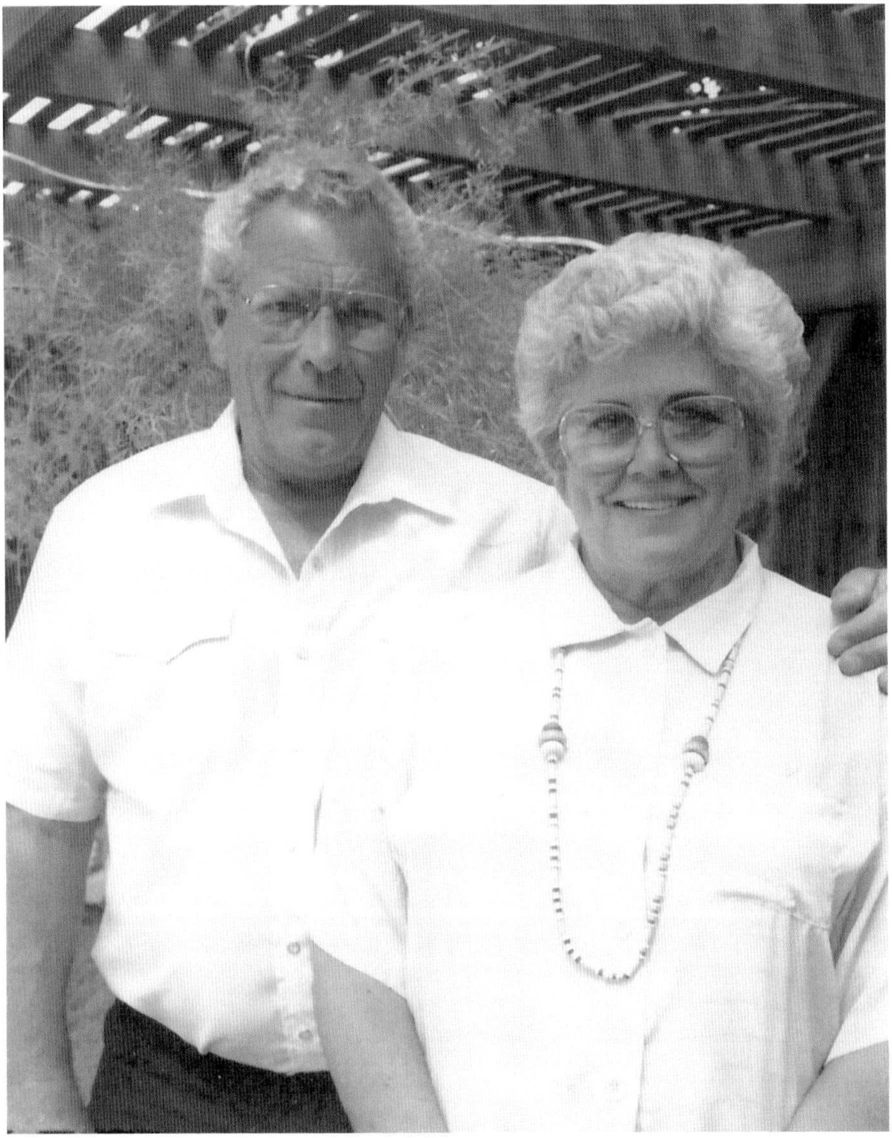

Gloria Thompson

Gloria and her husband, Oren Thompson, were the owners of Valley Paving. They worked together at this family-owned business for over 34 years. At the age of 70, however, Gloria wanted to try something new, and—having always enjoyed entertaining family and friends—she decided to open a party equipment rental service. Thompson's Party Rentals was a huge success and became the Ukiah area's source for anything and everything needed to entertain. Whether it was a barbecue, an elegant wedding, or anything in between, Gloria had it in her shop.

The Thompsons also made their spacious home and grounds available to local nonprofits looking to stage a fundraiser or host an award ceremony. Additionally, Gloria's parties and cooking skills were legendary. She was heavily involved with the Ukiah Sons of Italy, a member of Soroptimist International of Ukiah, and a founding member of Sews and Sews.

Gloria's energy level was amazing and showed everyone—of any age—that 70 could be the start of new adventures. (Courtesy of the Thompson family.)

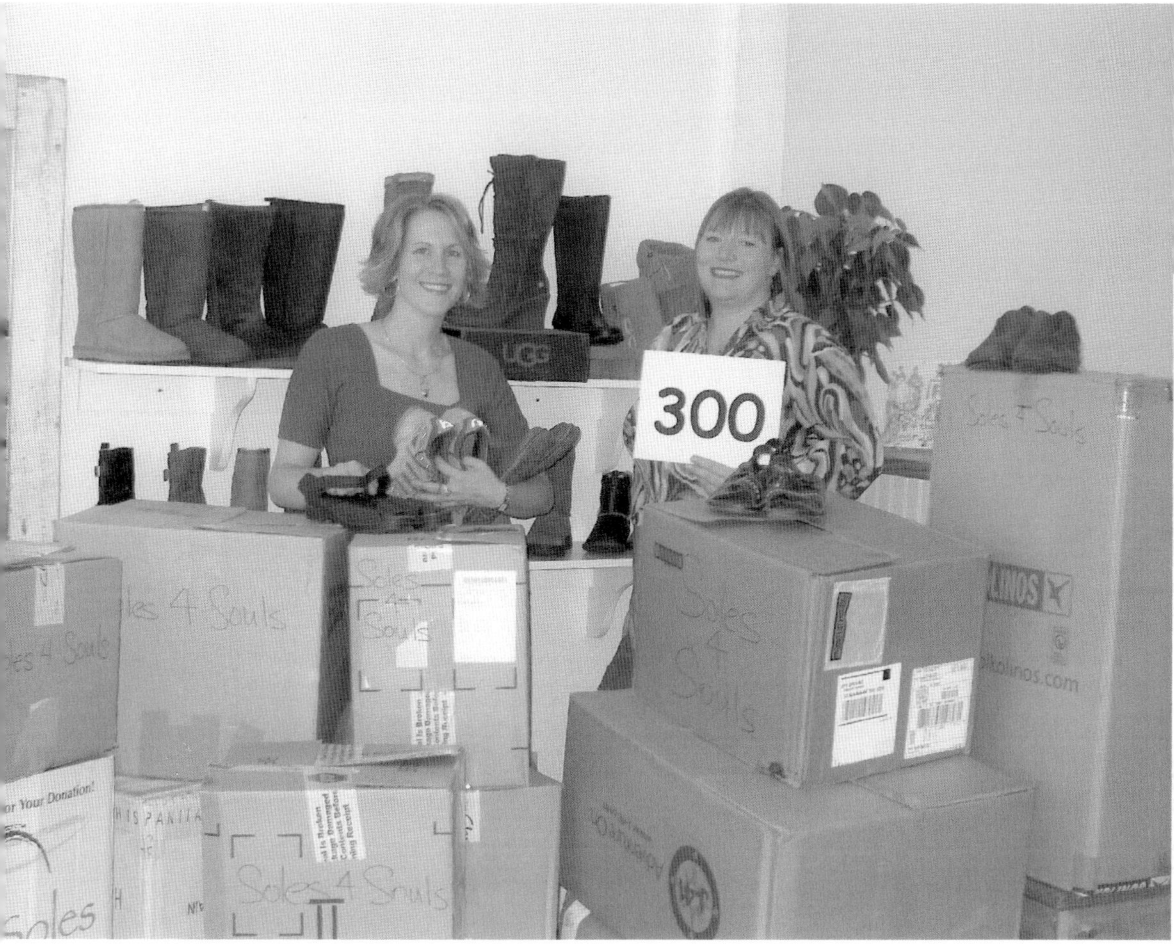

Shannon Riley and Cindy Sauers

Ten years ago, Shannon Riley and Cindy Sauers founded Shoefly and Sox on the idea that women wanted comfortable shoes and shoes that were still attractive—opening a store downtown. After a short time, the partners realized that there was a part of the population that did not have shoes at all—local homeless women and those who had to flee from domestic violence with only the clothes on their back. These women certainly did not have a pair of good, comfortable shoes.

Shannon and Cindy decided to start a drive that collected gently used shoes and distributed them to the homeless shelter and Plowshares—the local soup kitchen. To date, these two ladies have given away over two thousand pairs of good shoes to women in need—demonstrating that they really do care about Ukiah, their community, and helping those less fortunate. (Courtesy of Shannon Riley.)

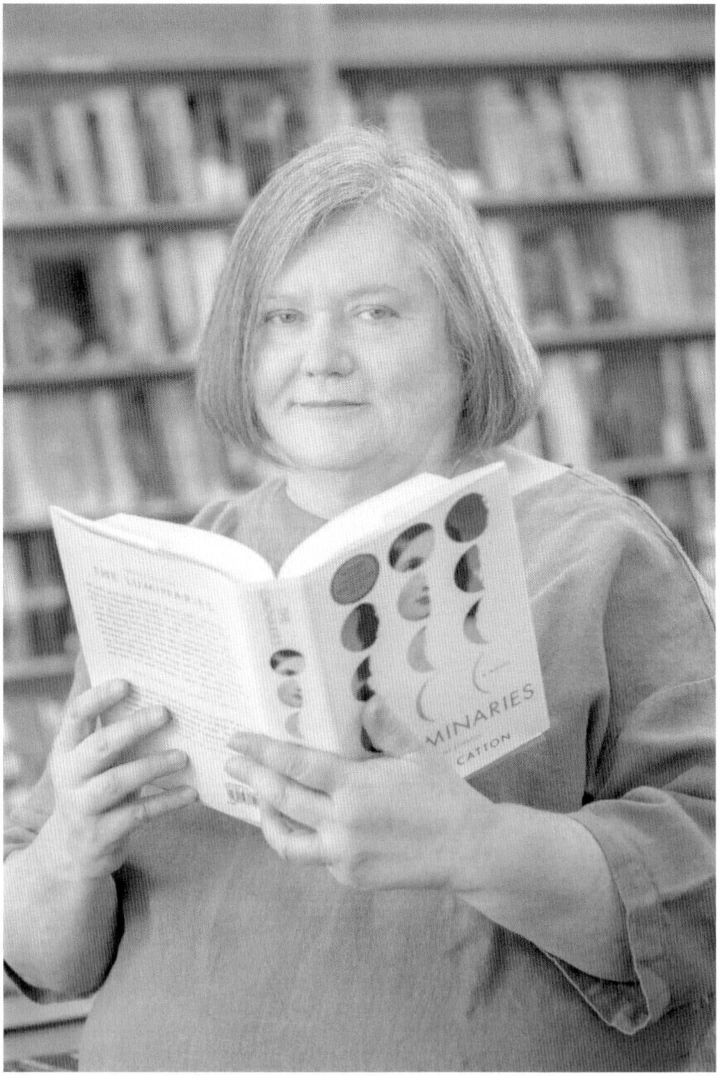

Ann Kilkenny

A Midwestern native, Ann Kilkenny settled in Ukiah several decades ago—purchasing a small bookstore here in town in 1983. Always a book lover, she thought that it was tome to make the plunge and take over the ownership of an existing store. Ann would be the first to tell you that she knew nothing about running a business, but she jumped into it with her whole heart and soul. More than 30 years later, the Mendocino Book Company is still here.

One of the great things about Ann's bookstore is the customer service. From ordering a book and giving the customer a call when it comes in, to giving someone a personal call because the employees know that they would like a particular text that just came in, they do it all. Ann is also generous enough to handle advance ticket sales for local art and entertainment productions—saving a patron from having to go on the Internet. Posters for upcoming events always find a home in her shop windows, and she hosts book signings for local authors while providing refreshments for all.

Ukiah is fortunate to have its own downtown bookstore. A place where someone can browse and enjoy the ambience—complete with a resident dog that oversees everything. (Courtesy of Ann Kilkenny; photograph by Nathan DeHart.)

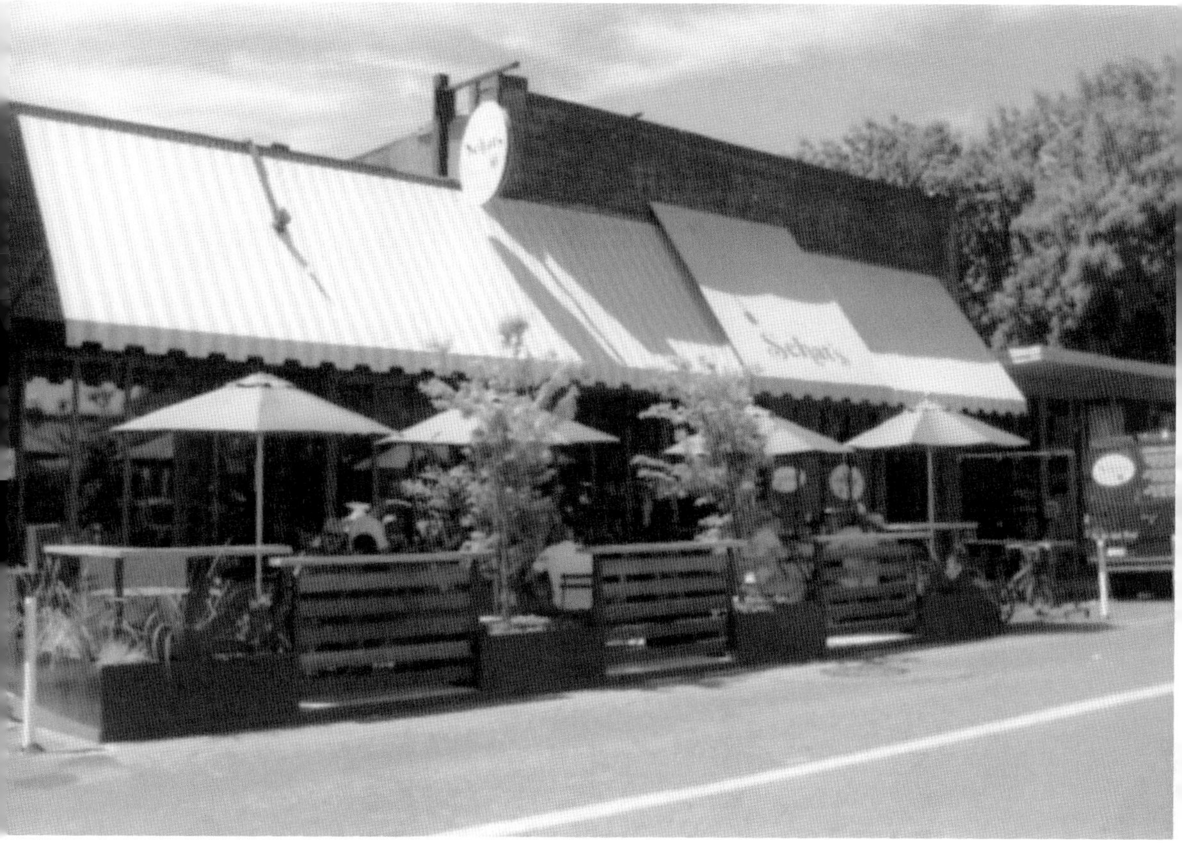

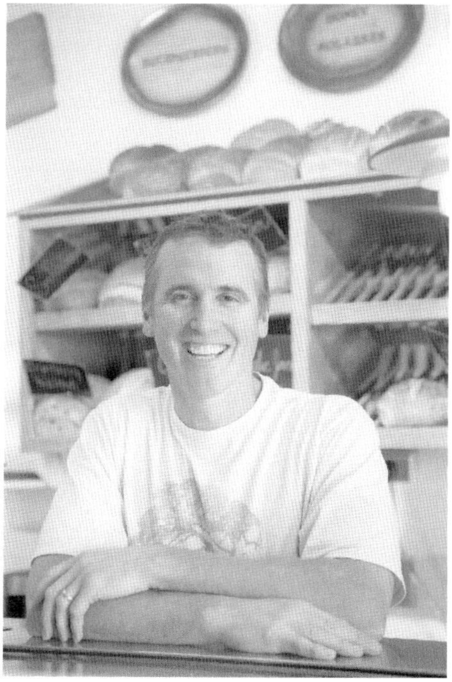

Zach Schat, Schat's Bakery
Schat's Bakery is located just across from the courthouse. You'll find anyone and everyone there at noon, and Zach Schat greets everyone like family—lending the place a feeling that you're at home and hanging out in mother's kitchen. The business was originally purchased in early 1990.

The Schat family has been backing since 1893, before they left Holland in search of the American Dream. Today, members of the Schat family are baking in Holland; Bishop, California; and Carson City, Nevada. There are currently three Schat's locations in Ukiah: at Mendocino College, the Courthouse Bakery, and inside Friedman Brothers.

Zach is always donating to local nonprofits and, many times, even delivers the baked goodies to the location himself, making it easier for those who are putting on the fundraiser. Christmas will find Zach and his family delivering rolls, bread, pies, cookies, and cakes around town by the van-full. Zach, like so many of the Ukiah business owners, is all about giving back to the community. (Courtesy of Zach Schat.)

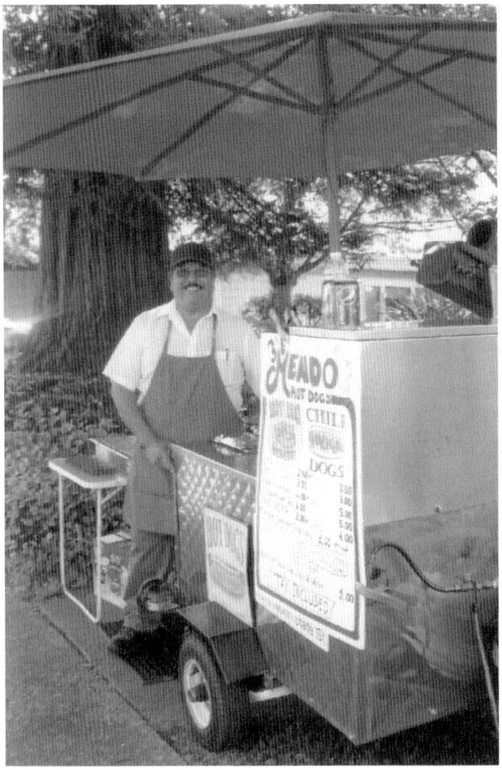

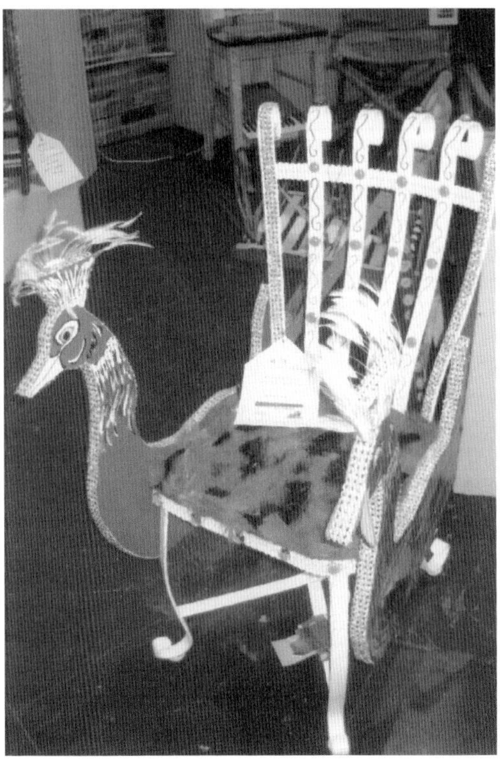

Jose Ramirez

For over a decade Jose Ramirez has been a fixture on North State Street. A former restaurateur, he set up his hot dog stand in front of Mendo Mill one day and there has been a crowd ever since. Jose has the ability to know exactly what a regular customer will order and always has it ready for them.

Jose always has a smile for everyone, but he will also burst into song on request—belting out popular music in English or Spanish, or an operatic aria. He is also a talented artist and recently had a piece of his artwork in a special showing at the Corner Galley. (Courtesy of Jose Ramirez and the Corner Gallery.)

CHAPTER THREE

Families

Families are the glue that holds a community together. Whether they have been in the area for several generations or only a decade, they are what make a town complete and welcoming. From the founding fathers whose children and grandchildren set down roots in this bucolic valley, to the farmers, loggers, physicians, attorneys, artists, and entertainers who found Ukiah to be the place where they wanted to spend their lives, they have all contributed to making Ukiah a place where the next generation can look around and decided that they have found their utopia.

Among the families that have provided this base for newcomers to build on and raise their families in are the Mayfields, the Cunninghams, the McCowans, and the Mannons. They have, for generation after generation, given back to their community.

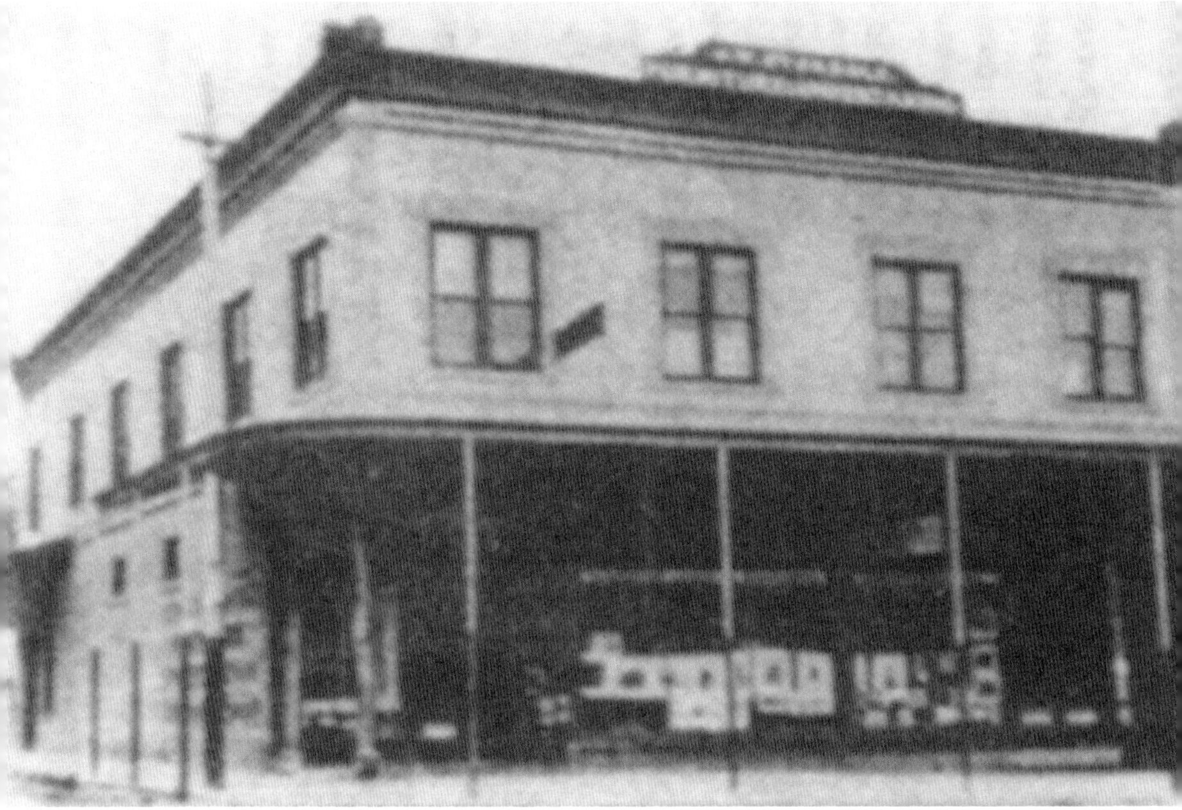

Eversole Family (ABOVE AND OPPOSITE PAGE)
The Eversole family has been in business for five generations and more than 120 years, making their company the oldest family-run mortuary in California. In the late 1800s, John Eversole moved to Ukiah from the Los Angeles area to make furniture and operate a general store. A few years later, a customer came to John and asked if it would be possible for him to build a casket. After that initial request, more and more Ukiah residents came to John Eversole with their mortuary needs, until he eventually started to perform the funerals too. He applied for the proper license and opened the mortuary. The Eversole Furniture Store was opened in 1890, and the first funeral was held there on July 13, 1893.

Eversole's first location was on the corner of West Smith and North State Streets, but the company moved to a larger facility on Low Gap Road in the mid-1960s. Younger generations of the family attended mortuary school and continued with the family business. This helped the Eversoles extend a certain hospitality to the families that come to them—not just as a business, but also as a supportive enterprise that helped mourners through a difficult time. They view their clients not just as customers, but as an extended family. Today, Rick Eversole and his son Edward represent the fourth and fifth generations to operate the mortuary. (Courtesy of Rick Eversole and the Held-Poage Library.)

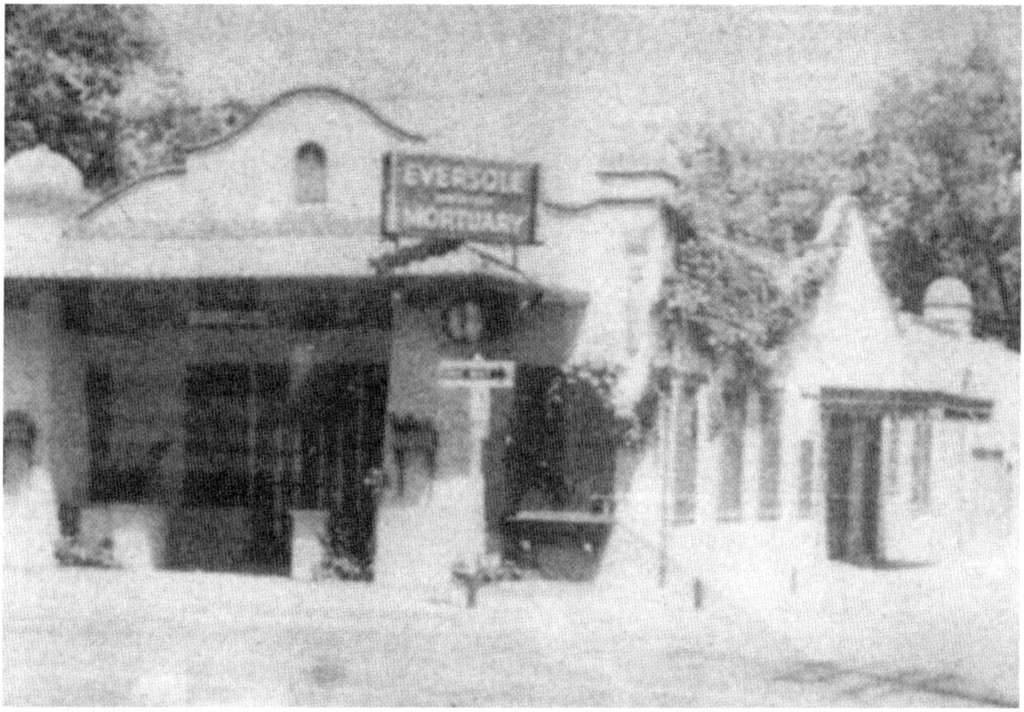
EVERSOLE
MORTUARY

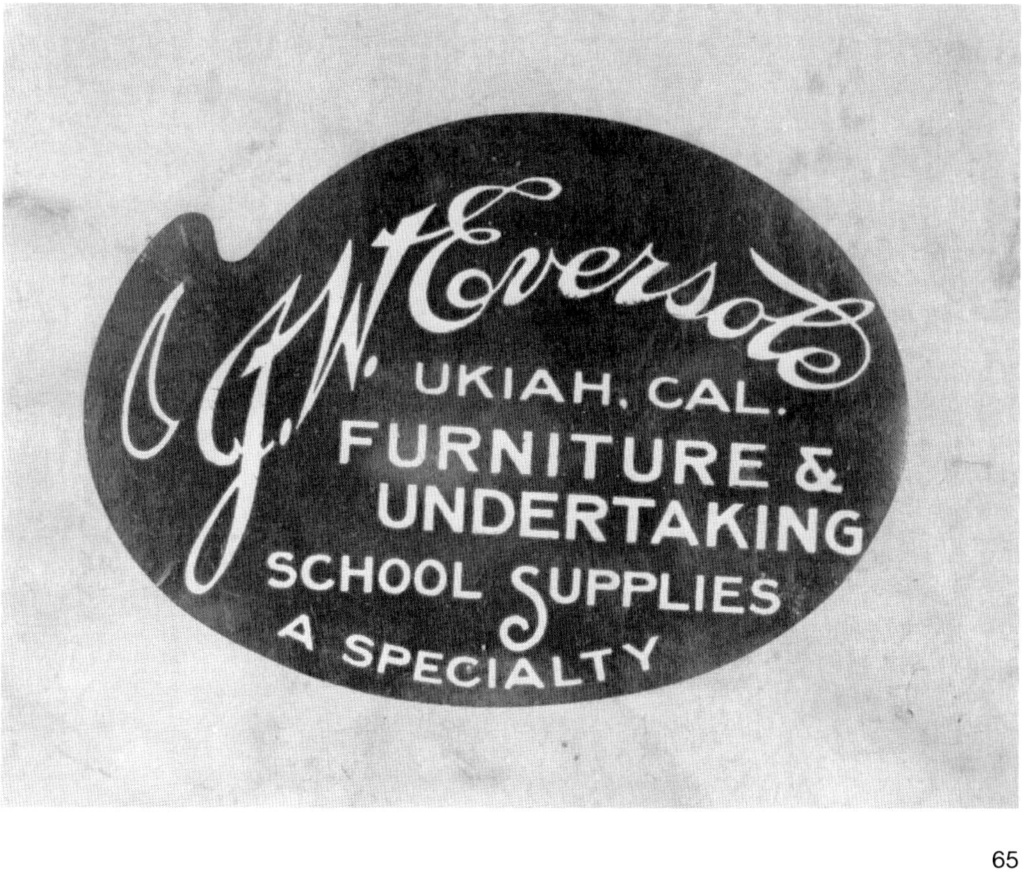
J.W. Eversole
UKIAH, CAL.
FURNITURE &
UNDERTAKING
SCHOOL SUPPLIES
A SPECIALTY

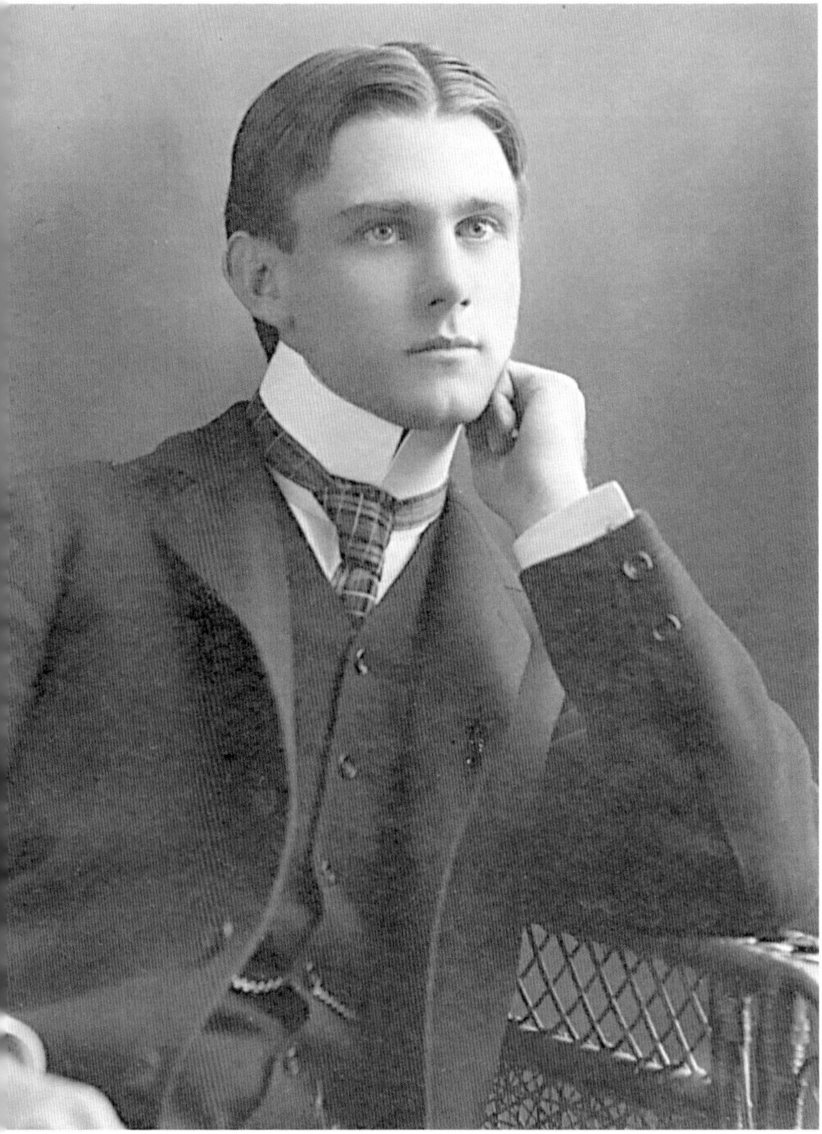

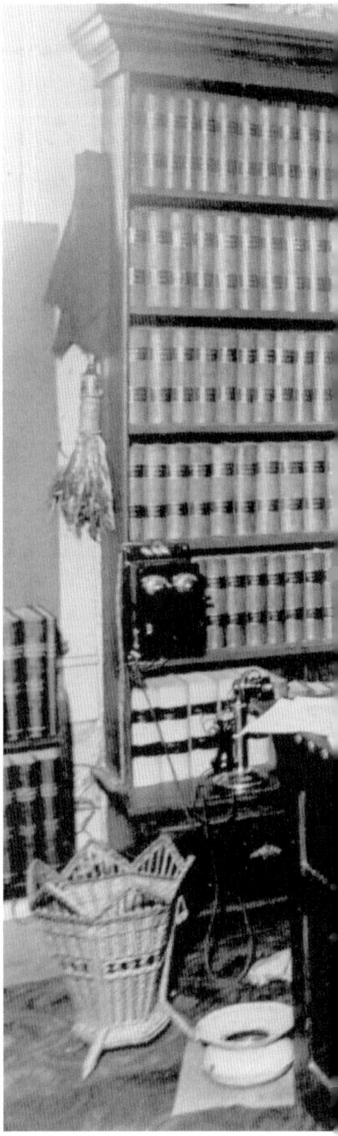

Mannon Family (ABOVE AND OPPOSITE PAGE)
Since Savings Bank of Mendocino County first opened its doors in December 1903, the Mannon family has been a part of its legacy—beginning with A.F. Redemeyer, a private banker, going to Judge J.M. Mannon to obtain a bank charter.

The bank grew by leaps and bounds, and in 1914 Judge Mannon became president of the bank. After he died in 1926, his son Charles M. Mannon—who had previously served as a bank director—was named the new president. He served in the role until 1957, at which point the post passed to people outside of the family until 1976. In 1976, Charles B. Mannon became president and served until 2011. He currently serves as chairman of the board.

Savings Bank has always been heavily involved in Ukiah and Mendocino County. The bank gives back to the community in many ways, from their annual free Fourth of July lunch to their sponsorship of PumpkinFest's Scarecrow City Contest. They also give generously to local nonprofits as financial sponsors. (Courtesy of Held-Poage Library.)

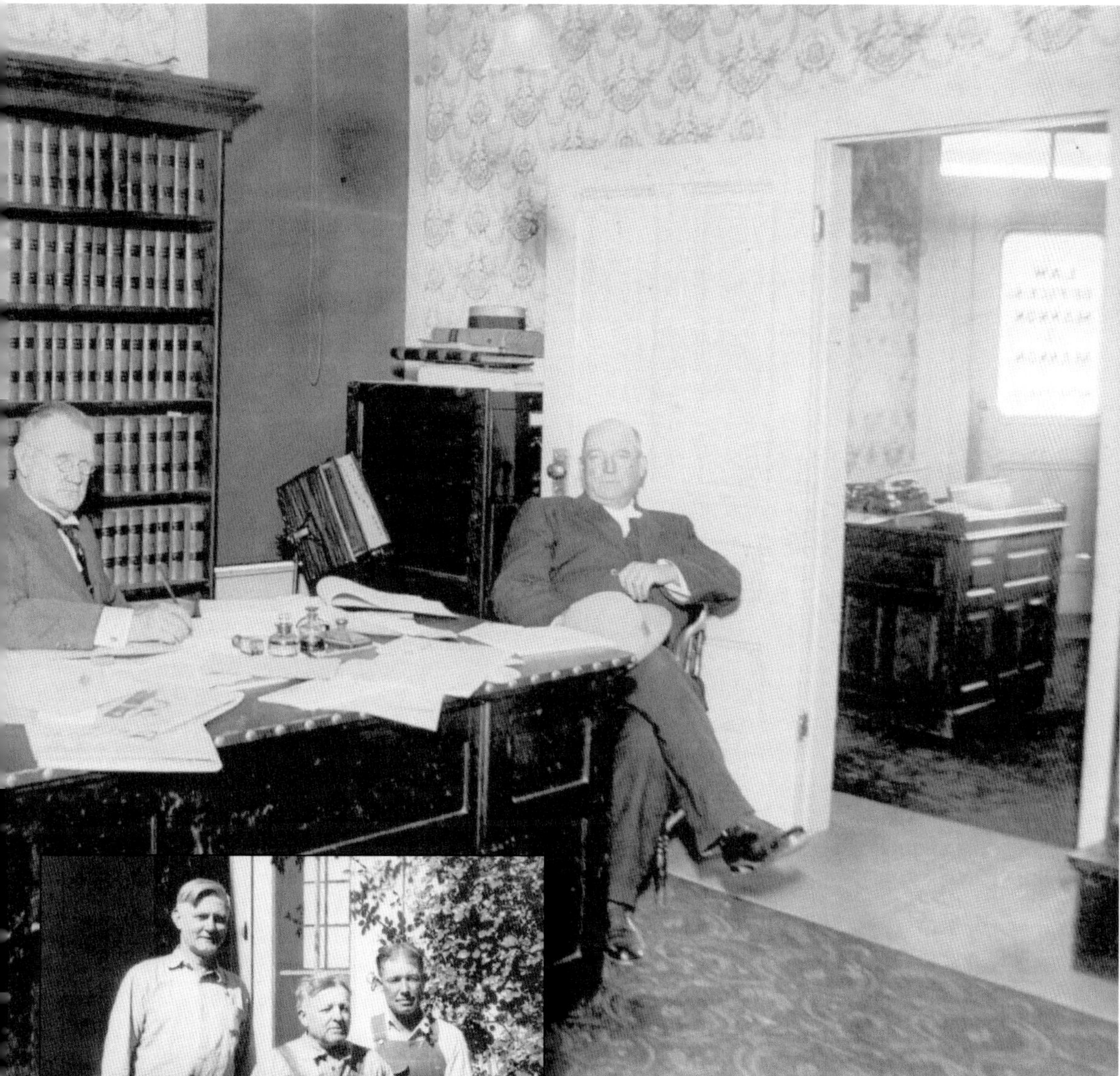

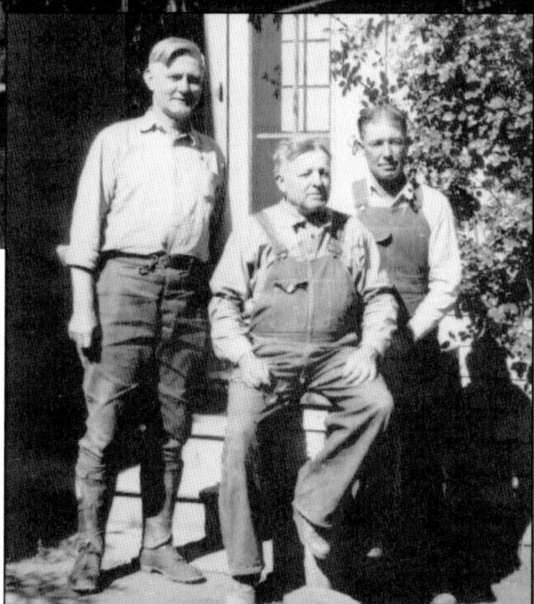

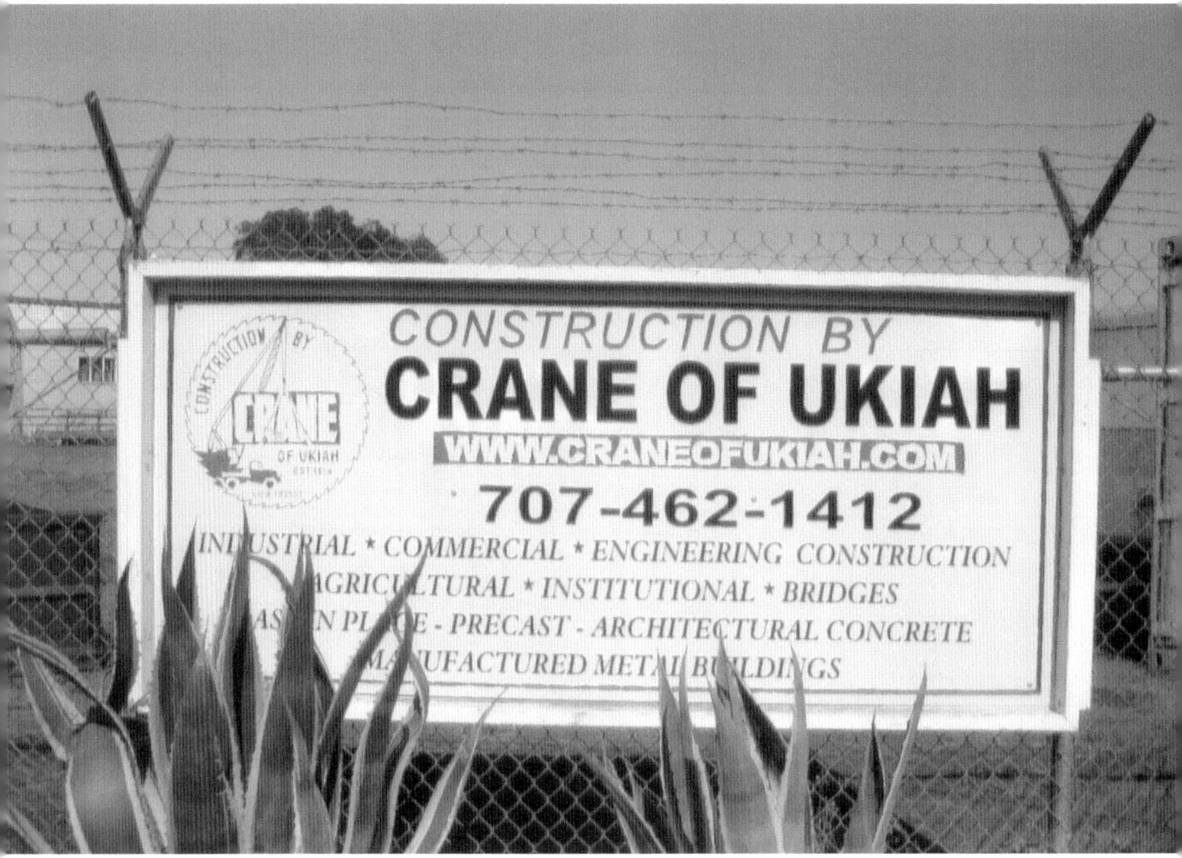

The Crane Family

Anywhere you travel in Mendocino County and Northern California, you will see where the Crane family has left their mark. Not just the builders of the Ukiah Civic Center and countless bridges, banks, homes, theatres, stores, and factories, Crane Construction is also responsible for the erecting of pipelines, sewer treatment facilities, steel buildings, and large industrial buildings. Today, Douglas Crane and his son, Eric, continue to operate the family business.

Not content to only build physical structures, the family is also heavily involved in the Ukiah and Mendocino County community. Doug Crane has served on the city council and was once mayor of Ukiah. This Rotarian has also served the community as the president of the Ukiah Rotary, the Ukiah Airport Commission, and the Mendocino County Government Streamlining Advisory Committee. Heavily influenced by his father, Frank Crane, Doug and his own son are also heavily involved with the Boy Scouts of America—donating funds and hundreds of volunteer hours to that group, and other area nonprofits.

The family also maintains the Frank and Maxine Crane Memorial Fund, which was established to give back to the community in even greater ways. The fund supports programs that teach, train, and assist young people—helping them to develop the skills and expertise that they need to become contributing members of the community. The fund has been divided several ways, so as to support vocational training, the performing arts, and Scouting. (Courtesy of Crane Construction.)

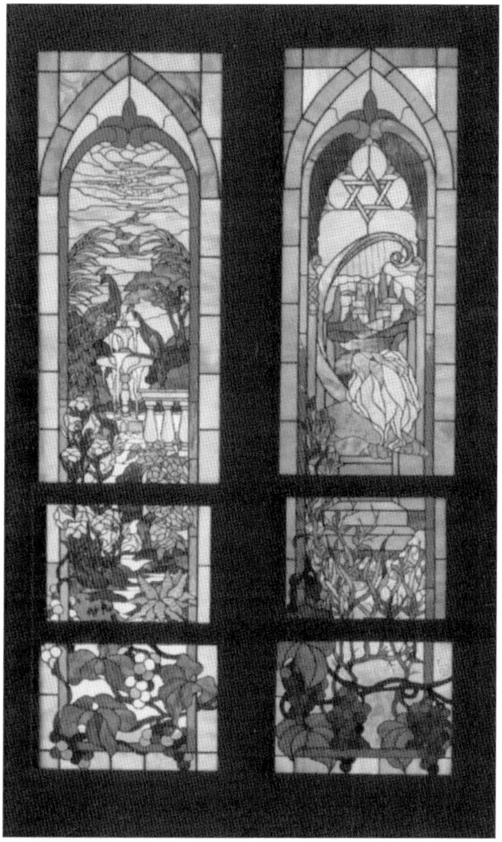

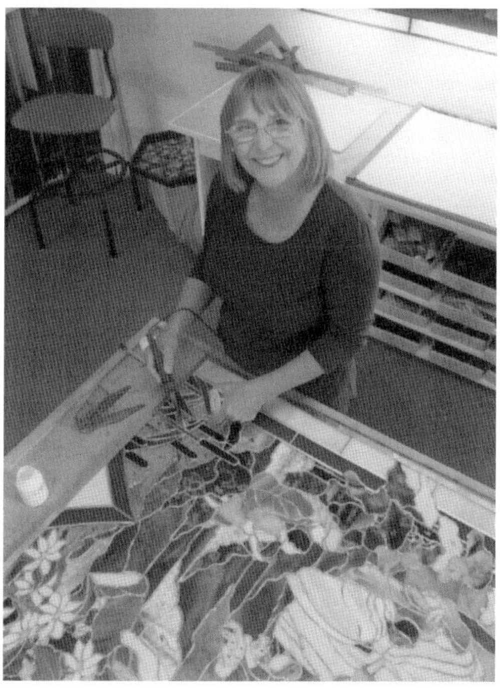

Jeanette Frey Carson

Jeanette Carson has been crafting beautiful stained-glass creations in Ukiah for over 35 years, and many of her windows are featured in local churches. She has been quoted as saying, "The nice thing about stained glass, is that it changes depending upon the hour of the day and the time of the year. The difference in the sunlight makes it even more interesting."

Jeanette enjoys participating in the artistic community and associating with her fellow artists. This led her to help found Corner Gallery Ukiah—an artist cooperative on State Street. She has also begun working in watercolors recently, which allows her to create art that enhances the people's experiences and allows her to express her own feelings.

Creative ability reigns in the Carson clan. Jeanette's son, Adam, is one of the original members of the band AFI, and her husband, Will, recently won first in group in the 2014 Brickyard Vintage Racing Invitational—an event held at the Indianapolis Motor Speedway. This invitational marked the first time that the legendary racetrack has been open to vintage automobiles. (Courtesy of Jeanette Carson, photograph by Ree Slocum.)

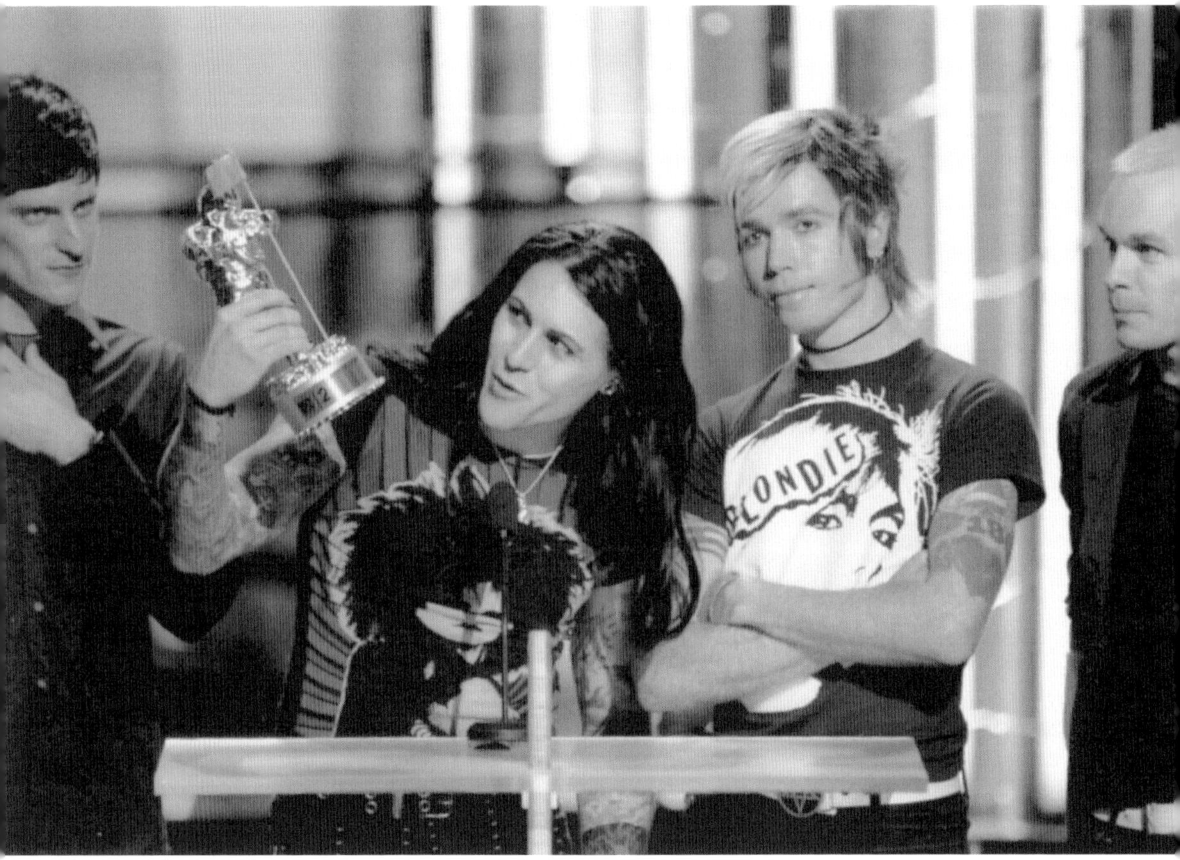

Adam Carson (BELOW AND OPPOSITE PAGE)

Adam Carson loved making music even as a small child, turning his mother's pots and pans into a drum set. Today, Adam is a drummer and backup vocalist with the band AFI (A Fire Inside). The group started out as a rock band in Ukiah in 1991, though Adam and Davey Havok are the only two remaining members of the original lineup. Over the years, he has also periodically played with the groups Tiger Army and Influence 13.

AFI's first full-length album was released in 1995, but they didn't find major commercial success until the release of 2003's *Sing the Sorrow.* The album reached the number five spot on the Billboard charts and remained there for 51weeks—a major accomplishment for a small-town band. In 2006, the band found greater success with *Decemberunderground*, which also hit the Billboard charts and has since been certified platinum. Their follow-up album, *Crash Love*, sold 52,000 copies in its first week of release.

Adam and the band have appeared on Saturday Night Live, and the group has provided background music for several films over the years. Regardless of their success however, Adam and his fellow band members have traveled all over the world doing what they love: making music. (Courtesy of Jeanette Carson.)

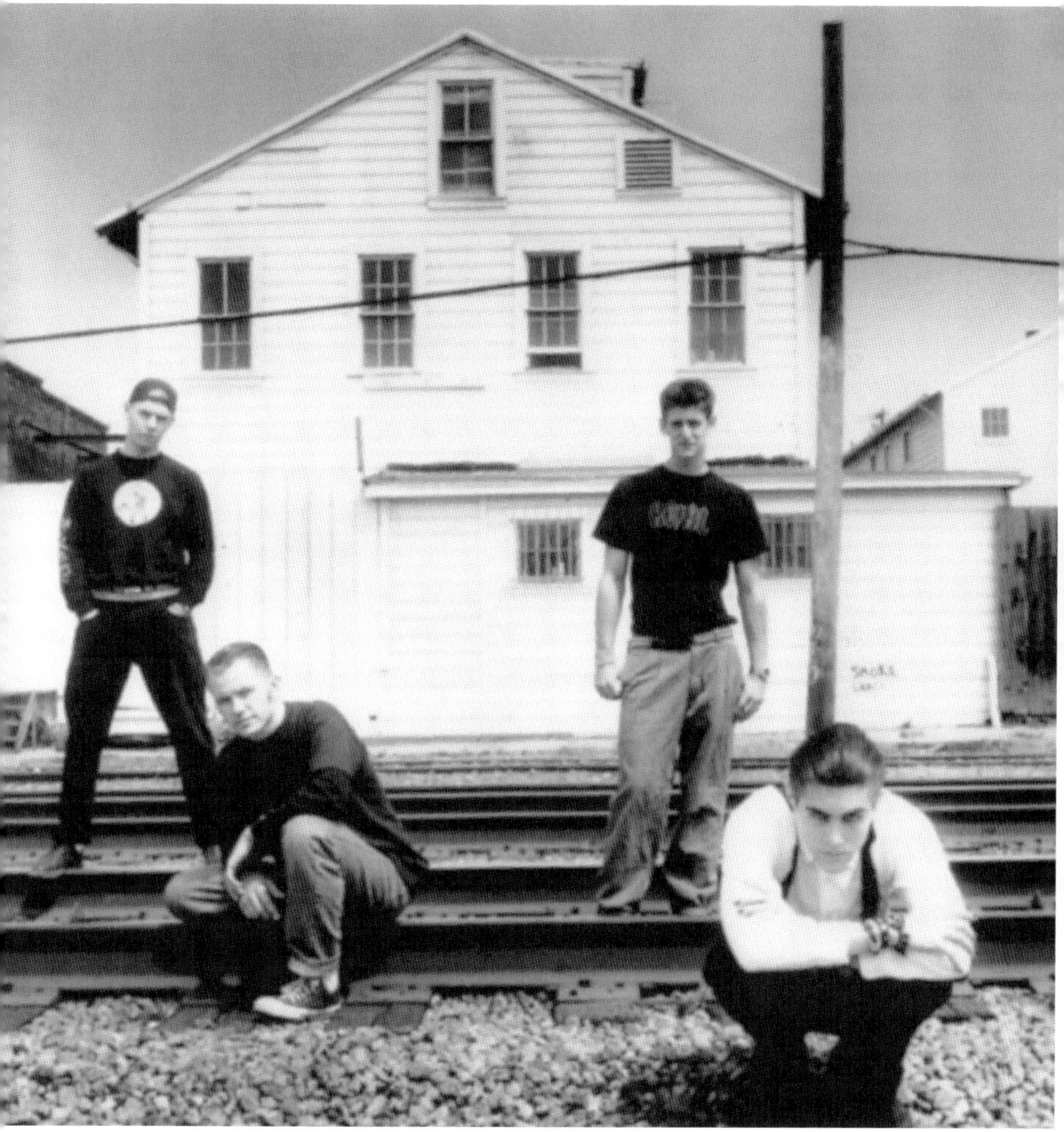

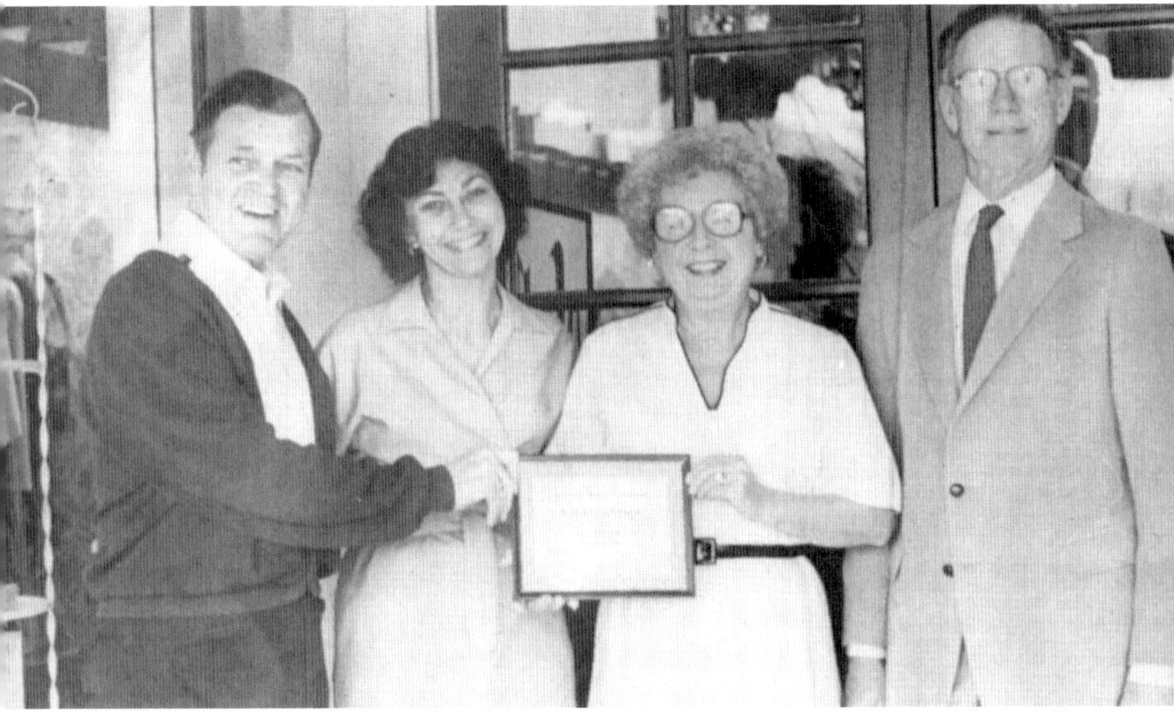

The Hansen Family (ABOVE AND OPPOSITE PAGE)
Paul and Dorathy Hansen opened the Palace Dress Shop, at the corner of North State and West Perkins Streets, in 1963 and operated it until 1998. For that span, it was the place to be for any Ukiah ladies in need of something special for a wedding, party, or other dressy occasion. It was also a frequent stop for any men who needed a tuxedo for prom or a wedding party. When the store closed, Ukiah lost its one and only upscale shop for women. (Courtesy of Rick Hansen.)

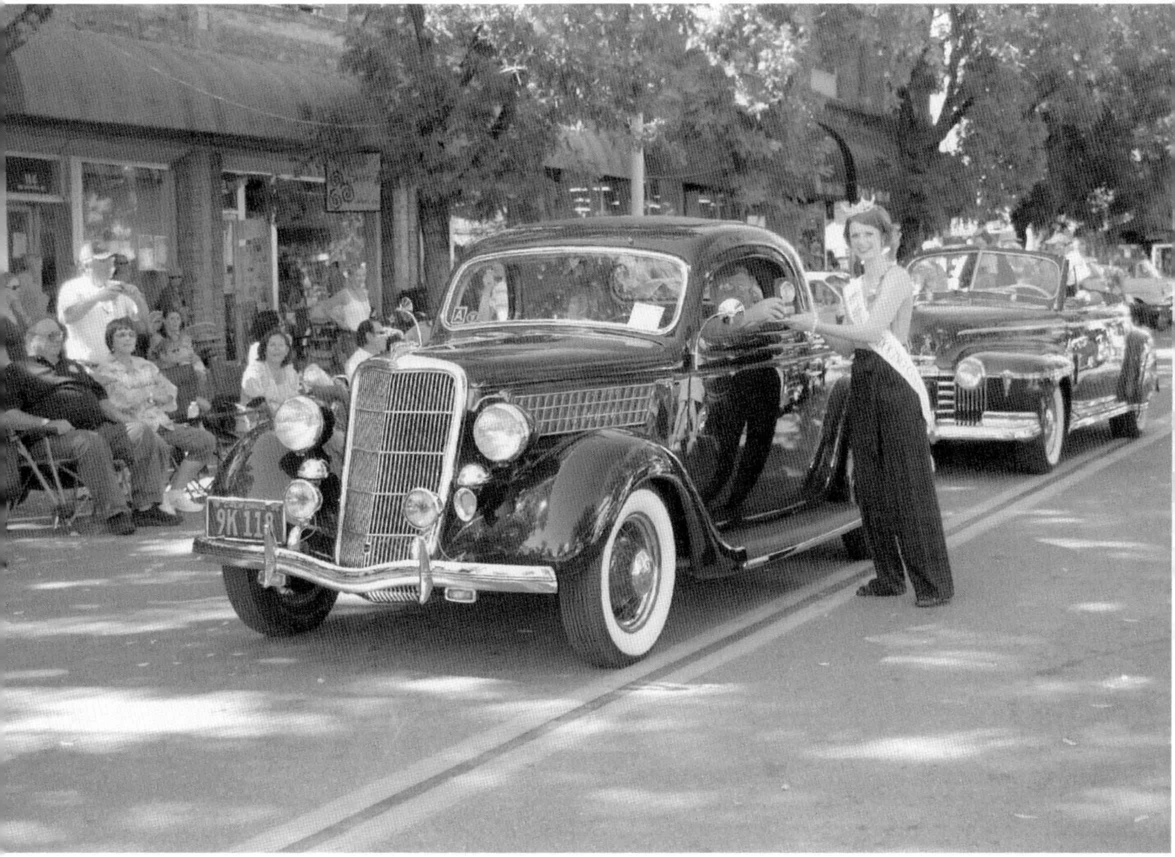
9K 118

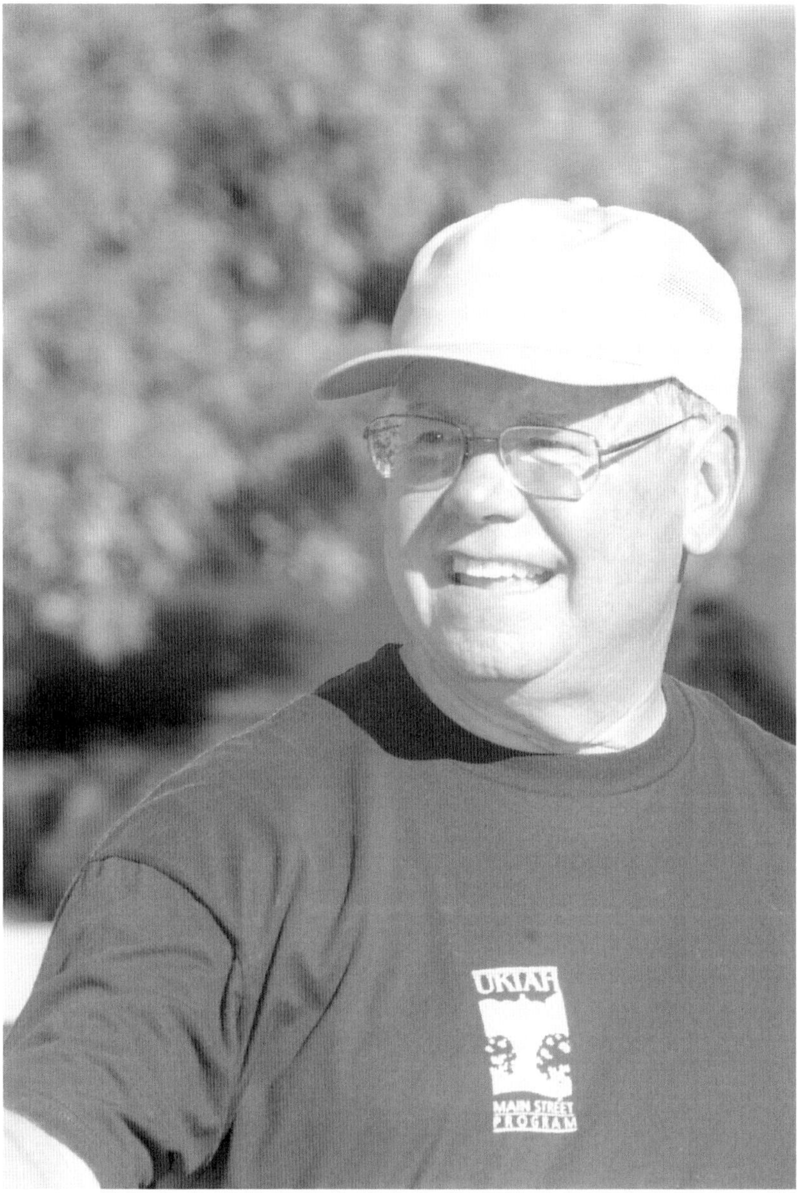

Rick Hansen

Paul and Dorathy's son Rick served as president of the Downtown Merchants Association for many years—in which time he was instrumental in starting the Fabulous Flashback Car Show. This three-day event has now been held each fall for more than two decades and features classic cars from throughout Northern and Central California, Oregon, Nevada and points beyond. Festivities include the Friday Night Bash Parking Lot Dance & Cruise-In, the Saturday Show-N-Shine Car Show, and Sunday's Poker Run.

In addition to Rick's involvement with the Downtown Merchants Association, he served on the board of directors of the Ukiah Main Street Program in a variety of capacities, including board president. In 2010, Rick was hired as the executive director of the Ukiah Main Street Program—the organization that hosts many of the community's events. The Ukiah Main Street Program's mission is the historic preservation and economic enhancement of the Downtown Business District. (Courtesy of Rick Hansen.)

CHAPTER FOUR

Artists, Musicians, and Entertainers

Ukiah is fortunate to be home to a plethora of artistic talent. Musicians, authors, and fine artists all have a place here—and their fair share of avid supporters. While other areas can have difficulty filling the house for performances, Ukiah's musicians and performers regularly play to sold-out crowds.

This small town is home to Grammy winners and nominees, musicians who have worked with Lucasfilm, and entertainers who are known on both a national and international scale. It is a place that hosts the Sundays in the Park free summer concert series, which draws some of the best known bands in the country. One of our high school bands has played at the Super Bowl and an Olympic opening ceremony, and has earned the title of best band in California for seven years in a row. We are also home to a well-known chanteuse who has twice been invited to perform at a special concert in Rome that features female singers from around the world.

The town also boasts a young man making movies in Hollywood, a SPACE graduate who is in New York performing on Broadway, a chef who has participated on television shows, and an artist who is painting and teaching at the age of 92.

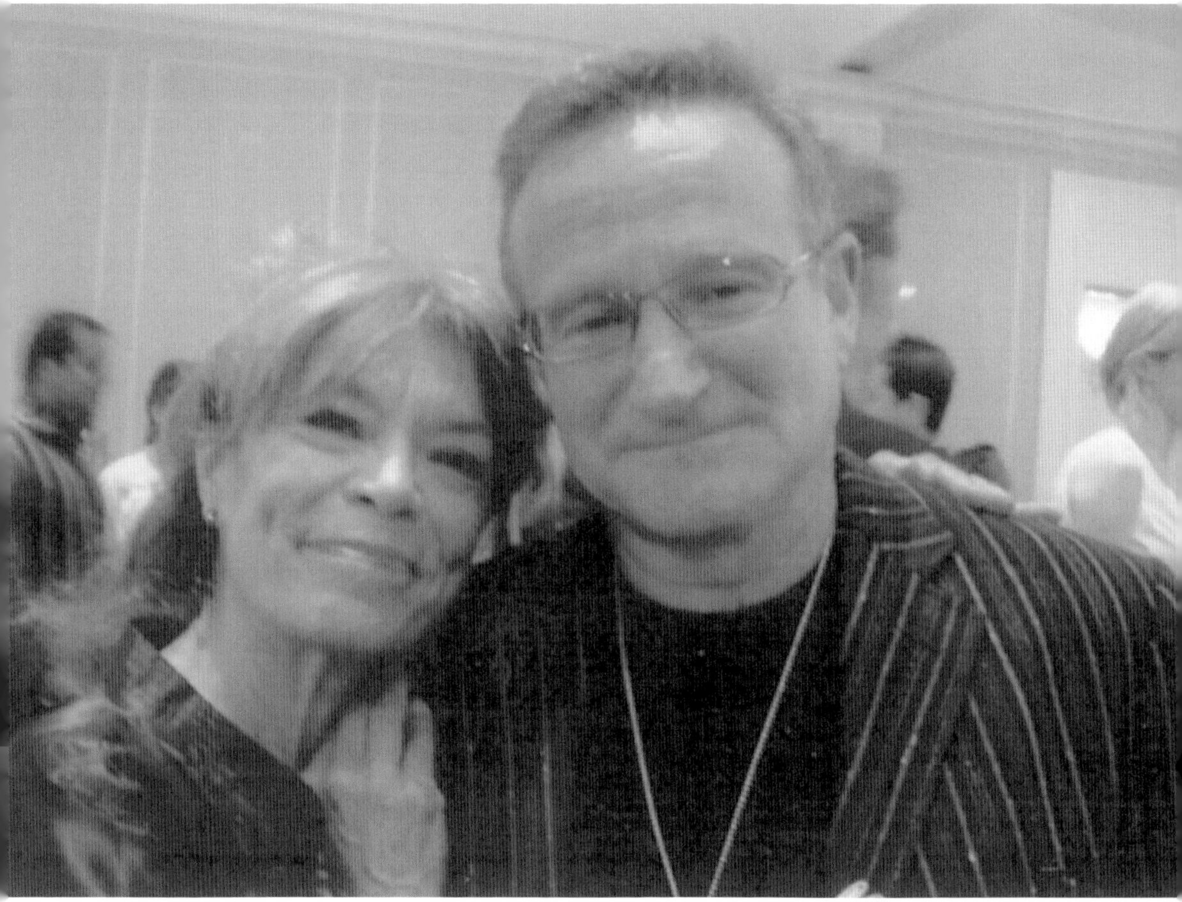

Paula Samonte

Paula Samonte is Ukiah's resident chanteuse. Whether she's singing smooth jazz or a Broadway showtune, it doesn't get any better than listening to Paula's sophisticated style. Be it in a small venue or a large concert hall, she has a stage presence that makes every member of the audience think that she's singing to them alone.

Paula's introduction to the arts took place at the age of six, when she started taking classical ballet. Within two years, she won a scholarship to Ballet Celeste in San Francisco, which toured California in productions of *Swan Lake*, *Giselle*, and *The Nutcracker.* Over the years, she has performed in a variety of settings, including at New York super clubs, Mondavi Summer Concerts, and with the Ukiah Symphony Orchestra. Paula has also appeared on television, both here in California and in New York.

Paula was involved with the National Academy of Recording Arts and Science during her time working as national promotions director for Grammy winner Paul Winter and the Narada record label. During that time, she received her second invitation to appear in Donne Musica in Rome—a special concert featuring women in music. Another of her appearances was at a benefit concert for Christopher Reeve, where she took the above photograph with Robin Williams.

Samonte is a founding member of the Ukiah Civic Light Opera and has received their prestigious Lifetime Achievement Award for her commitment and dedication to the community, due to her talent and creative efforts. (Courtesy of Paula Samonte.)

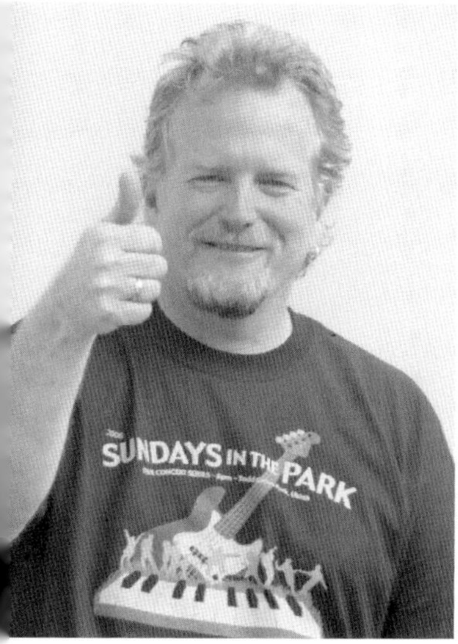

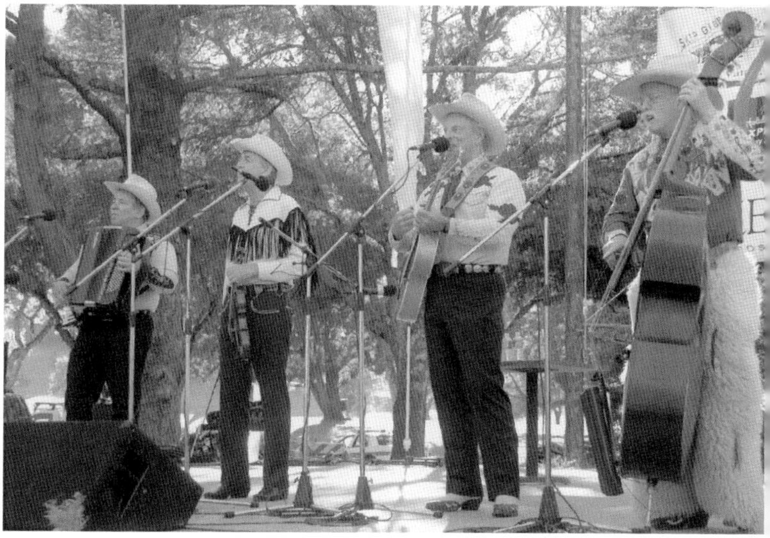

Spencer Brewer

If you hear great music in Ukiah, you can be sure Spencer Brewer is somewhere around. This composer, pianist, and performer has been involved in appearances all over the valley. He has Grammy nominations to his name and over 17 solo and duet albums to his credit, including a pair of number one hit records. His music has been featured in film and television and has been used as the theme for the Olympic Games. He's has also worked with George Lucas at Skywalker Sound. Spencer's music truly has been heard around the world.

In 1995, Spencer started Laughing Coyote Productions, a recording studio dedicated to recording for the acoustic market. Since then, he has produced over 200 recordings at the studio. He is one of the founding members of the Ukiah Educational Foundation—a group dedicated to supplying public schools and students with grants, funds, and scholarships—and a group of local pianists who perform at the Professional Pianists Concert every year, raising funds for scholarships. Spencer also started a rock camp for teens and young adults, allowing them to spend the summer making music, learning more about their craft, and advancing as artists.

Spencer opened the Ukiah Music Center in 2002 and won the Mendocino County Arts Business Champion Award in 2008. He has also created events like Acoustic Cafe, Guitars for Grades, Music for Youth Program, BandSlam, and the Treblemakers Event Center. Spencer believes in giving back to his community and, over the years, has donated dozens of private concerts for local nonprofit agencies. (Above, photograph by Roger Franklin, courtesy of Spencer Brewer; below, photograph by Spencer Brewer.)

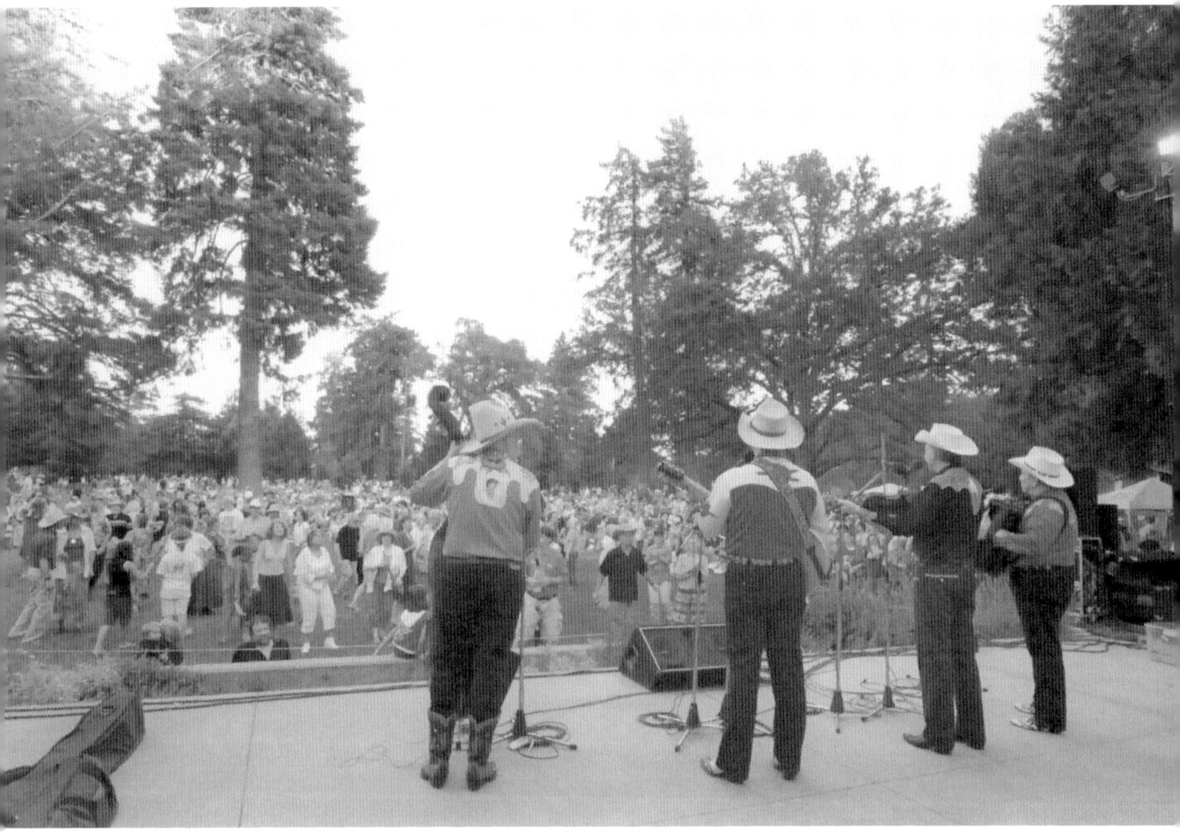

Sundays in the Park

Spencer Brewer is responsible for the creation of Sundays in the Park—a series of six free summer concerts that are attended by thousands of people. This top-notch entertainment has run for more than two decades, and Maria Muldare and The Red Hot Chili Peppers are among the amazing roster of artists that have performed there over the years. (Courtesy of Spencer Brewer.)

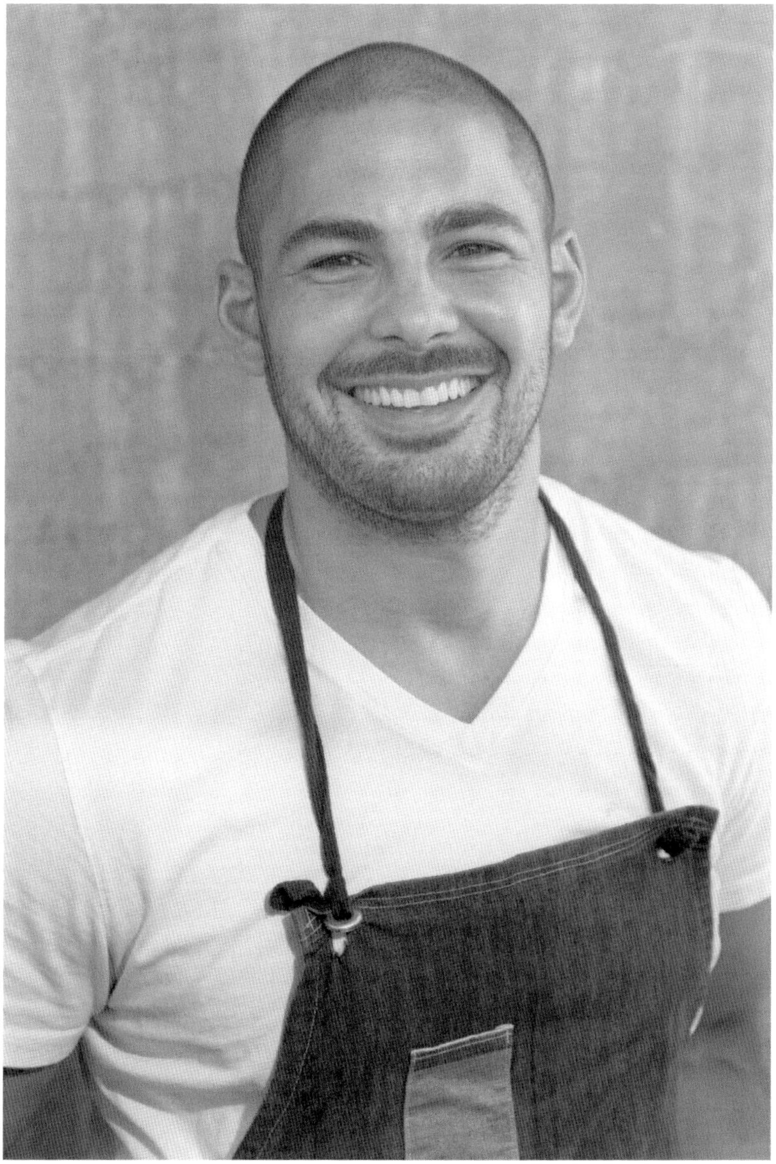

Louis Maldonado
Louis, a Ukiah High School graduate, decided at the age of 20 that he was interested in a career in the food industry. That led him to attend the California Culinary Academy in San Francisco. After receiving his training, he went on to work in several restaurants before ending up at the world famous French Laundry in Yountville, California. Louis was then offered a position in an upscale restaurant in Healdsburg. Not long after moving with his family to Healdsburg, he was approached by Bravo to appear on a season of *Top Chef.*

He agreed to join the show, which resulted in his spending several months filming in New Orleans. He went on to participate in Last Chance Kitchen and emerged with a dish that cohost Tom Colicchio said was the best he had eaten that season—quite a feat for a chef from a small town in Northern California. Louis currently runs two restaurants in Healdsburg: Pizzando and Spoonbar. (Courtesy of the Maldonado family.)

Quinn Van Antwerp

Ukiah's own Quinn Van Antwerp started his stage career in high school, doing backup singing for his aunt, Holly Near. During his time at the University of California, Irvine, he got his membership card with Actors' Equity Association and was booked at the Hollywood Bowl in *South Pacific*. There, he got to work with the likes of Brian Stokes and Reba McEntire.

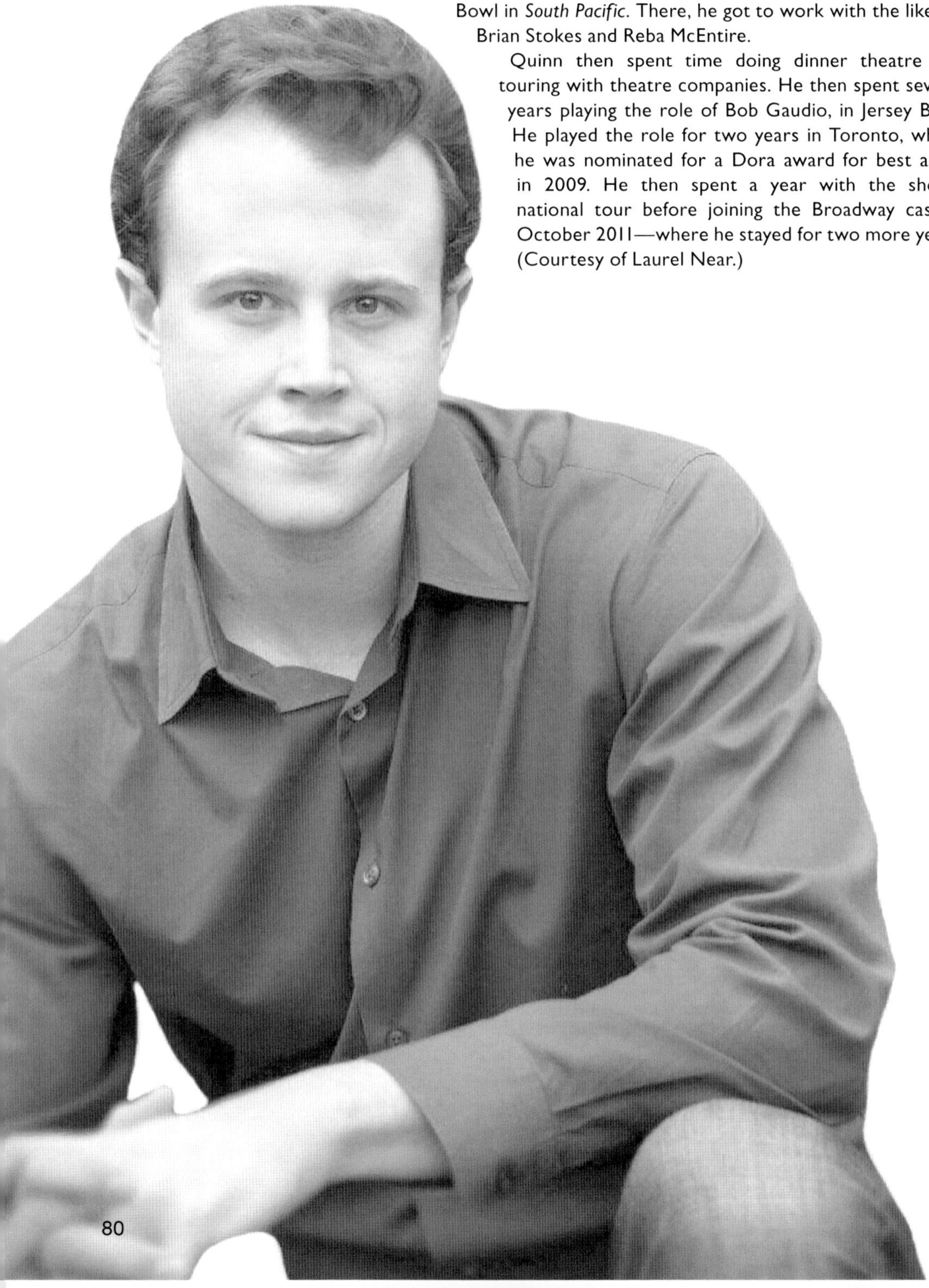

Quinn then spent time doing dinner theatre and touring with theatre companies. He then spent several years playing the role of Bob Gaudio, in Jersey Boys. He played the role for two years in Toronto, where he was nominated for a Dora award for best actor in 2009. He then spent a year with the show's national tour before joining the Broadway cast in October 2011—where he stayed for two more years. (Courtesy of Laurel Near.)

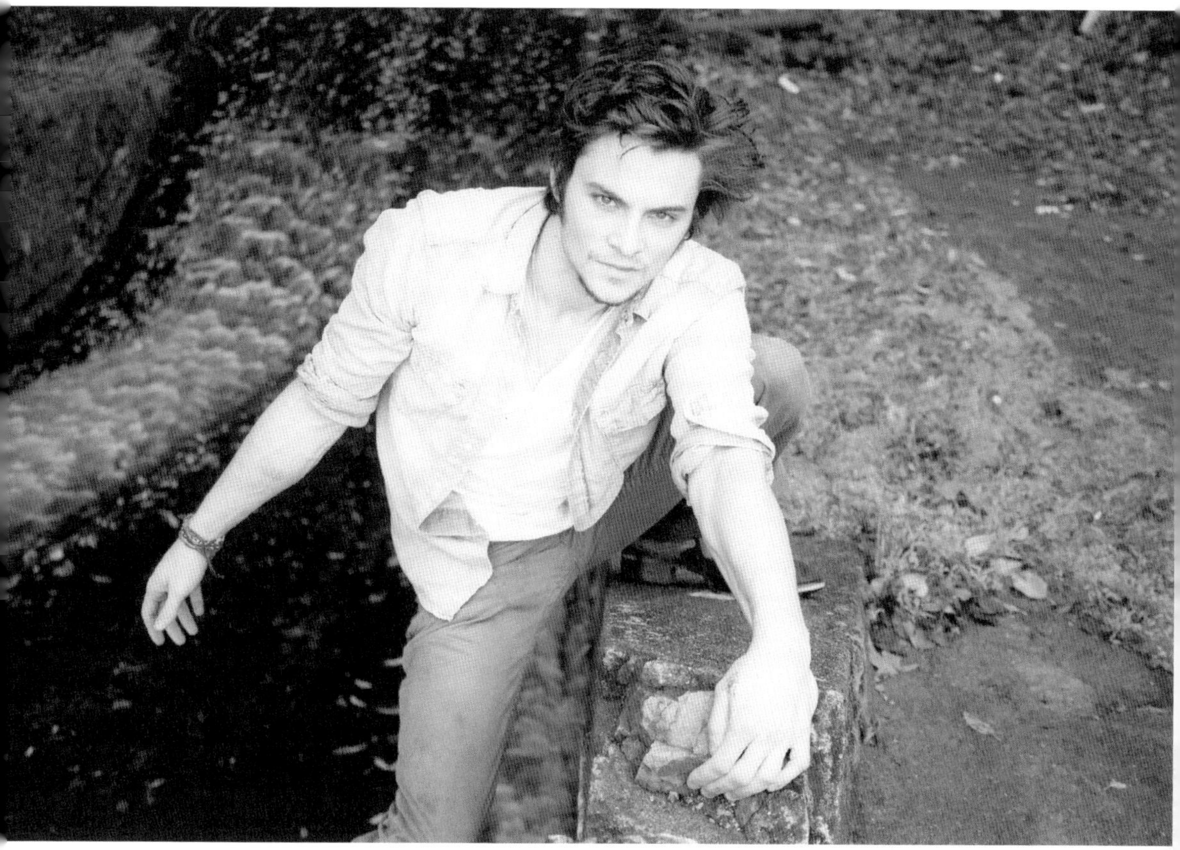

Shiloh Fernandez
Before making it to television and the silver screen, Shiloh Fernandez went from working as a dishwasher to working in the stock room of American Apparel. He was picked to be a catalog model and went on to be featured in an ad that was shown in New York City. He made his television debut in 2006, in an episode of *Cold Case*. He appearances took him to his big screen debut, when he landed the role of Edgar in *Interstate*. Most recently, he appeared as Phil in the film *White Bird in a Blizzard*.

Shiloh is quiet and down to earth—not the typical young television and movie actor. On his last visit home, he took time to meet with students who are studying acting. His ultimate goal is to try his hand at writing. (Courtesy of Sam Fernandez, photograph by Tyler Shields.)

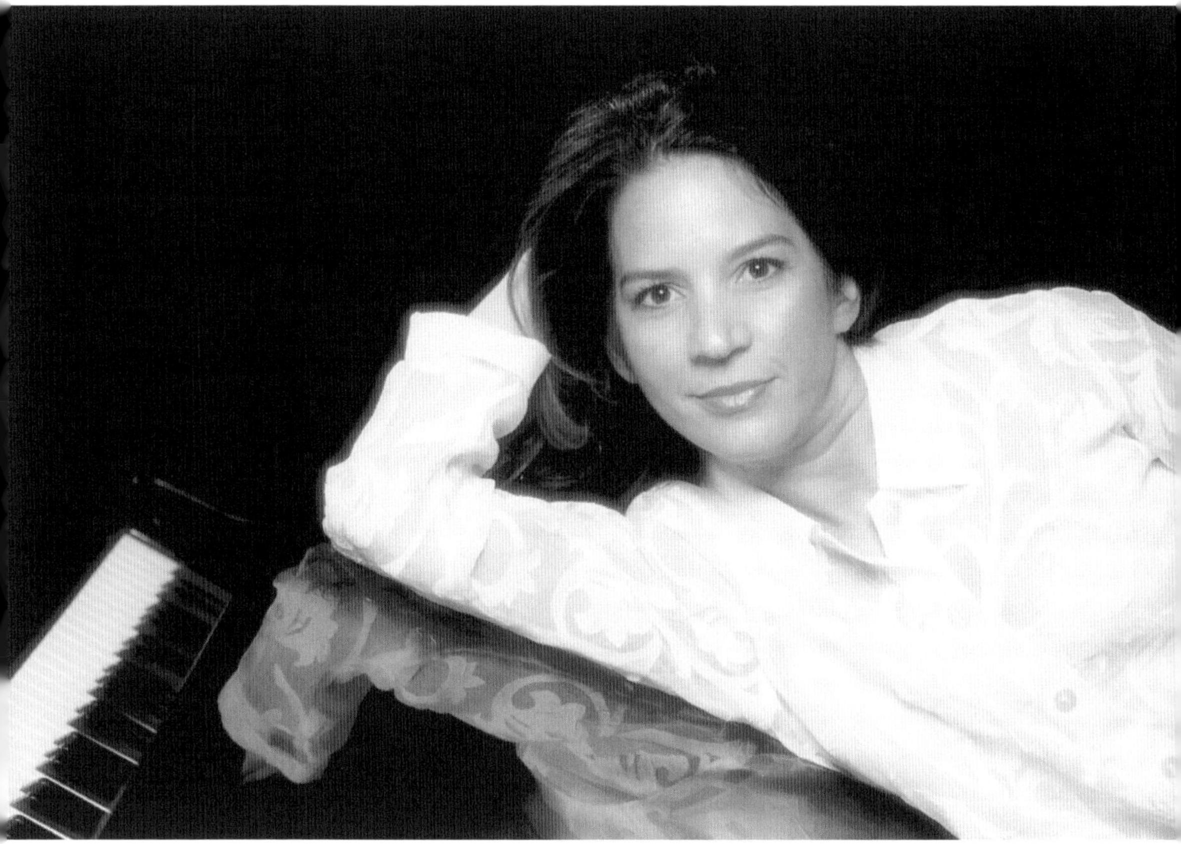

Elena Casanova

A Cuban native, Elena Casanova was born to be a pianist. She started piano lessons at a young age and, within three years, she was selected to enter the Music Conservatory in Havana. By the time she was 13, Elena had already performed major works by important composers including Bach, Beethoven, and Shubert. After she and her parents moved to the United States, she enrolled in the San Francisco Conservatory.

Her love of her native country's music has led Elena to record several albums, including, *Fuente Sin Igual*, which was a gift to her father. Recently she composed the music for *Still Life*, a short film that was accepted into the Cannes Short Film Festival. Elena has performed solo and with the Ukiah Symphony, live at the Acoustic Cafe and at sold out performances of the Professional Pianist Concert. The Professional Pianist Concert, of which Elena is an original member, raises funds to benefit the Ukiah Educational Foundation and the Allegro Scholarship Program.

Elena is very active in the community. She is president of the board of the Community Concert Association and donates her time to the school program and several other nonprofit groups can count on Elena to help them. She also teaches to better pass on her love of her native Cuban music. (Courtesy of Elena Casanova.)

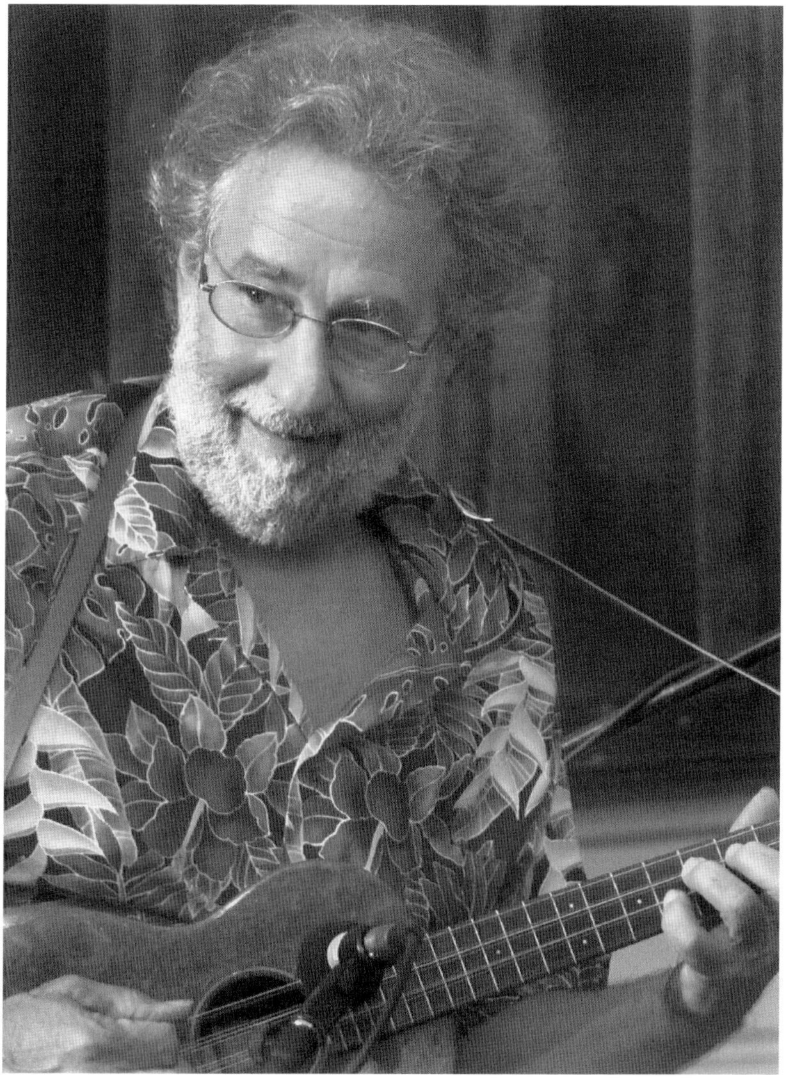

Will Siegel

Master guitarist and a founding member of Willy & the Nighthawks, Will Siegel came to Ukiah in the mid-1970s and has been playing and teaching in the area ever since. He and his wife, Ellie, started out playing folk, bluegrass, and Western swing for audiences in Ukiah and Mendocino County, but that's far from all that they do.

No one can bring musicians and an audience together like Will Siegel. In the 1990s, you could always find him playing at the Hopland Brewery. In 1995, the band recorded an album of original material, titled *The Nighthawk Strikes*. In 2004, Will joined with Ukiah Players Theatre to direct, act in, and play music for their production of *Woody Guthrie's American Song*. In 2007, he recorded a soundtrack CD for the documentary film *Fearless Mountain*, which focuses on the Abhayagi ri Buddhist Monastery in Redwood Valley. He has also spent the past 10 years teaching guitar at Mendocino College.

Will and his friends have played at Ukiah Players Theatre, the Mendocino Botanical Gardens, and the Acoustic Cafe. It has been said that, "Will Siegel and Friends is the only band accomplished enough to play jazz for Sunday Brunch and rhythm and blues for a full dance floor on Blue Monday." (Courtesy of Will Siegel.)

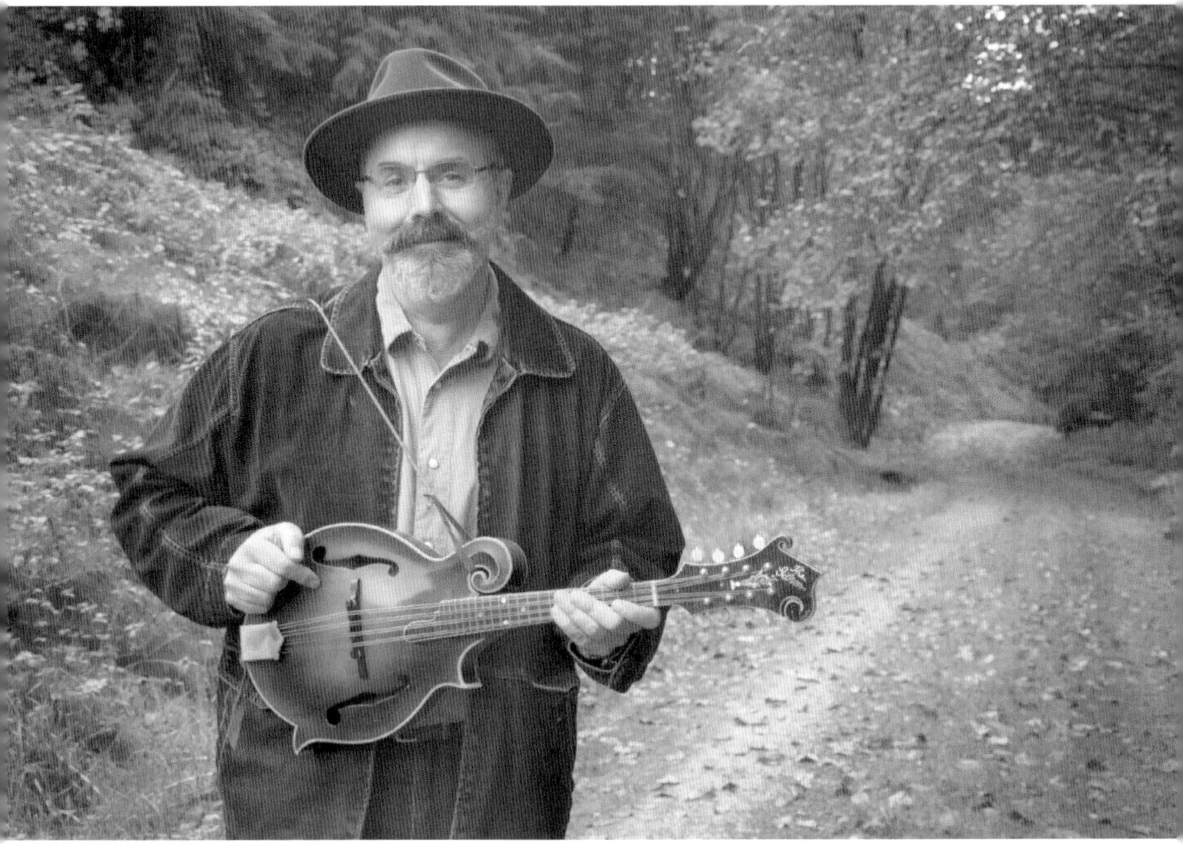

John Reischman (ABOVE AND OPPOSITE PAGE)
A native son who made it big in the world of bluegrass music, John started playing guitar at the age of 12 and, by the age of 17, had discovered the mandolin. As an adult, John spent more than two decades performing in the San Francisco Bay Area, where he was an original member of the Tony Rice Unit. His reputation as an outstanding musician was only enhanced by touring and recording with the Good Ol' Persons. He then moved to Vancouver in the early 1990s to begin a solo career.

Today, John is one of the acoustic world's top-ranked mandolin players and composers. His expertise has led him to be nominated for awards by the Canadian Folk Music Organization, as well as nominations for the Juno Award—the Canadian equivalent to the Grammy. *Acoustic Musician* magazine described him as "One of the most tasteful and accomplished mandolinists anywhere," while the *Vancouver Sun* once lauded him as "The Bluegrass master. Reischman's lightning-fast hands were a miracle to behold." (Courtesy of John Reischman.)

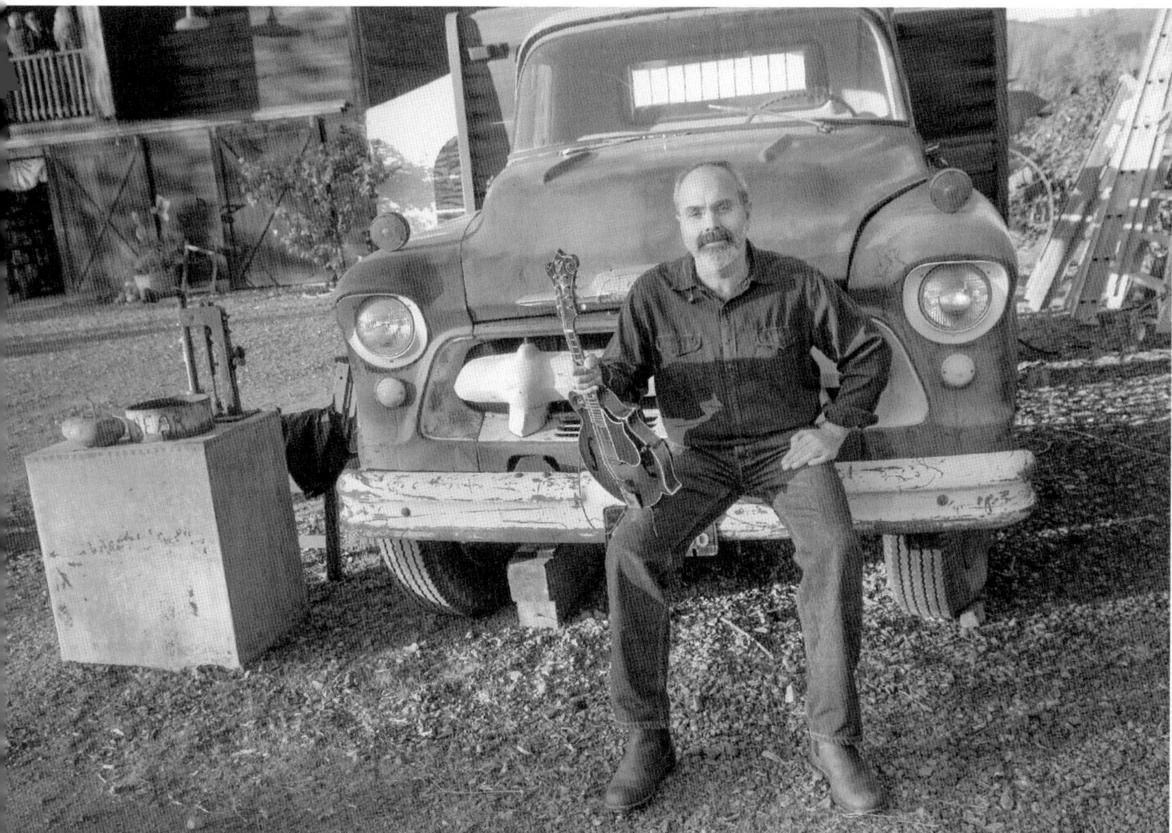

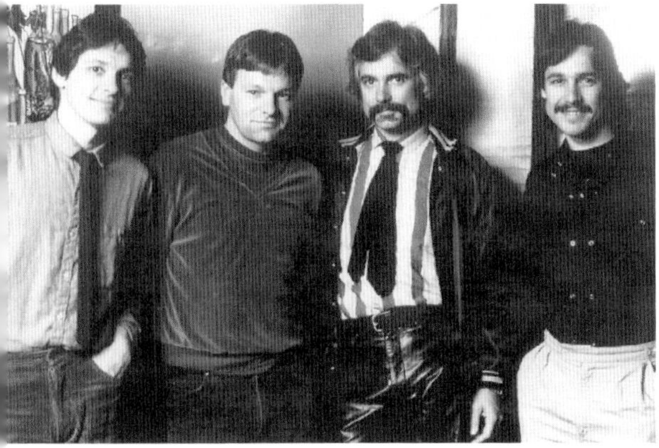

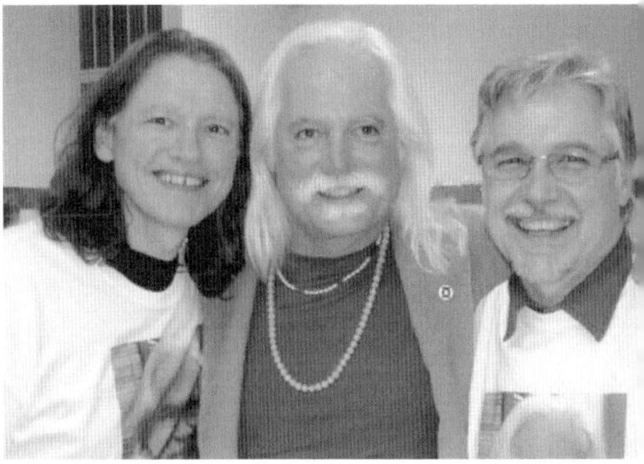

Ford Blues Band

Patrick, Mark, and Robben Ford were raised in a musical family. Both parents played piano, and their father played the guitar. Patrick was the first to begin playing in a band, when he and some friends started a surf band in eighth grade, but Robben soon picked up the guitar. By the time Patrick was a senior in high school, the brothers were in a band together.

In the mid-1960s, Patrick and Robben began exploring the blues and it changed their lives forever. Mark, upon hearing Paul Butterfield's harmonica playing went to the local music store to buy a harp of his own—effectively kick-starting his career in music. In the early 1970s, all three brothers had assembled into The Charles Ford Band, which was named after their father. Although this blues act lasted only a year, it has a cult following to this day and their 1972 recording still sells. Robben has gone on to an exceptional career, making his own Grammy-nominated recordings and touring or recording with artists like Miles Davis, Joni Mitchell, George Harrison, Jimmy Witherspoon, and more.

Patrick stayed firmly rooted in the blues, touring and recording with artists like Charles Musselwhite, Brownie McGhee, and Lowell Fulson. He formed the Ford Blues Band in 1988, and they continue to tour around the world. Mark has limited his time in the music business but has two solo releases—which have been best sellers—and has toured Europe with both his own band and the Ford Blues Band. (Courtesy of Patrick Ford.)

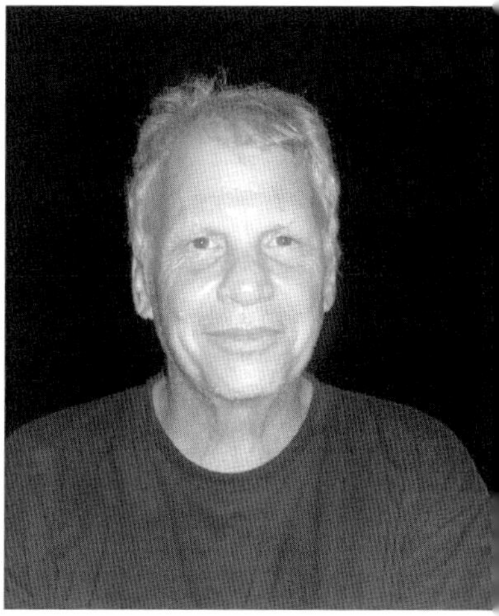

Barry Melton

Our very own, Barry "The Fish" Melton is the guitarist for Country Joe and the Fish. For a time, the Berkeley-based group was known for its opposition to the war in Vietnam. In their day, Barry and County Joe played alongside Jimi Hendrix, Jefferson Airplane, and the Grateful Dead.

A fan of Clarence Darrow, Barry knew he wanted to be an attorney someday. When he was on tour, he would spend his offstage hours poring over law books. While he never officially went to law school, Barry passed the bar exam, got his bar card, and eventually came to Mendocino County to take the position of chief public defender.

While working for the county, Barry organized accredited continuing education classes for the other attorneys in the office. Terence Hallinan, once the San Francisco district attorney, said of Barry, "He's the kind of person interested in causes, he's a sweetheart of a guy, always there to help the underdog." (Courtesy of Barry Melton.)

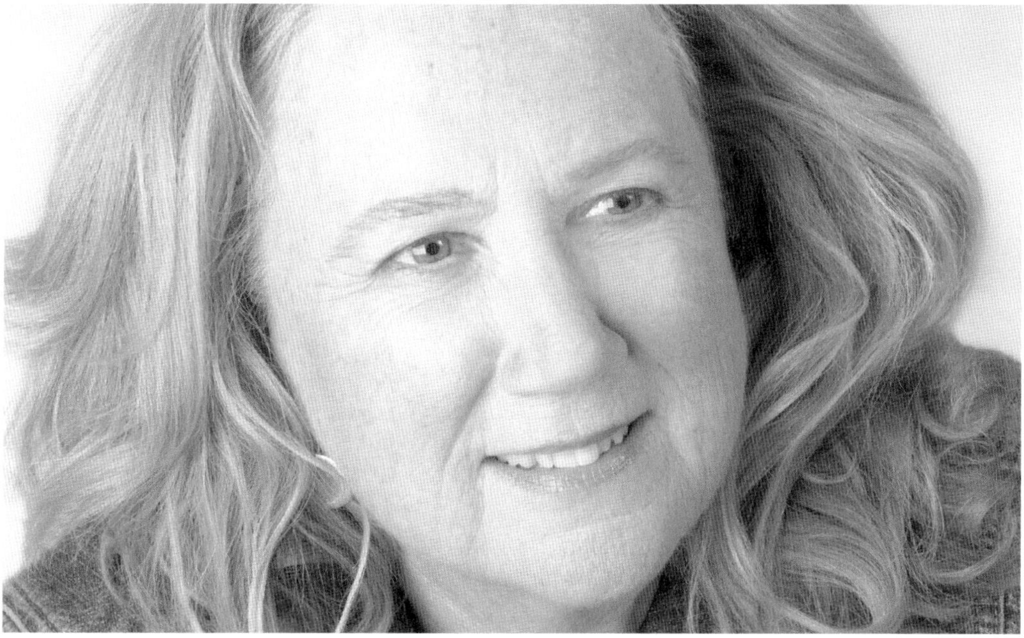

Holly Near

This Ukiah native has done it all . . . and still is going strong. Holly began performing in high school before moving on to television acting—appearing in *The Mod Squad* and *The Partridge Family*—and eventually acting and singing in the hit Broadway musical *Hair*.

In the early 1970s, Holly decided that she wanted to dedicate her life to writing music, singing, and teaching. In 1972, she started Redwood Records, which was one of the first woman- and artist-run recording labels. Along the way, she has sung with Arlo Guthrie, Pete Seeger, Bonnie Raitt, Harry Belefonte, Jackson Browne, and others. She has been an activist as well, joining an anti-Vietnam road show that featured the likes of Jane Fonda and Donald Sutherland.

Holly has received honors from the ACLU, the National Lawyers Guild, the National Organization for Woman, and the National Academy of Recording Arts and Sciences. *Ms.* magazine named her Woman of the Year in 1985, and in 2005 she was voted one of the 1,000 women who should be considered for a Nobel Peace Prize. (Courtesy of Holly Near.)

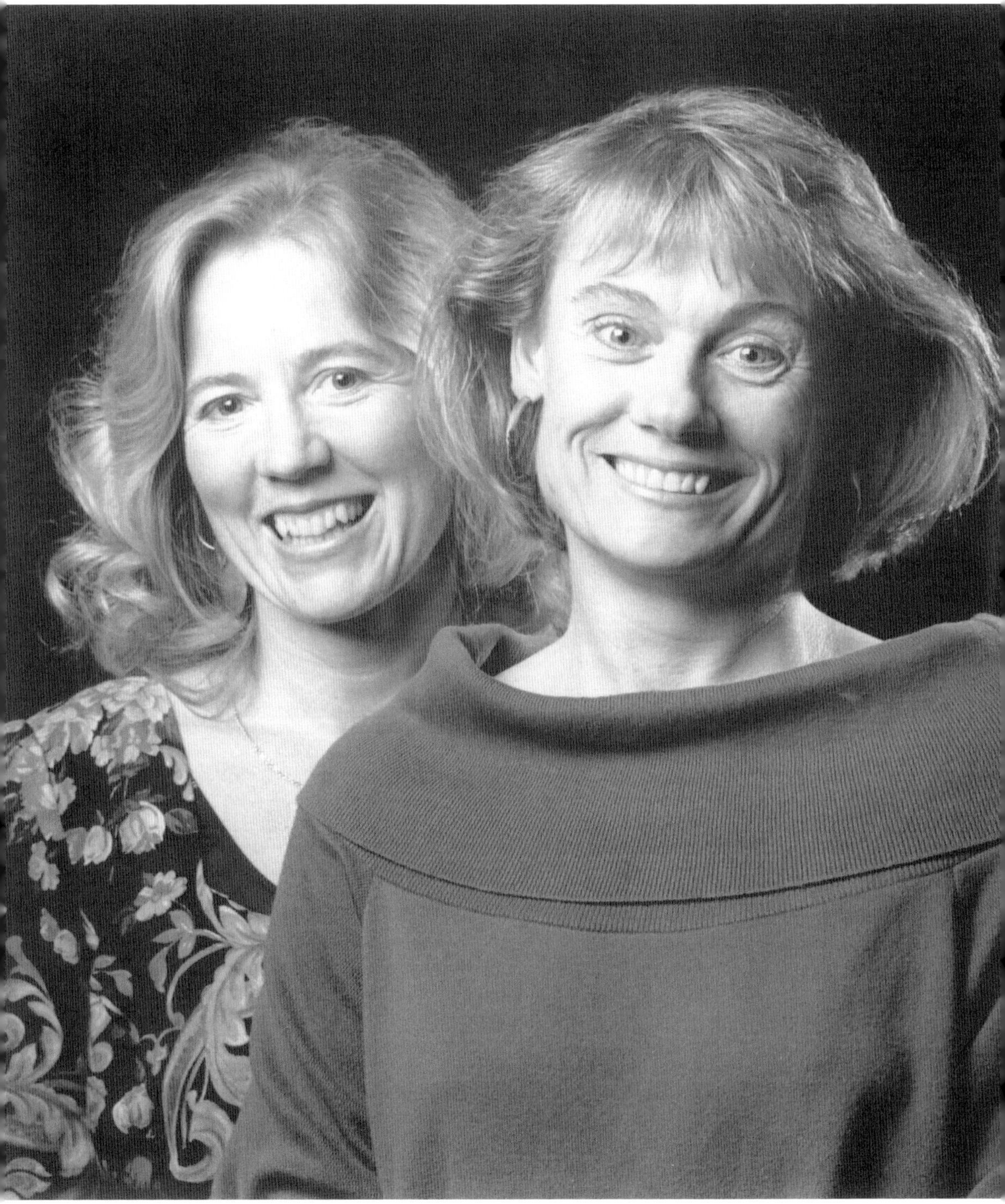

Paulette Arnold and Laurel Near (OPPOSITE PAGE)
In 1995, Paulette and Laurel fulfilled their dream of creating a place where young people could learn about both the performing arts and the cultural diversity of Ukiah. This shared vision came to fruition as SPACE—the School for the Performing Arts and Cultural Education.

Paulette is a director, playwright, and performer. She received her education at Duke University and, for three years, was an artist in residence in California. She wanted to use the performing arts to interrupt racism and give young people the opportunity to express their feelings, but she was looking for a partner with the same dream.

Laurel Near has a similar background and comes from a well-known musician and activist family. She studied modern dance and theatre. Her feeling was that, in order to work successfully with children, the families that raise them—and the community in which they live—must be included in the education.

Laurel and Paulette's founding of SPACE has been a huge boon to the Ukiah community—using the performing arts to interrupt racism and give young people the chance to express themselves in their own way. In 1999, SPACE was able to move in to the old St. Mary's Church, enabling them to offer many more classes. A teacher-training seminar is also offered to high school students for the advancement of the performing arts in the community. (Courtesy of Laurel Near and Paulette Arnold.)

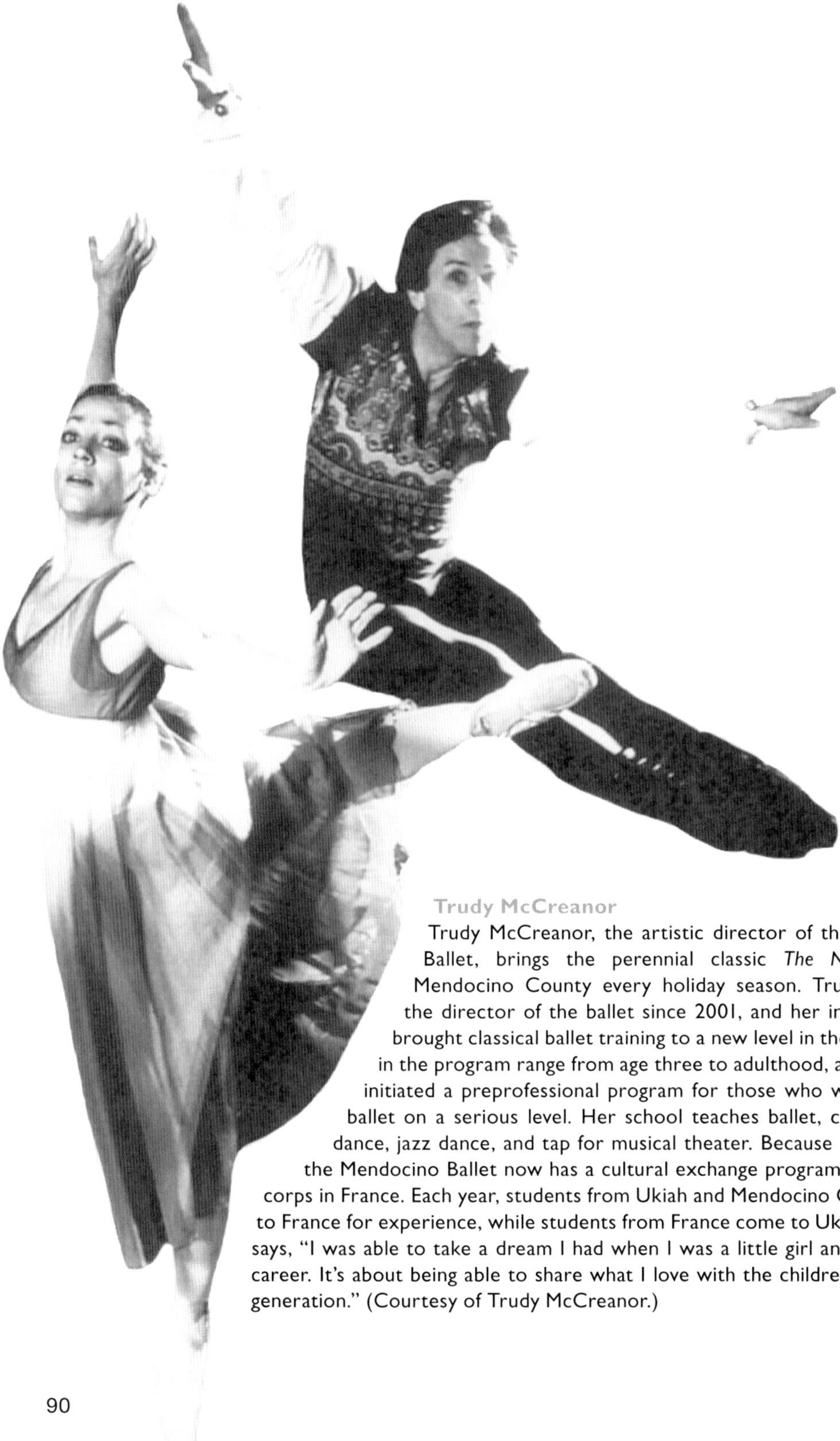

Trudy McCreanor

Trudy McCreanor, the artistic director of the Mendocino Ballet, brings the perennial classic *The Nutcracker* to Mendocino County every holiday season. Trudy has been the director of the ballet since 2001, and her innovation has brought classical ballet training to a new level in the area. Those in the program range from age three to adulthood, and Trudy has initiated a preprofessional program for those who want to study ballet on a serious level. Her school teaches ballet, contemporary dance, jazz dance, and tap for musical theater. Because of her vision, the Mendocino Ballet now has a cultural exchange program with a ballet corps in France. Each year, students from Ukiah and Mendocino County travel to France for experience, while students from France come to Ukiah. As Trudy says, "I was able to take a dream I had when I was a little girl and make it my career. It's about being able to share what I love with the children of the next generation." (Courtesy of Trudy McCreanor.)

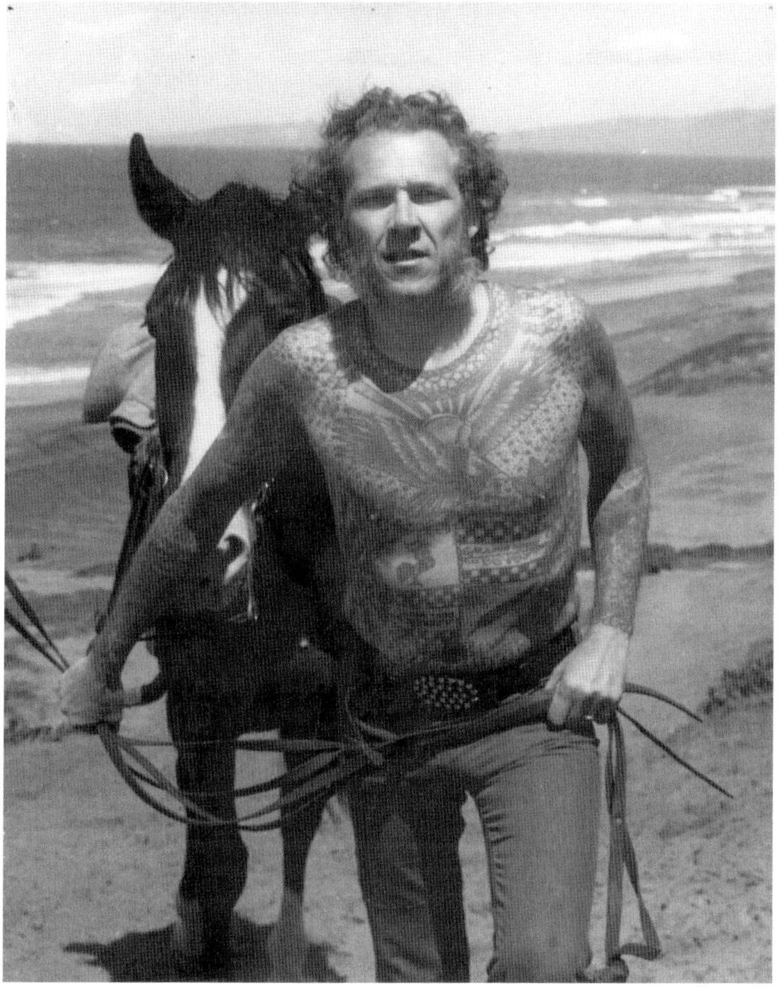

Lyle Tuttle

From Ukiah, to San Francisco, to all around the world, everyone knows Lyle Tuttle. A tattoo artist extraordinaire, Lyle's artwork appears on everyone who's anyone in rock and roll. Cher, Janis Joplin, the Allman Brothers band members, Joan Baez, Henry Fonda, and thousands of others have all appreciated and enjoyed his talent.

Lyle got his first tattoo at the age of 14, after a bus trip to San Francisco—a heart within a banner that read "Mom" that even his own mother couldn't stay angry over. He opened his first studio in 1954 in San Francisco. As his artistry became more and more well known, he was asked to appear on *The Late Show with Johnny Carson*. That led to the cover of *Rolling Stone* magazine in October 1970, where he was photographed by the famous Annie Leibovitz.

Although he officially retired in 1990, Lyle still travels the world, teaching seminars on tattoo machine maintenance and construction. He considers tattoos a form of travel sticker—just on the body instead of luggage. They mark an important event in someone's life. When he was asked what has brought tattoos in the mainstream, he said women's liberation and said that he felt it was empowering for women and brought them a newfound freedom.

In January 2014, Lyle took a trip to South America, making it the seventh continent on which he tattooed. It has been said that, over his career, he has tattooed more people than all other tattoo artists in the world combined. (Courtesy of Lyle Tuttle.)

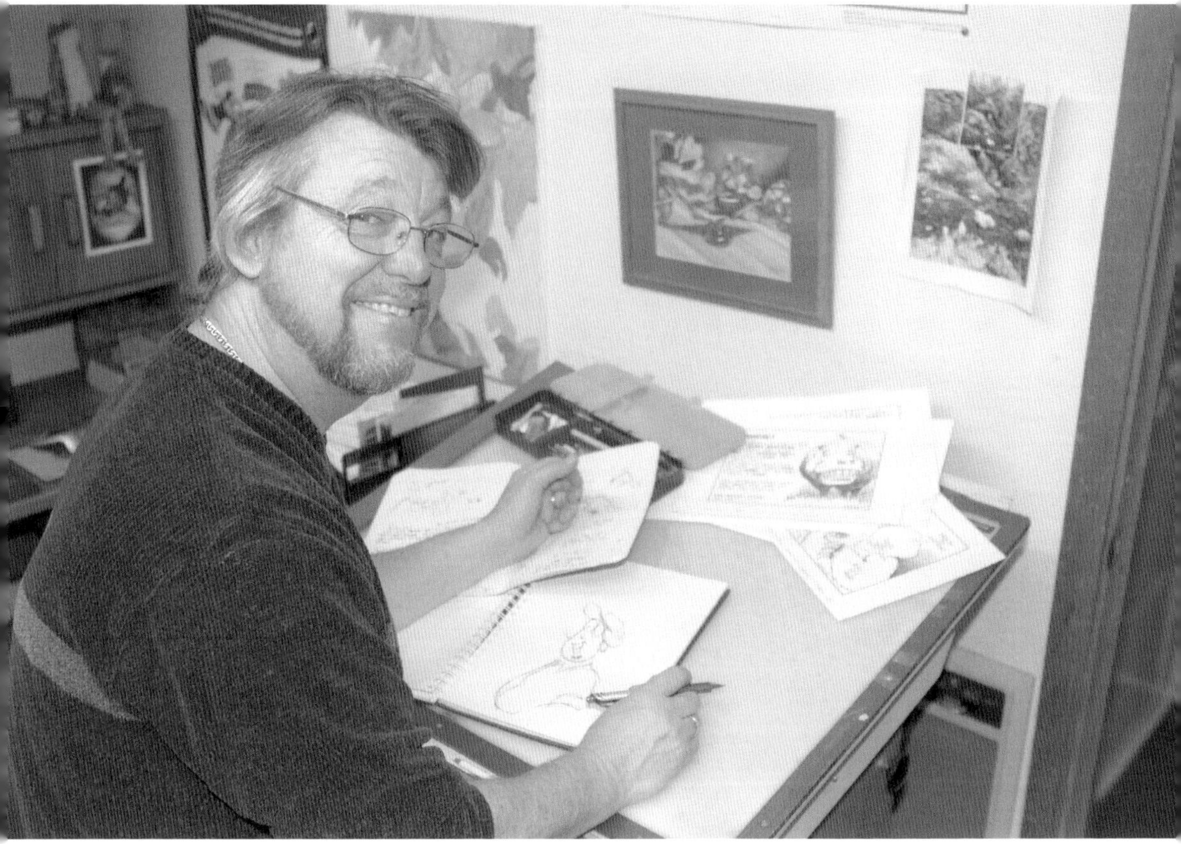

James Kester (ABOVE AND OPPOSITE PAGE)
What could be better than a slice of life cartoonist who makes you laugh, and think too? James Kester is an illustrator and cartoonist for the *Ukiah Daily Journal*, where his column has been running since 1977. James designs have been commissioned by every local business from Granite Construction to Retech, and the Konocti Rod and Gun Club to the local Humane Society. His work is thought provoking but humorous.

James once did a caricature of Marvel Comics pioneer Stan Lee for the Comic Scene, New York convention. When Stan saw it, he called James' editor and asked for the original. Kester sent it in and, a few weeks later, received a copy of *The Marvel Encyclopedia*, signed by Stan himself. The inscription reads, "To Jolly James, who's done the best caricature I've seen." (Courtesy of James Kester.)

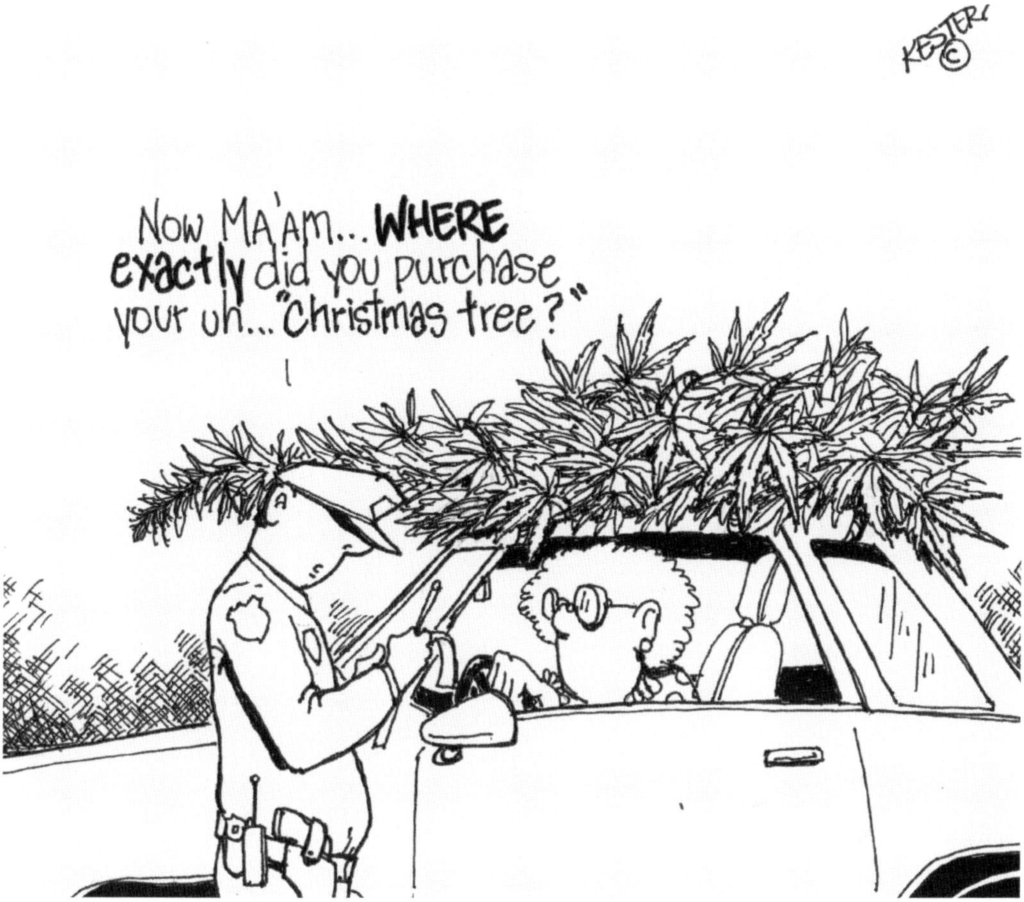

CALIFORNIA NEWSPAPER PUBLISHERS ASSN. AWARD

Daily Journal cartoonist honored

Ukiah Daily Journal

James Kester, longtime editorial cartoonist in The Ukiah Daily Journal, this month won Second Place of editorial cartoons in the Better Newspapers Contest of the California Newspaper Publishers Association.

In the small newspaper category, Kester's cartoon about the government shutdown in the fall of 2013 swayed the judges.

"James has been drawing great editorial cartoons for us for a couple of decades and before that he was featured in our sister newspaper in Fort Bragg," said UDJ Editor K.C. Meadows. "He is an extremely talented artist with a goofy sense of humor, but also a big heart. The cartoon he drew recently in honor of Deputy Ricky Del Fiorentino, for the slain deputy's memorial, was extraordinary."

The Daily Journal also won kudos from the CNPA judges for reporter Justine Frederiksen's story about local downtown property owner Kevin Brogan and for photographer Nathan DeHart's photo of a young 4-H girl and her obstreperous goat and the accompanying story by reporter Tiffany Revelle.

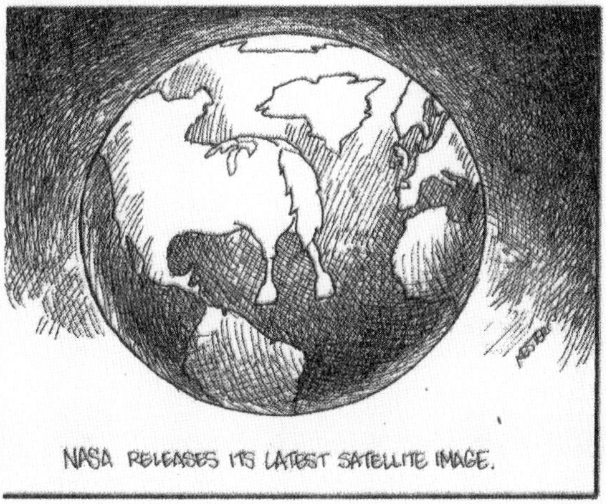

Follow James Kester on Twitter @kesterkartoon

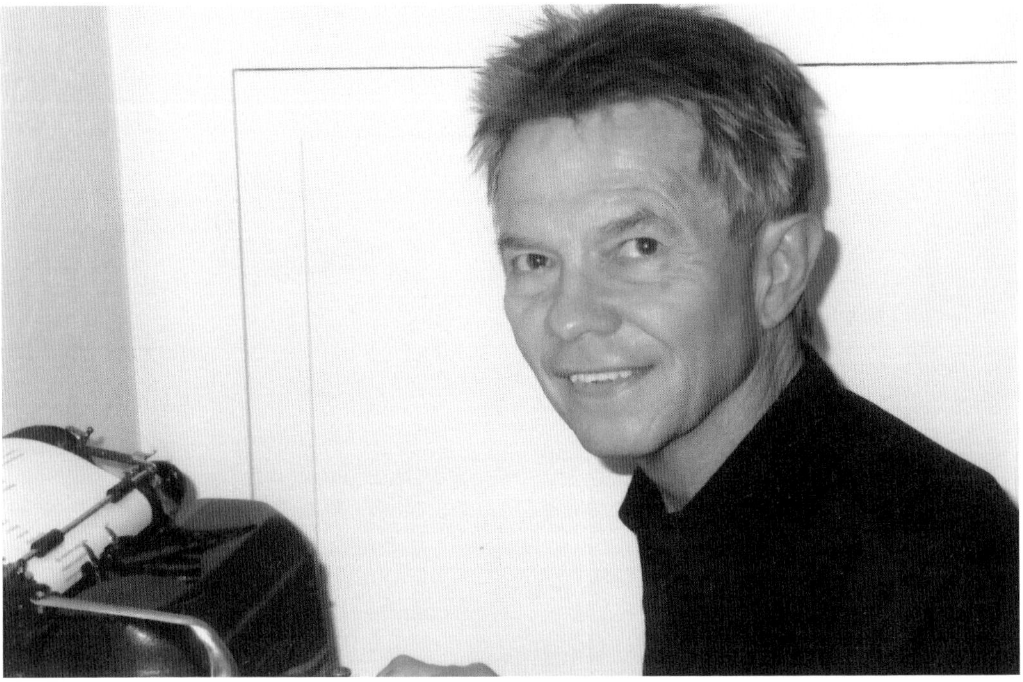

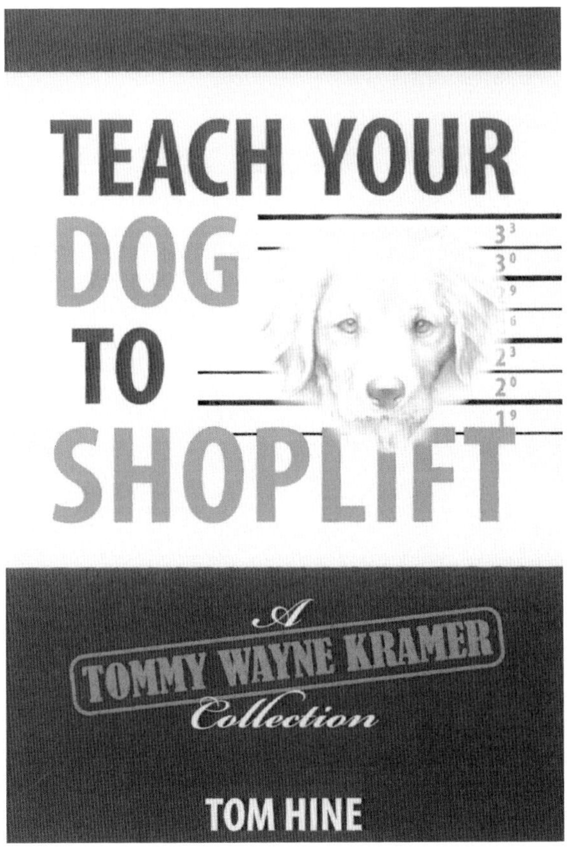

Tom Hine
Ukiah's resident satirist, Tom Hine plies his trade under the alias Tommy Wayne Kramer. His column has appeared in the Sunday edition of the *Ukiah Daily Journal* for almost a decade. Insulting the town, the people, and sometimes himself, Tom keeps Ukiah in stitches. To quote Tom, "My writings are not universally admired, and the paper's Letters to the Editor section provides ample proof that many find me divisive, polarizing, and annoying. But sometimes funny, most admit."

Tom's book, *Teach Your Dog to Shoplift – A Tommy Wayne Kramer Collection*, describes him as a "bitter critic marooned in a Stepford Land of New Agers." In his work, he regularly targets social workers, therapists, teachers, artists, and anyone he suspects of once having been a hippie—though he does concede that he was once a hippie himself. Tom spent over three decades as a journalist and conducting criminal defense investigations for the public defender. (Courtesy of Tom Hine.)

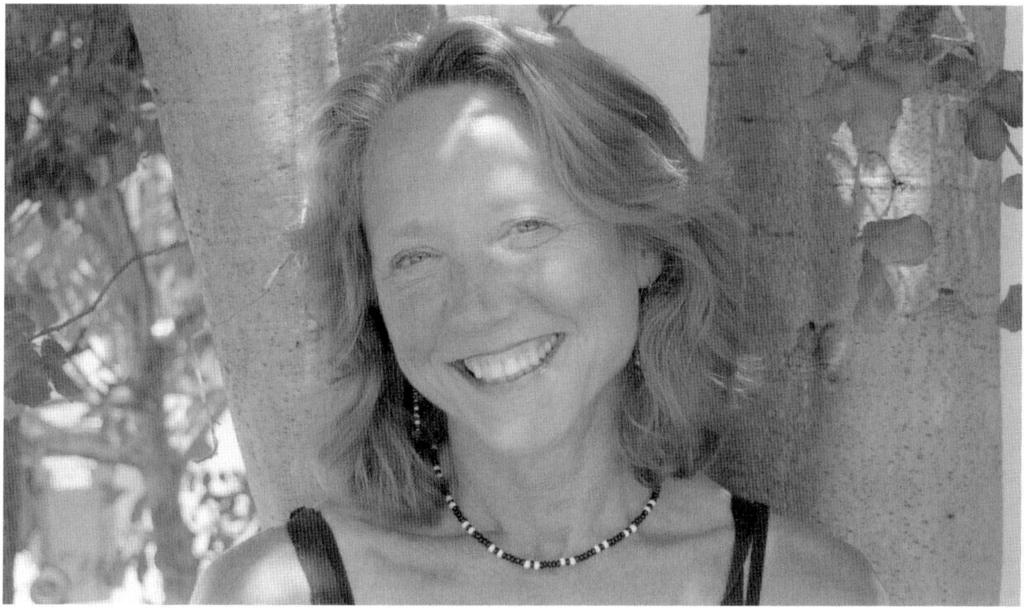

Kate "Babcock" Magruder
Kate developed a love of writing, directing, and acting for the theater during her school days in the Midwest. After moving to California, she studied theatre at UC Irvine's drama department, which fueled her love for the theater even more.

In 1973, Kate and a friend moved to Ukiah to become part of the "back to the land" movement. After few years, she had met other theatre lovers who shared her desire to put on a show, and the Ukiah Players Theatre (UPT) was born. The community rallied to support this effort and its promise of ongoing productions, and in 1982, the Ukiah Playhouse was built by dozens of dedicated volunteers, on land donated by the City of Ukiah.

Kate has been instrumental in guiding the direction of UPT since its birth—serving as an actor, director, administrator, playwright, teacher, and board leader. Her passion has been focused on helping the community tell its stories, both historic and personal. Over the years, she has created several storytelling projects, including *Telling the Truth in a Small Town* and *The 'Good War' Project*, which are designed to enlighten the audiences and help them see things from a different perspective. (Courtesy of Kate Magruder.)

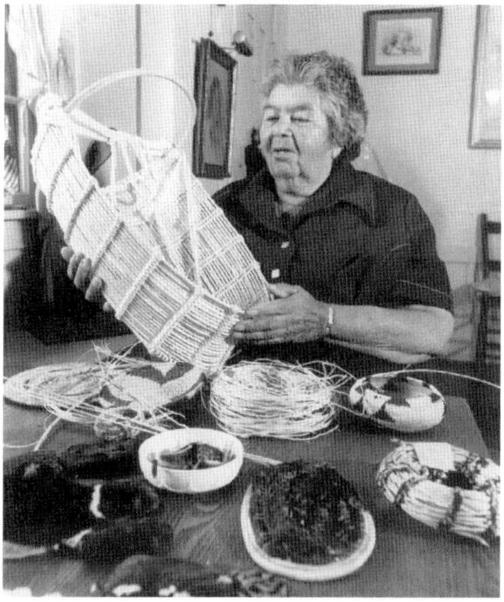

Elsie Allen
Elsie Allen was a Native American Pomo basket weaver. This nationally known weaver of baskets was only able to devote herself fully to her craft when she was in her 60s—previously putting it aside to raise her four children. She passed on her knowledge to others, so that the traditions of weaving would not be lost. Today, many of her baskets are on display at the Grace Hudson Museum. Her baskets are considered priceless and are sought after by both museums and collectors throughout the country. (Courtesy of Grace Hudson Museum.)

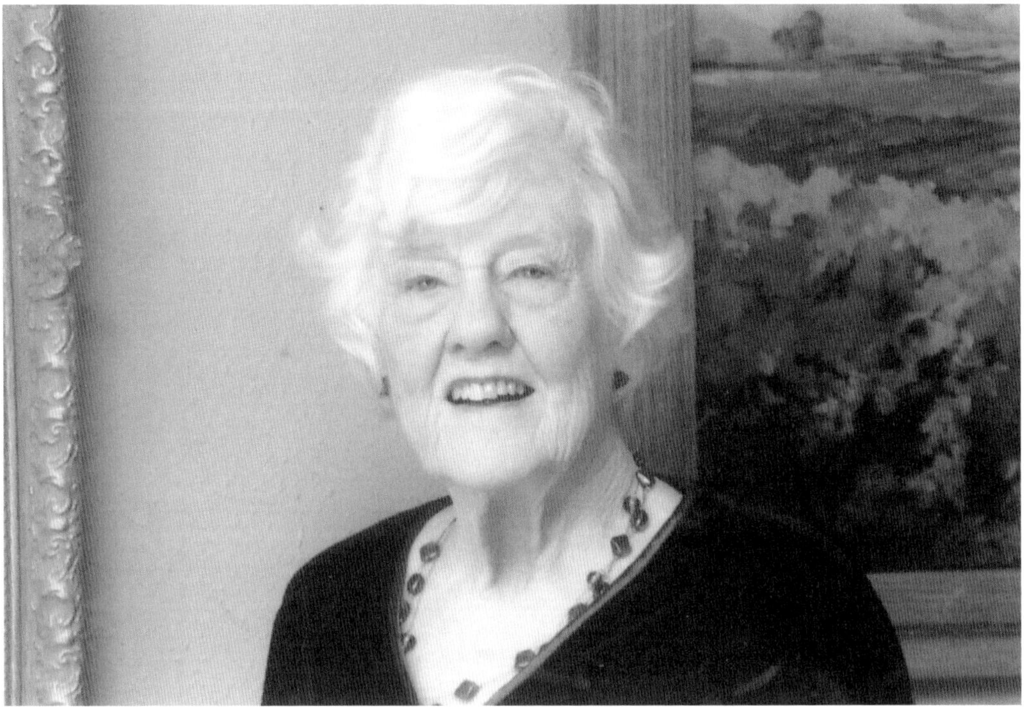

Adele Pruitt

An artist, art conservator, and teacher, this amazing woman is still practicing her craft and teaching at the age of 91. Even in the first grade, her artistic talents were evident, and her teacher asked her to do a mural for the classroom. Adele came by her talent naturally as well—her mother was an illustrator and her grandmother a painter.

Upon arriving in Ukiah in the late 1960s, Adele opened a gallery and began teaching art at Mendocino College. There, she developed a unique restoration process and was sought out by clients from all over the area who were looking to conserve their treasures.

She has been meeting with a small group of local artists at her studio since the 1970s, where they collaborate and to enjoy each other's company. Adele is living proof that if you find something you love to do at an early age, it will enrich your life and keep you young. (Courtesy of Adele Pruitt.)

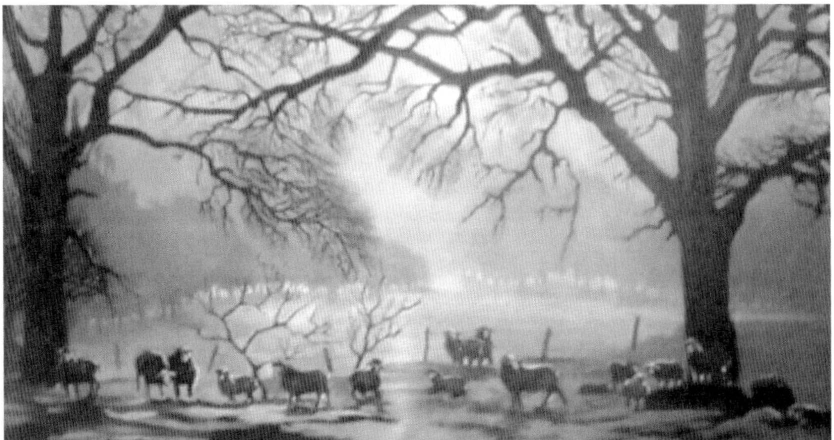

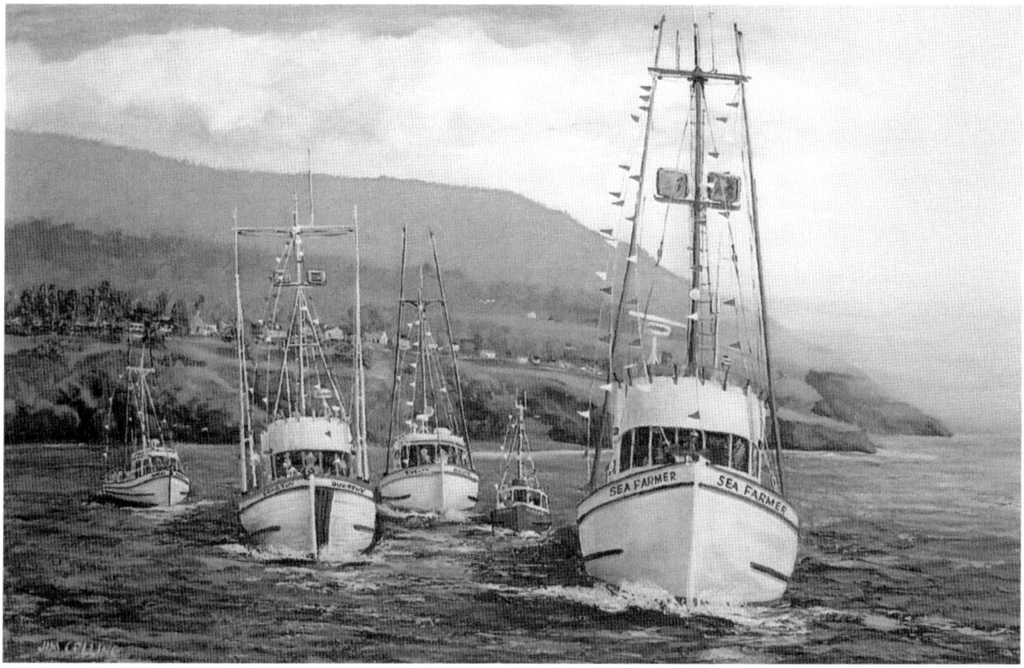

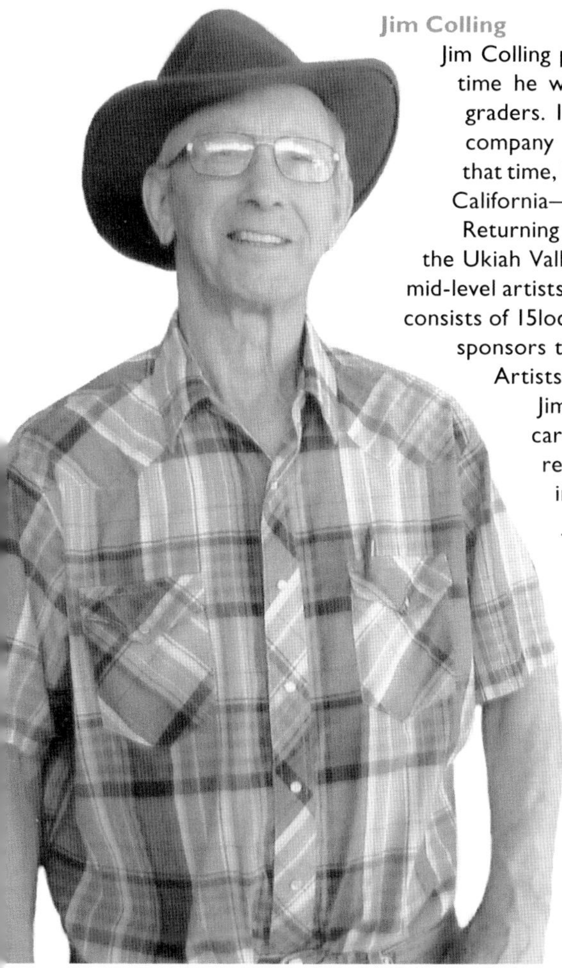

Jim Colling

Jim Colling painted his first picture at the age of nine. By the time he was in high school, he was teaching art to third graders. In the late 1990s, this owner of a building supply company decided to pursue his art career full-time. Since that time, his paintings have been hung in galleries throughout California—from Palm Desert to Fort Bragg—and Oregon.

Returning to his roots in Mendocino County, Jim helped form the Ukiah Valley Artists Co-op. He believed that emerging and mid-level artists needed an outlet for their work. The cooperative consists of 15local artists and is located in the Pear Tree Center. It sponsors the Annual Art Faire, Artoberfest, and the annual Artists Studio Tour.

Jim Colling is proof that a person can start a new career at any time in their lives and pursue what they really enjoy. His paintings can be found on display in local banks and other venues. (Courtesy of Jim Colling.)

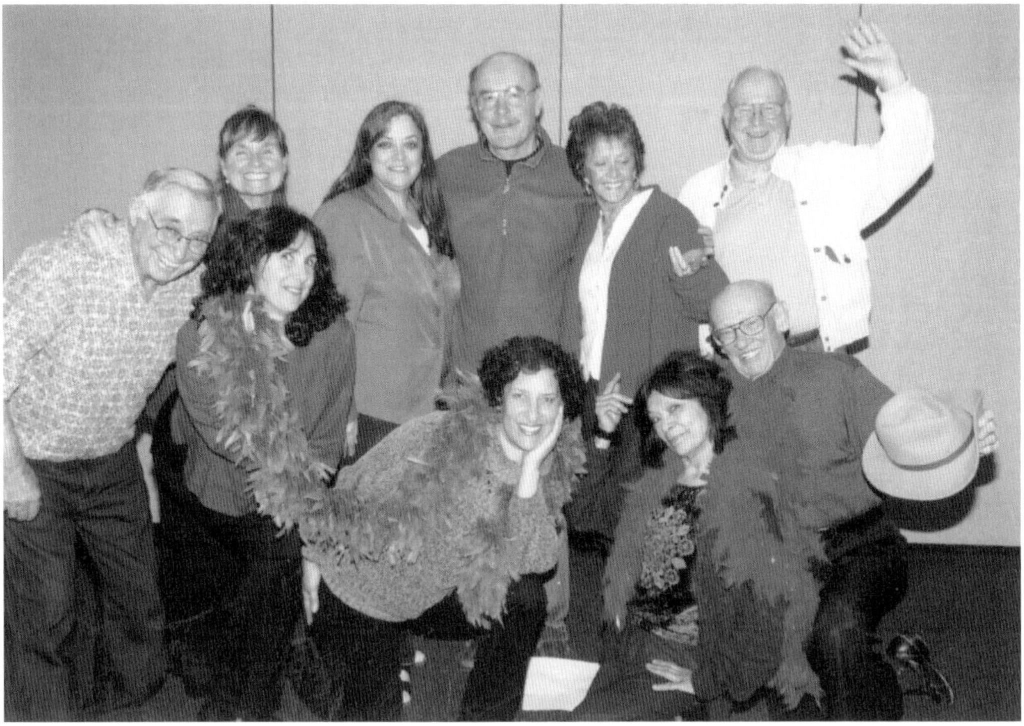

Tom Segar and Jo and Bill McMorris

Tom was Ukiah's true Renaissance man. His father, Elzie, was the creator of the comic strip *Thimble Theater* and its Popeye character, and Tom was his inspiration for the character Sweet Pea. Born in Hollywood, Tom found his way to Ukiah Valley after getting married. Tom started a number of companies before he retired and—never one to just sit on the porch swing—inevitably became involved in several other enterprises. In the 1980s, he purchased Soda Creek Ranch and turned it into a nature preserve. The name Soda Creek was later used for Tom and Lucinda's publishing company, Soda Creek Press.

One of Tom's first ventures into publishing was the creation of Mysteries by Mail—a quarterly catalog that featured hundreds of paperback books, audiocassettes, and videos. Several years later, a romance catalog was added that offered out-of-print romance and mystery titles at a reduced price. Tom also dabbled in acting, taking roles in several local theater productions. Along the way, he became interested in ceramics. He was one of those rare people that really enjoyed life and lived it to its fullest. If you saw a red Corvette around town, you knew Tom was somewhere close by.

Most of all, Tom will be remembered for his philanthropy. He was always there to help nonprofits, the Ukiah Players Theatre, Plowshares, or St. Mary's School, and he was a sponsor of many productions at SPACE.

Bill and Jo McMorris are East Coast transplants who chose Ukiah to be their home over two decades ago. Bill spent his career as editor of *Boys' Life*, the Boy Scouts of America publication based in New York City. He authored books on camping, boating, and scouting, as well as a host of children's books.

Jo was involved in Democratic politics and was chairman of the Democratic Party of Mendocino County. She was also the president of the board of directors of the Ukiah Civic Light Opera and was responsible for coordinating productions at Mendocino College. Bill acted in many of these sold-out productions, which he thoroughly enjoyed.

They were both involved in fundraising for local nonprofits. Each New Year's Eve, they held a party that ushered in the new year with musicians and artists from their neighborhood, and the police had to come by to see what was going on a couple of times. That's quite a lot of fun for two people who were in their 70s at the time. (Courtesy of Paula Samonte.)

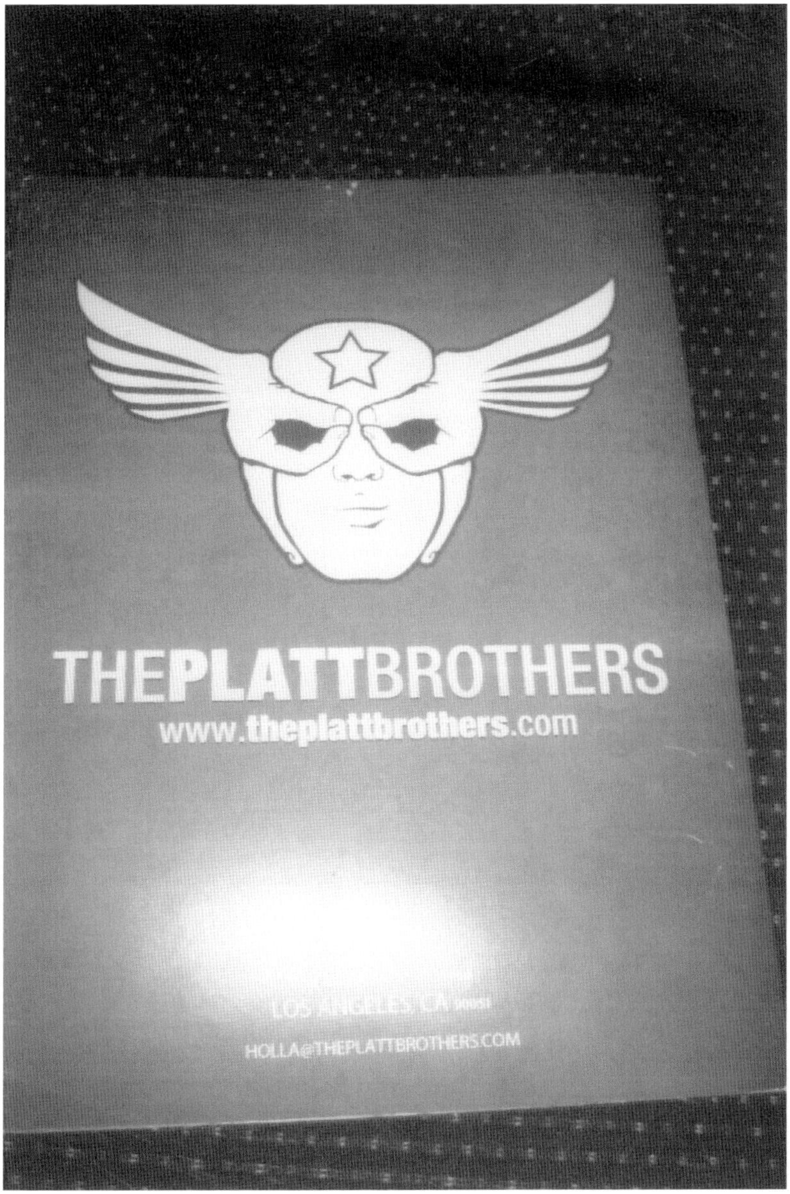

Platt Brothers

Comedians Cy, Boone, and Cheetah Platt started out in Ukiah and ended up appearing on *America's Got Talent*—becoming quarterfinalists. They have performed with Cirque Du Soleil and on the Chabad Telethon and have toured from coast to coast. Raised without television, the brothers had to explore their own creativity through make believe adventures and the games that they created to entertain themselves and their family.

The brothers' act is a fun blend of acrobatics, dance, comedy, and music. They have received much acclaim for their family-oriented shows and were once voted the Best Live Comedy in San Diego. The group has performed for companies like Disney, Universal Studios, and Microsoft, and at the Rose Bowl Parade. They are also strong advocates for education and for kids channeling their creative abilities. (Courtesy of SPACE.)

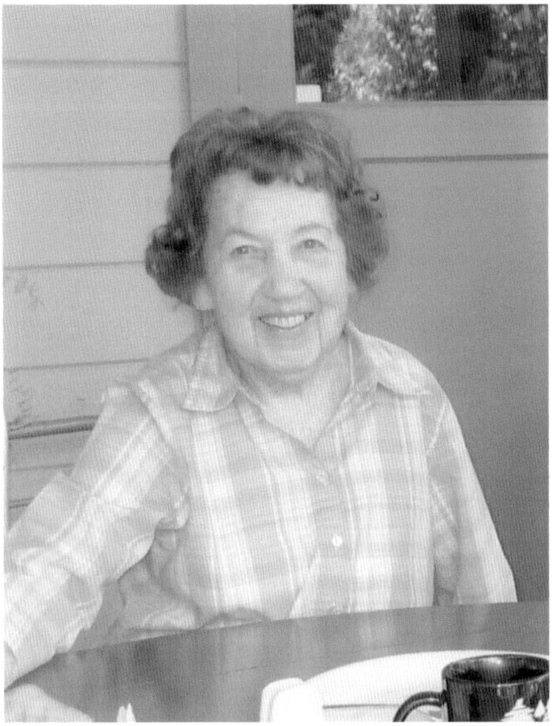

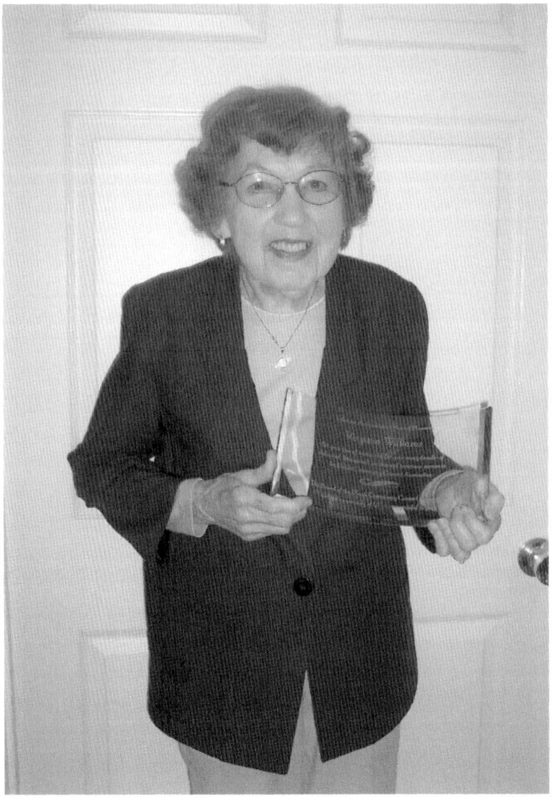

Virginia McFarland Williams
One of the treasures of Ukiah's art and music community, Virginia came to California with her family in 1921. The family settled originally in Riverside. During World War II, Virginia trained with the CAA as an air traffic controller and was stationed at many locations around the western United States.

In 1950, she moved to Ukiah to help her sister open a yard goods store—Fabric Lane—which flourished. A short time later, she met James Williams—whose family had lived in the area for several generations. The two of them were married for over 54 years. Virginia worked at the local Pacific Gas & Electric office until her retirement.

After retirement, she became active in several local nonprofits and was one of the founding members of the Ukiah Community Concert Association. Virginia devoted 60 years to the organization and became its first female president. Through her efforts, the association was able to secure a permanent location as a venue. The group brings in talent from around the United States and Europe. Virginia was also a gardener and a member of the Ukiah Garden Club for over 50 years and her interest in politics led to a long membership in the League of Women Voters. (Courtesy of the Williams family.)

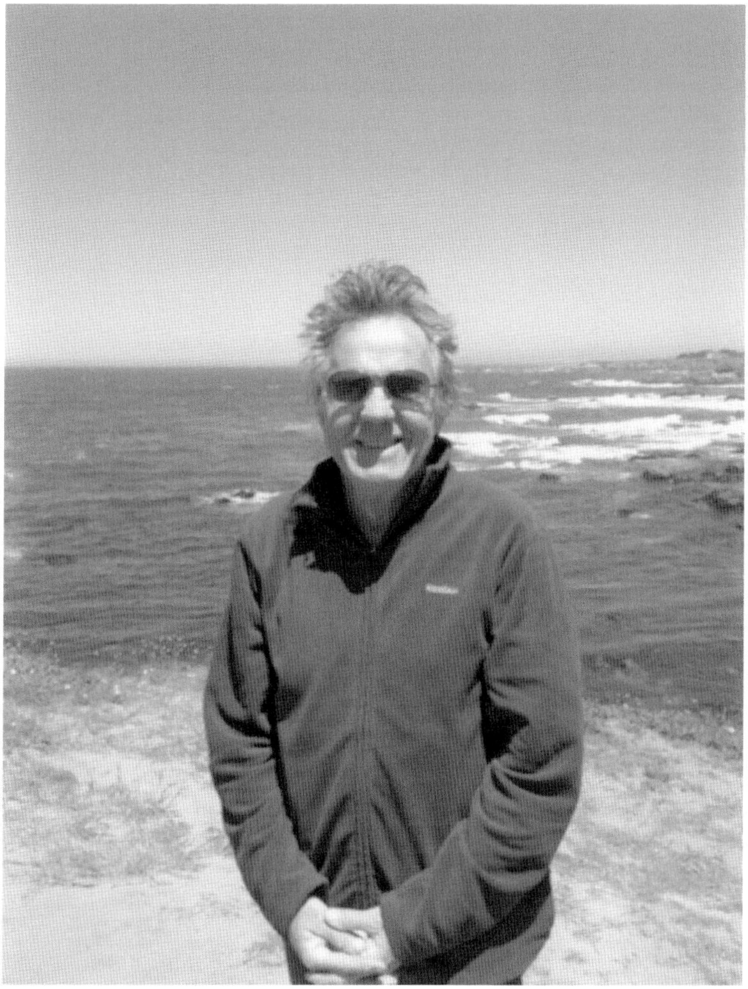

George Husaruk
George started on his musical journey in life at the age of six—learning from his older brother, Eugene, who went on to become concertmaster of the Montreal Symphony Orchestra. By nine, he was studying at the Royal Conservatory of Music with the famous flutist Marion Duschenes. After his family moved to Southern California from Montreal, George continued his studies on the flute with the principal flutist of the Los Angeles Philharmonic Orchestra.

While attending UCLA, George played in a rock band and started listening to Wes Montgomery. Since settling in the Ukiah area, he has performed with Will Siegel, Barry Melton, Elena Casanova, Barbara Curtis, and a score of others. Now he divides his time between teaching music and mathematics and performing in Mendocino, Sonoma, and Lake Counties, and around the Bay Area.

Although George was primarily a band teacher, he decided to learn the math curriculum and attended classes that allowed him to teach that subject as well. He currently teaches at Bacchtel Grove Middle School, where he acts as the band director. He has been instrumental in organizing many fundraisers for kids who could not otherwise afford to rent instruments and pay for other things that are necessary to be in a band. To quote George, "It's a meaningful thing helping people less fortunate." George has been nominated teacher of the year by his fellow staff, and when asked about his teacher, a student said, "He rocks!" George also serves as president of the Ukiah Community Concerts Association's board. (Courtesy of George Husaruk.)

Steve Baird (OPPOSITE PAGE)
An opportunity to play with local jazz legends Barbara Curtis and Rod Pacini set Steve off on a path that merged his early training with band and small ensemble experience. He's now part of Ukiah's vibrant local music scene.

For more than 30 years, Steve has been playing bass and horns, and singing in musical groups around Mendocino County. Whether it's jazz, rock, blues, Broadway, or classical music, Steve's involved. Many times, he can be found with his compatriot and mentor, guitarist Will Siegel, making sweet sound for the community. (Photograph by Tom Zamaria, courtesy of Steve Baird.)

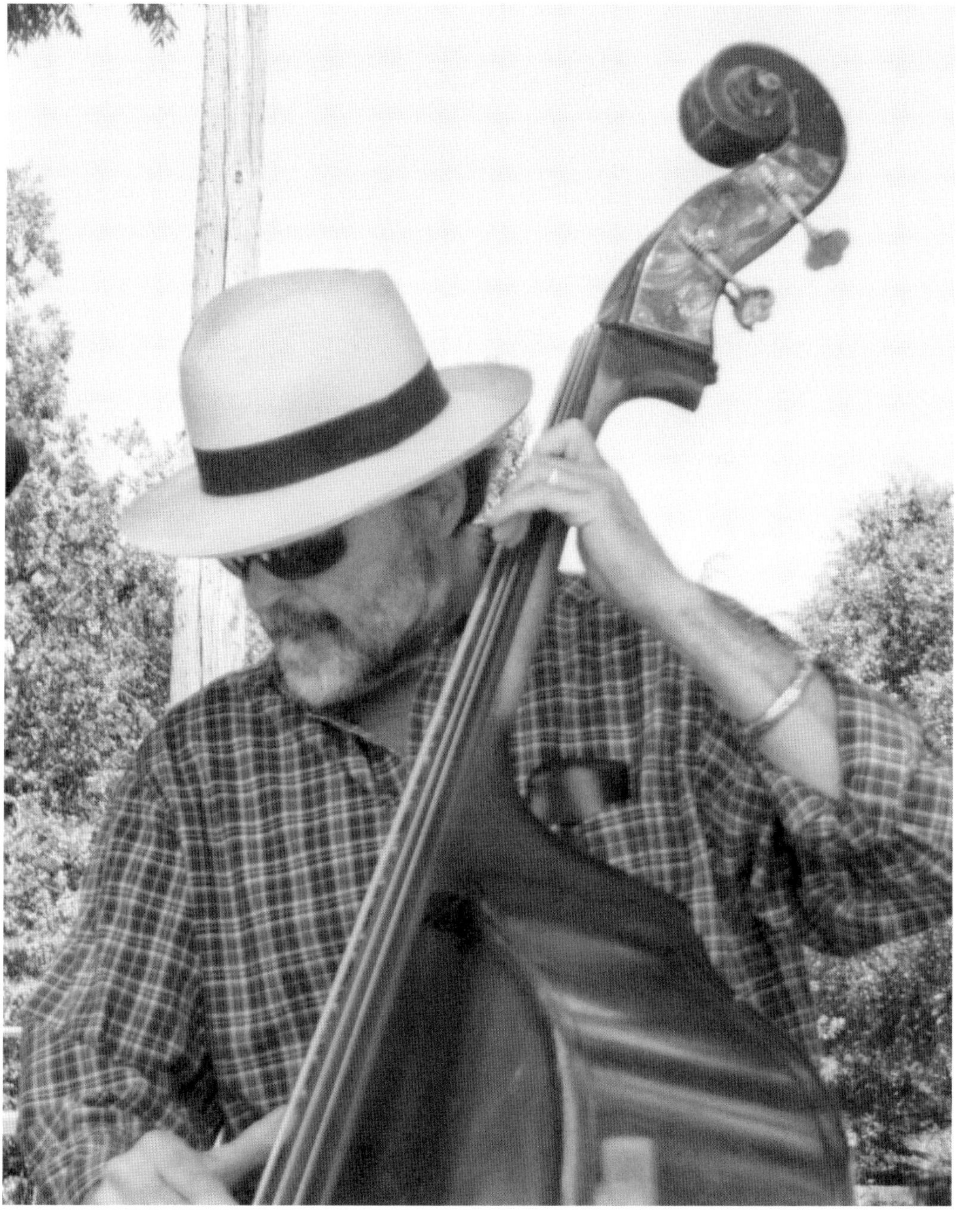

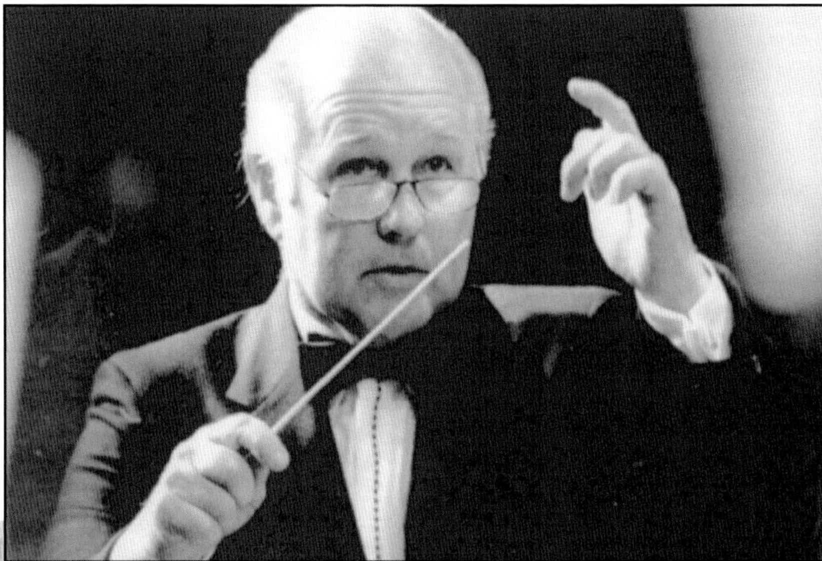

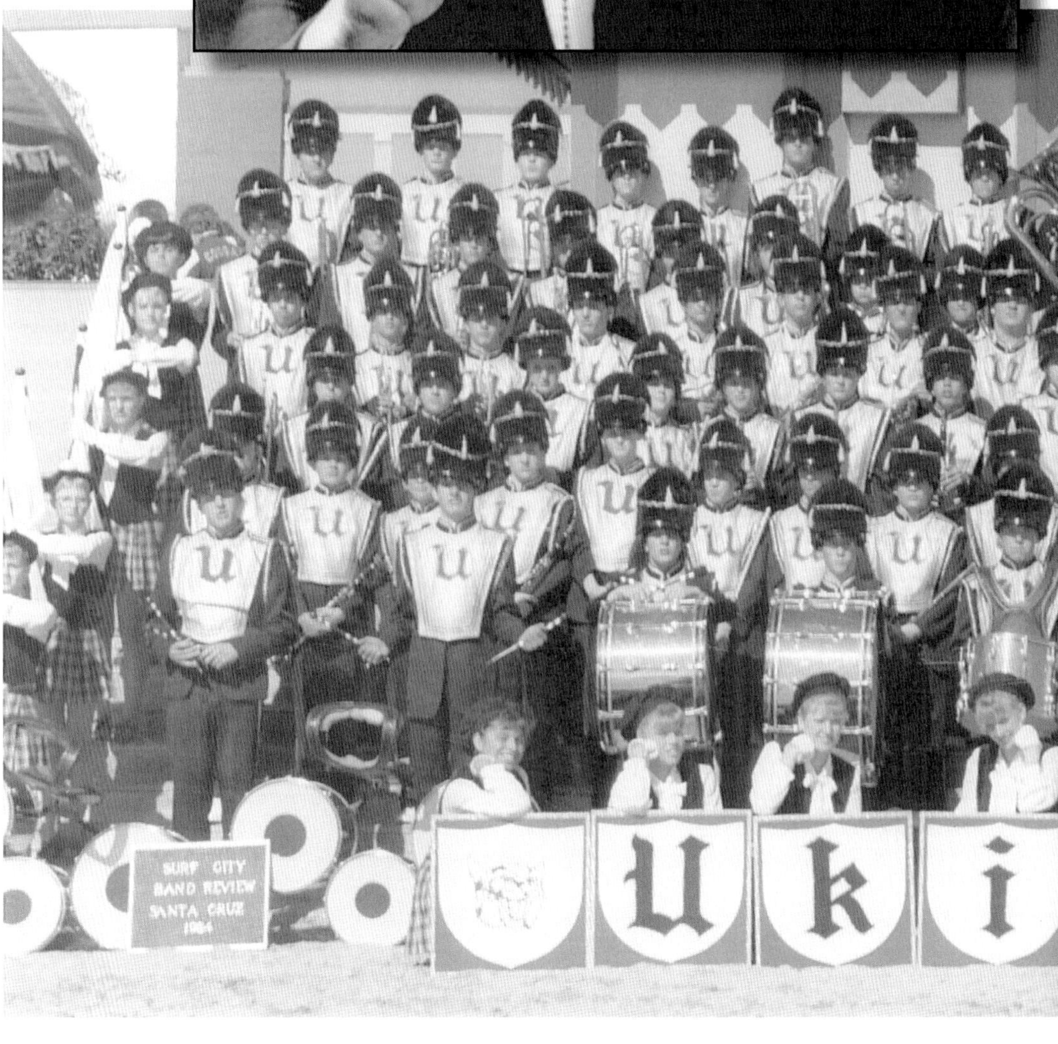
SURF CITY
BAND REVIEW
SANTA CRUZ
U k i

Roland Nielson

Of Roland Nielson and his legacy, former commissioner Tom Cropp said, "Wherever the man goes, or wherever you go, you hear Ukiah identified with 'that outstanding high school band.'"

Before his 1994 retirement, Roland spent 29 years building an outstanding music program for the Unified Ukiah School District—taking his students to perform at a nationally televised concert in Europe and at the 1985 Super Bowl XIX pregame show. While there, the Ukiah High School band made up just a portion of the more than 1,200 marchers who formed a human flag as they marched into Stanford Stadium. Under his direction, the Ukiah High School band was also involved in many special performances in Canada, the Tournament of Roses, the Fiesta Bowl, and more. Roland was also the founder of the Ukiah Band Review, which brought together over 30 high school and junior high marching bands. Even after his retirement, he has continued to teach music to kids throughout Northern California.

In 2009, Roland was presented with the Community Achievement of the Arts award at Sundays in the Park. Upon receiving the award, he said, "Music is the heart of everybody's soul . . . I'll never stop playing." (Courtesy of Roland Nielson.)

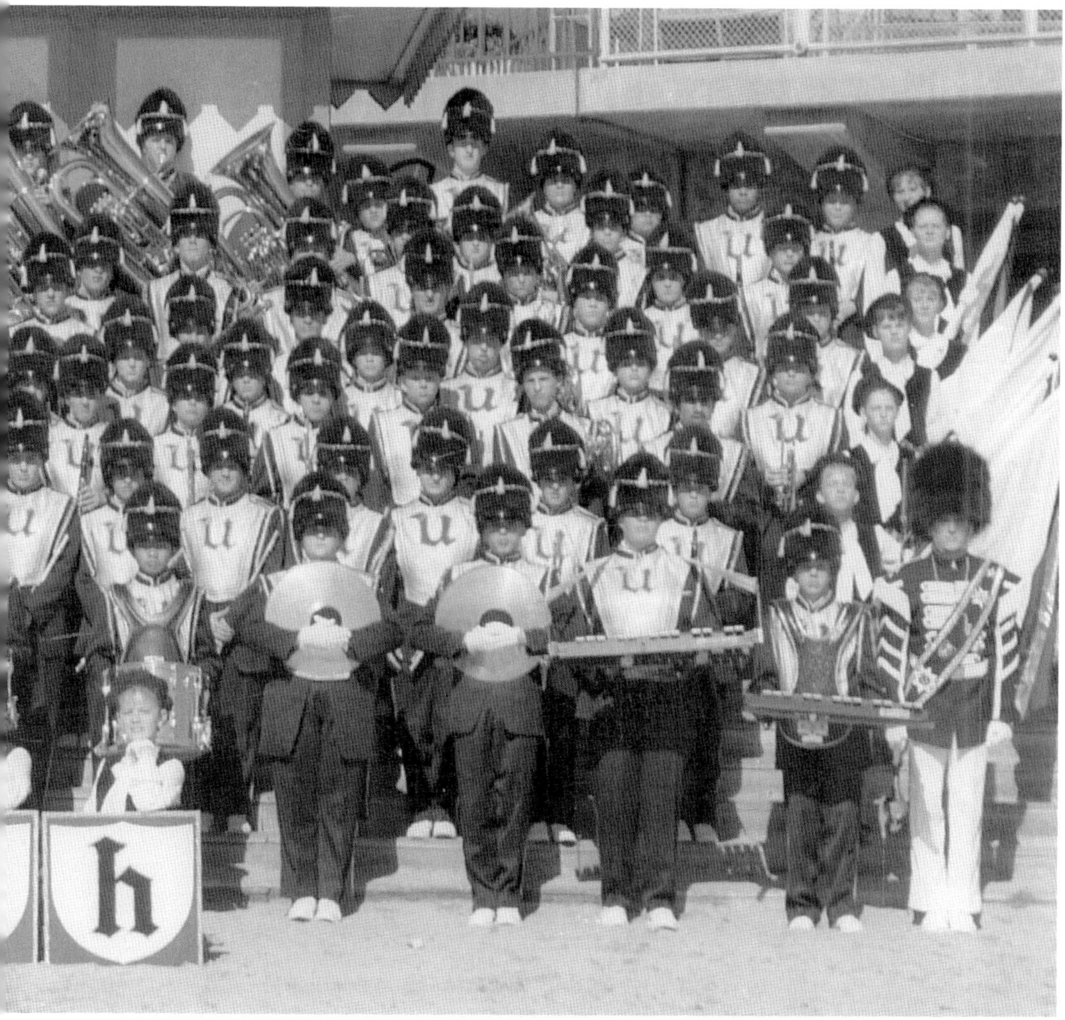

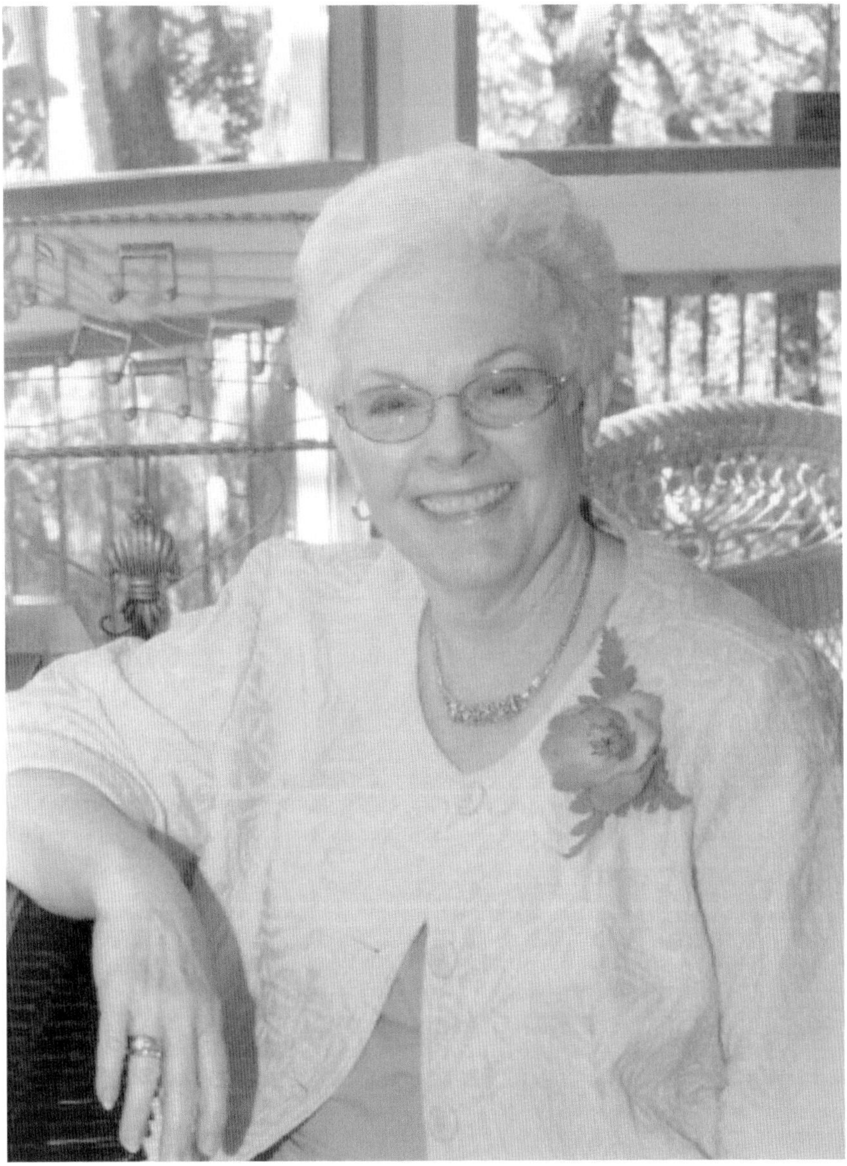

Carole Hester

If you hear music and laughter in Ukiah, it's a safe bet that Carole Hester is somewhere nearby. Carole has had a lifelong interest in anything musical and grew up surrounded by great classical music. As an adult, Hester has been a music leader in churches—directing choirs, organizing ensembles of varying sizes, and singing in each. Locally, she has performed with the Mendocino College Masterworks Chorale, the Ukiah Children's Theatre, Ukiah Players Theatre, the Ukiah Civic Light Opera, and the Ukiah Symphony. Carole also sings lead in the women's gospel quartet, Voices of Grace.

For many years, Carole has written regular columns for the *Ukiah Daily Journal*—keeping local residents informed on what is going on in town. Whether writing about musical performances, or giving kudos to an accomplished fellow resident, Carole is the one who always knows what is going on in the area. She is always ready to roll up her sleeves and help with promoting a project for local nonprofits, and everyone refers to her as the "go-to lady." (Courtesy of Carole Hester.)

CHAPTER FIVE

Rebels with a Cause

Every city, town, and village has unsung heroes who help their neighbors. These amazing individuals provide assistance wherever it is needed and with no thought for recognition. Whether volunteering to dive disabled veterans to their doctor appointments, or showing up at the home of a family that have just suffered a major fire, they care about their community and go above and beyond what is expected. The people in this chapter deserve to be recognized, though that is never their goal.

By the very nature of their lives, they inspire others to pitch in and go the extra mile to help their neighbors and their town. They are Ukiah's rebels with a cause and—be that cause working at the library sorting books, raising money for the library, spearheading a fundraising campaign for the Boys and Girls Club, or anything else—the cause is what's important. Ukiah is fortunate to have many individuals who qualify for the title.

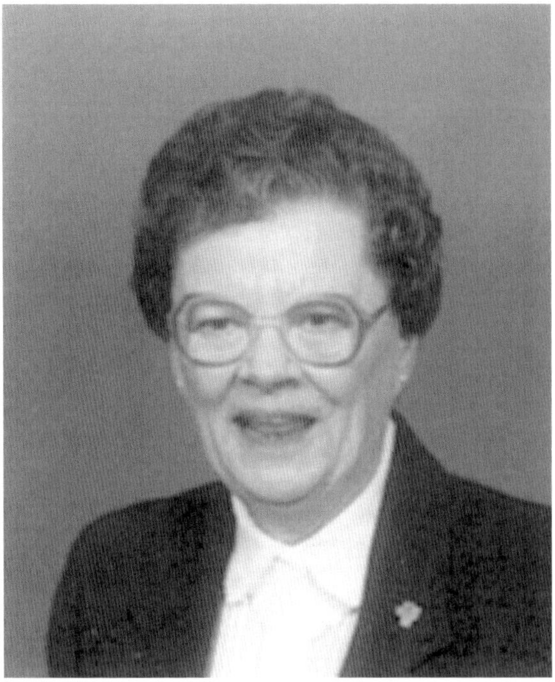

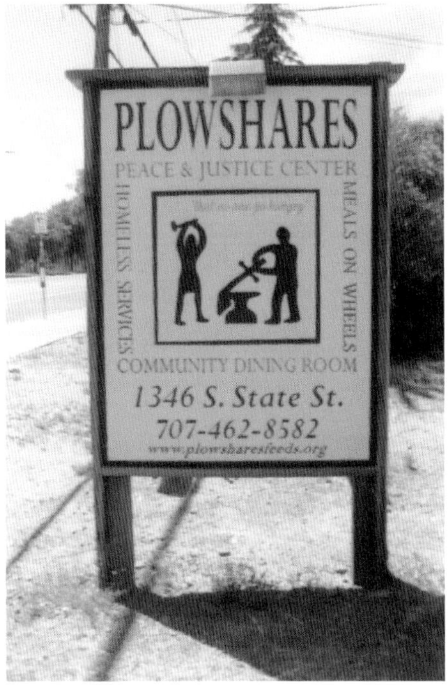

Sister Jane Kelly (ABOVE AND OPPOSITE PAGE)
Ukiah had its own Mother Teresa in Sr. Jane Kelly. She came to Ukiah on behalf of the Sisters of the Presentation Convent in San Francisco in 1973 and has stayed with us ever since. Her original objective was the organization of St. Mary's of the Angels Parish School of Religion—an institution designed to be separate from the St. Mary's Grade School.

This mission led to her expanding outreach to the Native American community, visiting reservations, advocating for families, and leading her to serve for a time on the board of the nonprofit Senior Indian Nutrition Center. One of her primary interests was the opening a soup kitchen for the homeless, which eventually resulted in Plowshares—a community dining room that she opened with a group of young activists. Plowshares opened its doors on November 15, 1983, and those disadvantaged who use the facility had no harder working or more vocal advocate than Sister Jane. Over the years, the original community dining room has evolved into a place where someone can get a good hot meal, get their hair cut, shower, and receive their mail.

Since Sister Jane left Ukiah in January 2008, even more services have been added—including a community garden and an area where people can bring their dogs. Today, even more things are planned to provide assistance to those in need. Sister Jane is Ukiah's own saint, and everyone in the community misses her. (Courtesy of Mary Bell.)

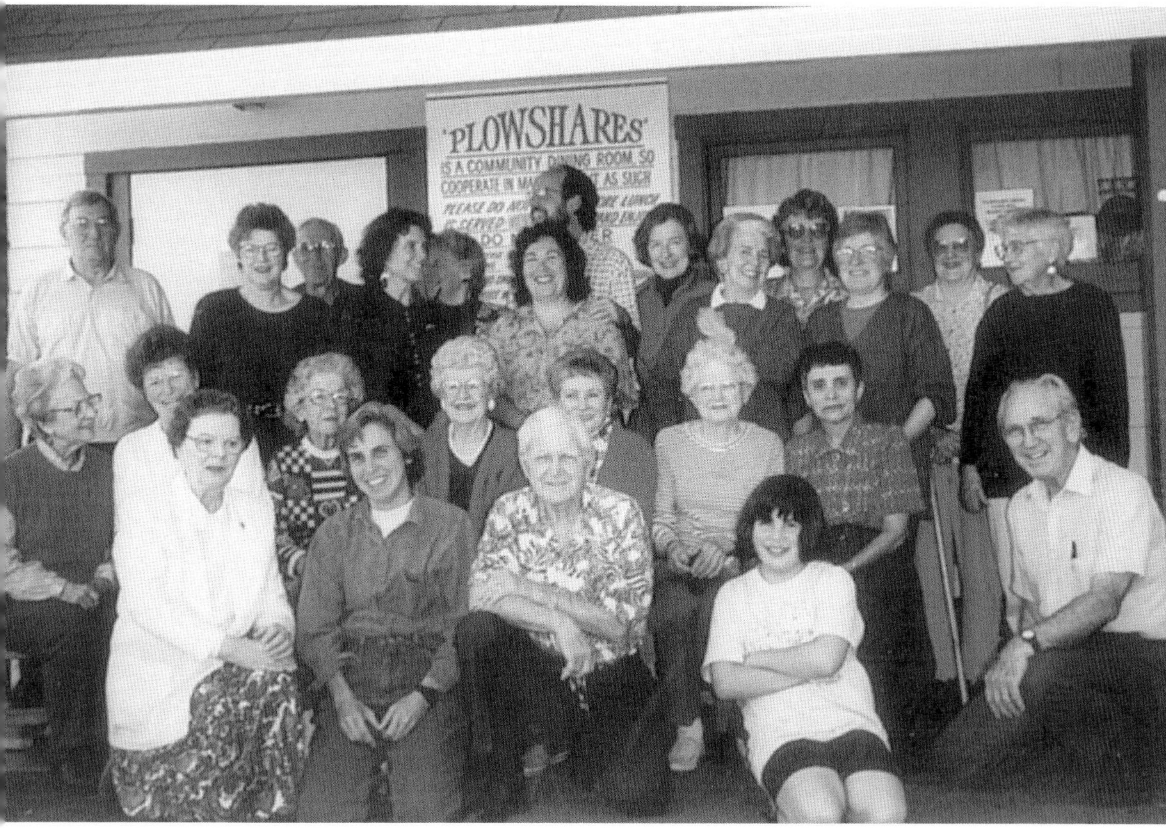
'PLOWSHARES'

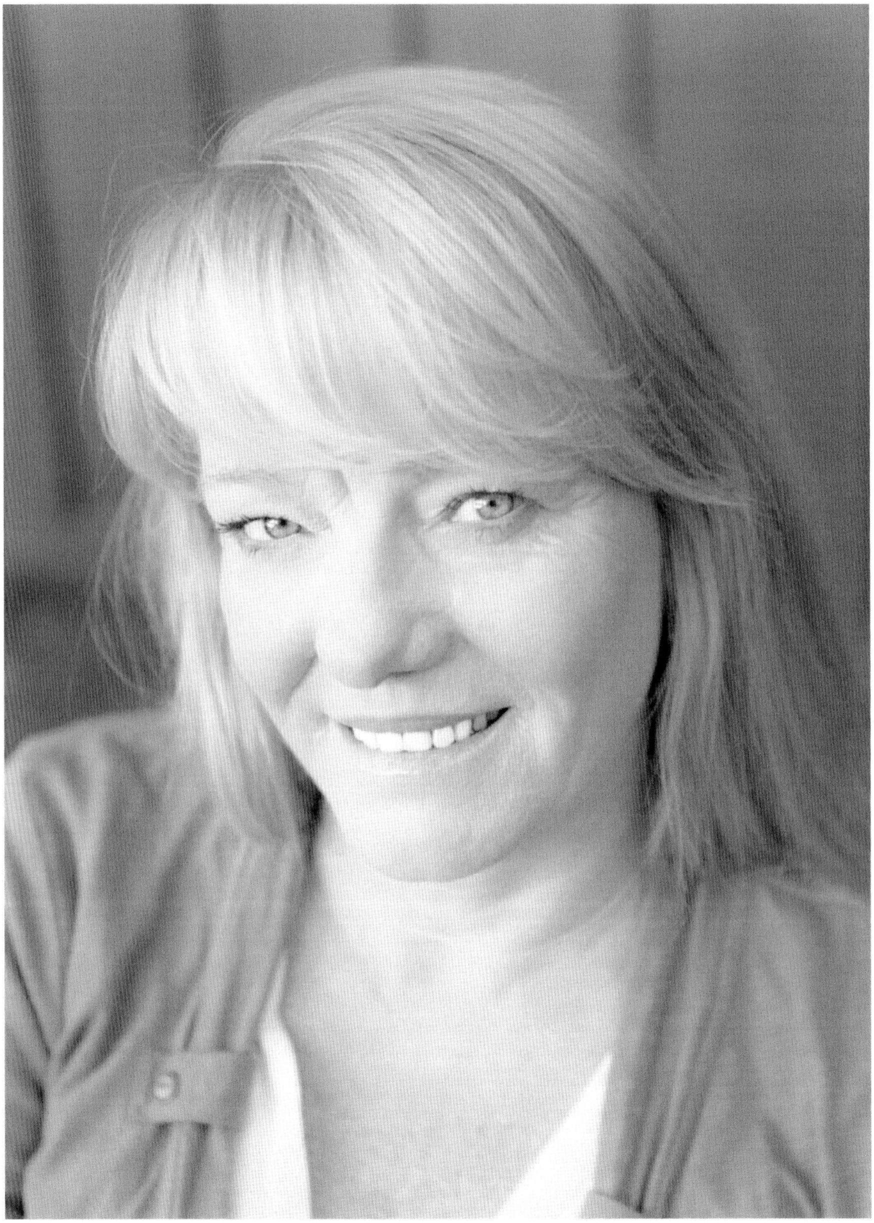

Camille Schraeder

Camille Schraeder is "the children's friend and protector" of Mendocino and Lake Counties. She is the founder and director of Redwood Children's Services, and through her tireless efforts, Redwood Children's Services has grown to a multi-level organization that assists foster and at-risk children. Their mission statement says it all: "The mission of Redwood Children's Services, Inc., is to improve the lives of at-risk children and families by providing community support and quality therapeutic services."

Camille founded Redwood Children's Services in 1995 to provide specialized care and programs for foster children and their families in Mendocino and Lake Counties. Their programs include support systems for foster parents, group homes for severely emotionally disturbed foster youth, transitional housing placement, and children's therapeutic services. (Courtesy of Camille Schrader.)

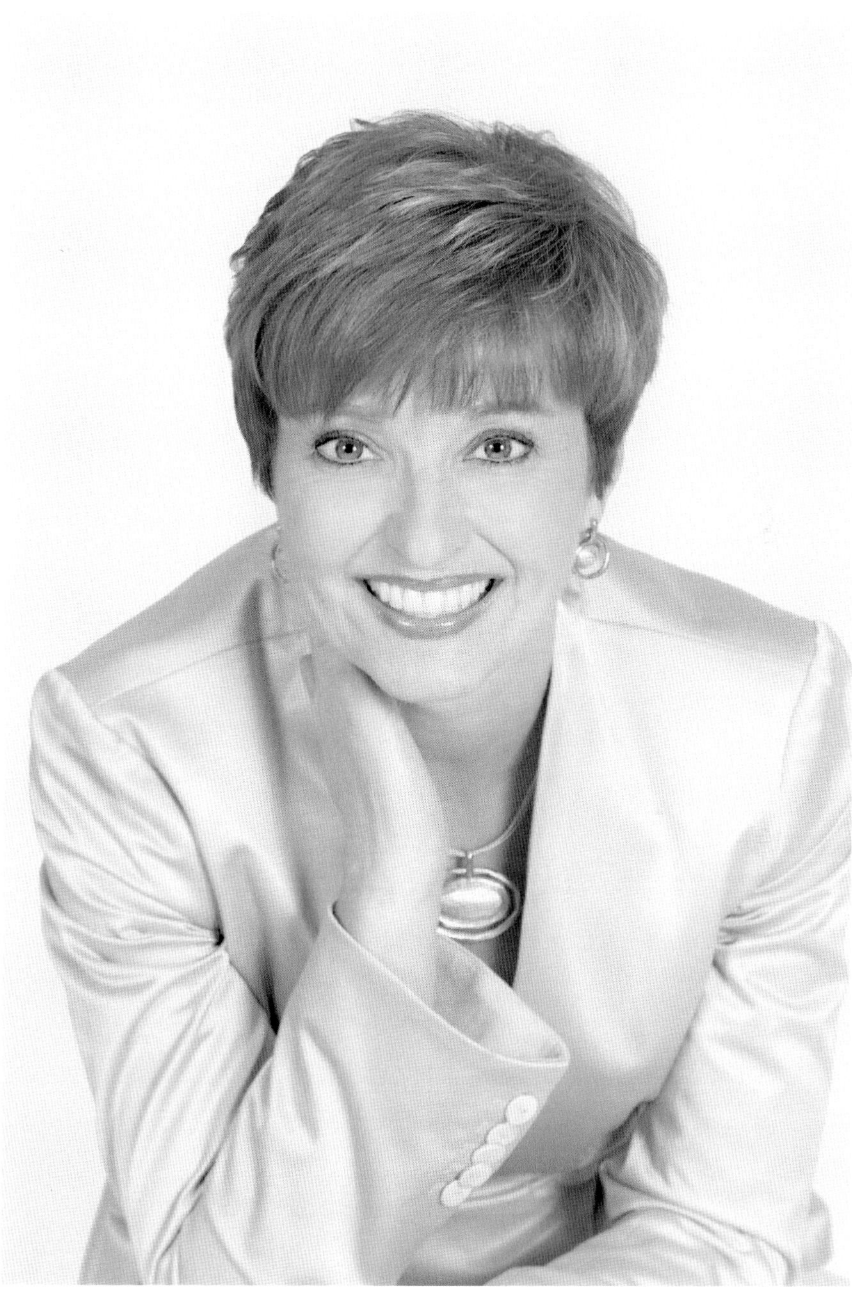

Barbara Marshall

An author, businesswoman, and television personality, Barbara Marshall is a Dutch native who came to Ukiah and started a nondenominational organization. She hosts a weekly television program that is filmed in Ukiah and features guests who cover a wide range of topics with their interviews, testimonies, and inspirational messages. This weekly television show is viewed by several hundred people in the Ukiah area and its surroundings. Barbara has also been an international speaker since 1993, is the author of several books, and still continues to host seminars centered on "Loving Yourself from the Inside Out." Her seminars are focused on strategies for successful living. (Courtesy of Barbara Marshall.)

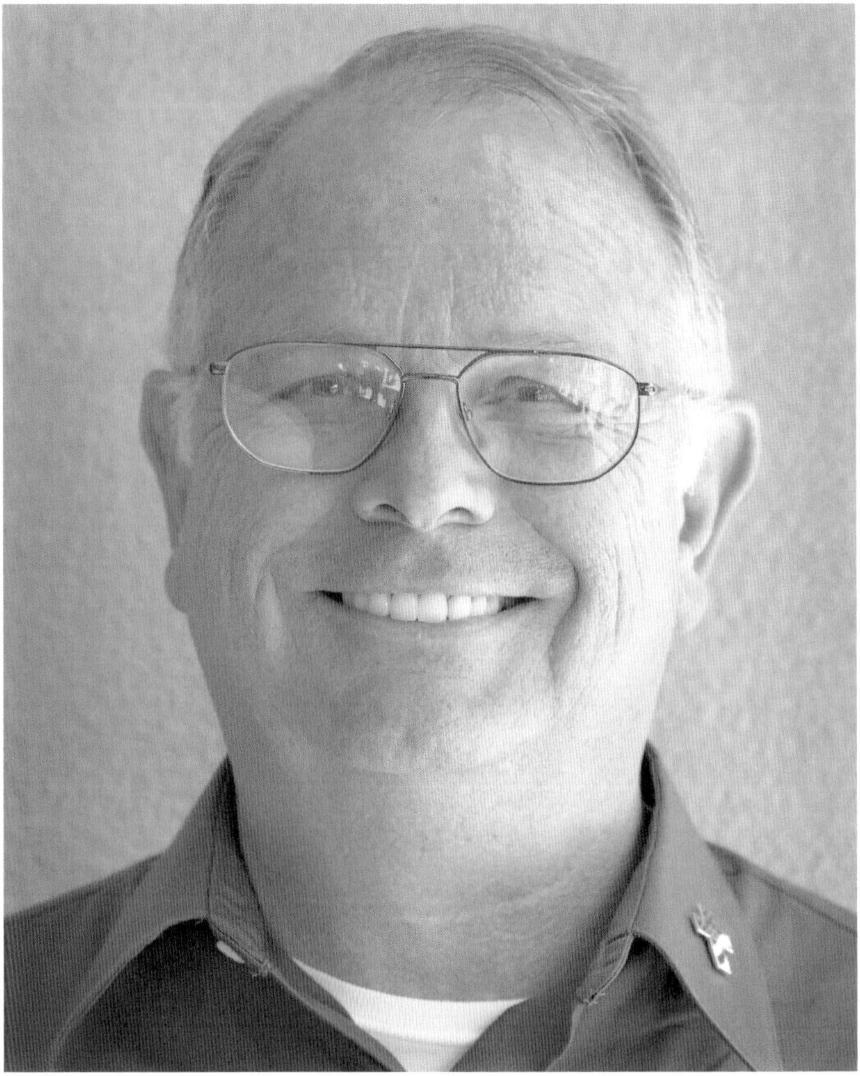

Rick Paige

Rick Paige needs a red cape to wear with his regular clothes. After heading up Emergency Services in the South Bay, he and his family moved to Ukiah. Here, Rick served as the director of emergency services for Mendocino County for almost a decade and has gone on to serve as a volunteer disaster response supervisor since 1979. When Hurricane Sandy hit the eastern United States in 2012, this Ukiahan was on the scene—setting up shelters as one of the six volunteers from the area. While there, he served as a government liaison manager and oversaw the efforts of government departments in eight counties.

Whenever there is a local emergency, Rick is the first one on the scene. A major house fire in Ukiah found Rick helping the family with everything from shelter, food, and clothing, to assisting with the filling out of forms so the insurance claim could be expedited.

In his spare time, Rick is the director of the nonprofit organization, YES (Youth Emergency Services). Every year, the group sets up a camp to teach young people how to respond to an emergency situation. Whether it's a fire, a flood, or another disaster, these young people are trained to survive and assist by Rick Paige and his team. They are trained in first aid and CPR certified. This is one of only many ways that Rick gives back to his adopted community. (Courtesy of Rick Paige.)

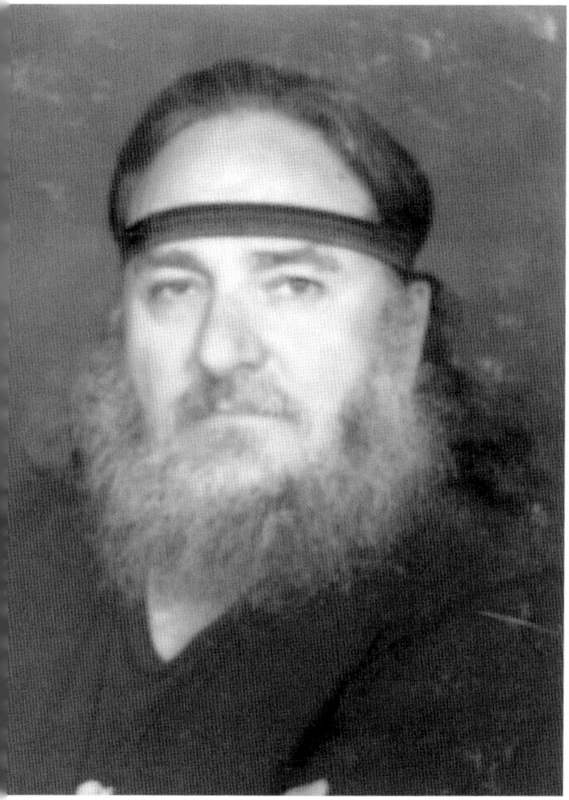

Utah Carl "Trench" Haley

"Living Wake"

Veterans Memorial Hall
293 Seminary Ave., Ukiah, CA, 95482
7pm to 9pm Wednesday night, March 27, 2013

All are invited to the living wake for Utah Carl "Trench" Haley. Per his wishes, we will not morn his passing, ***we will celebrate his life!***

There will be plenty of great food and exotic drink (if someone brings it) live entertainment (if some-one does it) deep discussions on a wide range of subjects related to a ***Life Well Lived*** (for one who has ***lived*** it). There will be an open mike, video recorder, guest books and note books to give you a last chance to say something to him. After the wake, these books, notes and messages will be read to him. ***I know he will not hear them, but do believe he will feel them.***

This celebration will close with Amazing Grace by Charly Ellis, and, again per his wishes,

A primal yell to warn the next world that a man is coming from this world!

If you have food or drink, bring it.
If you have words for him, say them
If you have a bike, ride it!

wake **noun** [formally of Scand origin (ca. 1547)": the track left by a moving body, but herein both a **verb transitive and verb intransitive** [of American origin (Trash ca. 2013): as defined by the life of Utah Carl "Trench" Haley] *a ripple in the fabric of space/time and all that is within it caused by the passing of something enormous*

Utah "Trench" Haley
Utah was born in Oklahoma and moved with his family to Ukiah. As a young man, he joined the military and served as a guided-missile technician in Germany during the Cuban Missile Crisis. After his tour of duty, he returned to Ukiah and worked as a mechanic and professional driver.

In his later years, Trench devoted his time to the Disabled American Veterans Association. He spent thousands of hours driving veterans to their appointments at Fort Miley—a veterans' facility in the San Francisco Bay Area. He was a firm believer in helping those less fortunate. Utah was also involved in many community and charity programs—especially Ukiah's Annual Toy Run—and on Valentine's Day, he organized a group to ensure that the veterans he helped would get valentines and know that they were appreciated and remembered. Utah was truly a man who had a smile and an encouraging word for everyone he met.

His friends and the community organized a living wake for him at the Veterans Memorial Hall, celebrating a man who lived each day to the fullest. As at the flyer for the wake said, "A primal yell goes out to warn the next world that a man is coming from this world!" (Courtesy of the Haley family.)

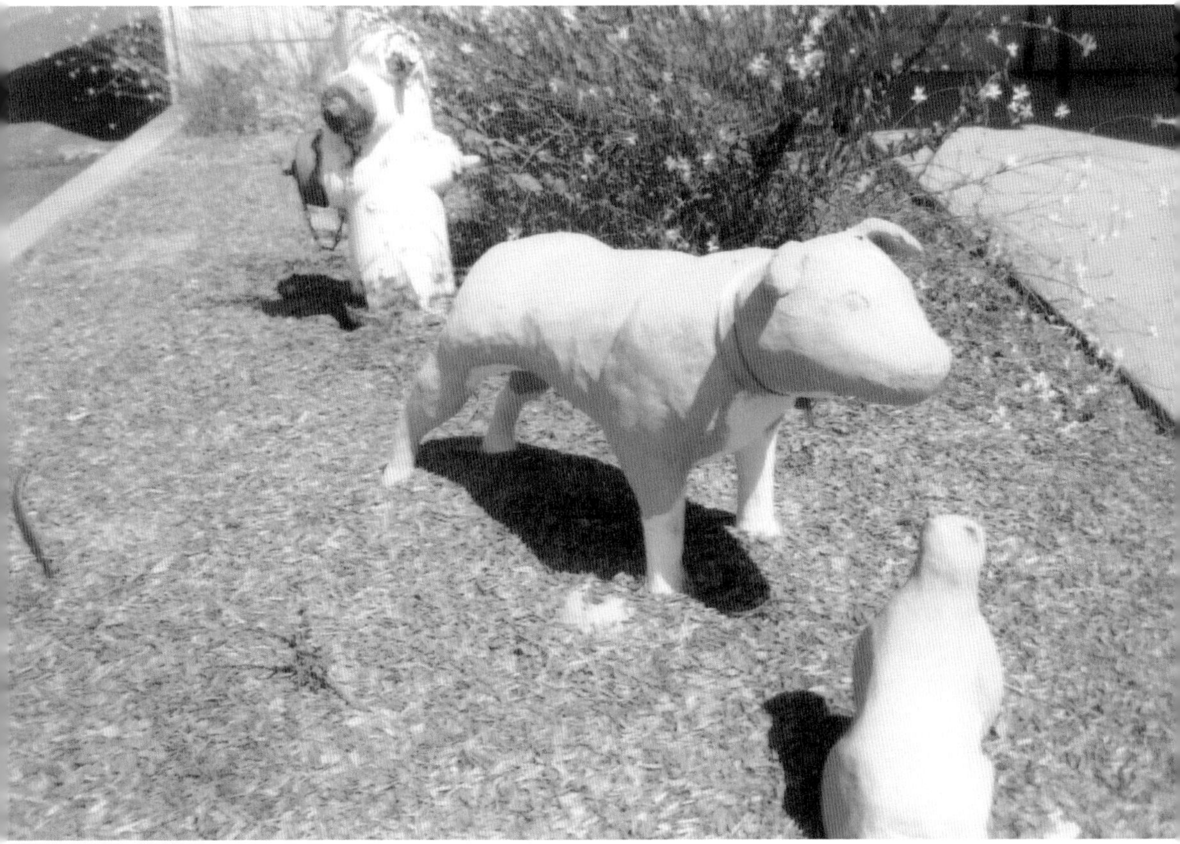

Sage Mountainfire (ABOVE AND OPPOSITE PAGE)
Sage has been a volunteer with the Mendocino County Animal Shelter for almost a decade. She worked with the *Ukiah Daily Journal* to develop a program that photographed the animals and showed them in the newspaper. The feature also includes the animals' stories, including where they were found and their personalities—making you want to run right out, meet your new best friend, and take them home.

Sage also oversaw the development of a website for the shelter, which helps people to locate missing pets. Sage also heads up a volunteer group that comes in each day to walk the dogs and socialize them, so they're comfortable with people. She also started a foster care program that enables people who don't have the ability to adopt a pet to still enjoy time with an animal. The teenagers who volunteer at the shelter learn about how to care for the animals and pick up valuable life skills about responsibility.

One of Sage's funniest stories about the shelter happened on a hot July day. Just before closing time, a truck pulled up with a large crate in the bed. Sage said that all she could see in the crate was fur, from all angles. The driver explained that he was moving out of town and the people who had originally said they would take the dogs couldn't, due to a family emergency. Sage asked her staff to stay late, and out from the crate, came one large dog after another. There were five in all, and none of them weighed less than 60 pounds. Happily, Sage found homes for all five of them in a very short time. (Courtesy of Sage Mountainfire.)

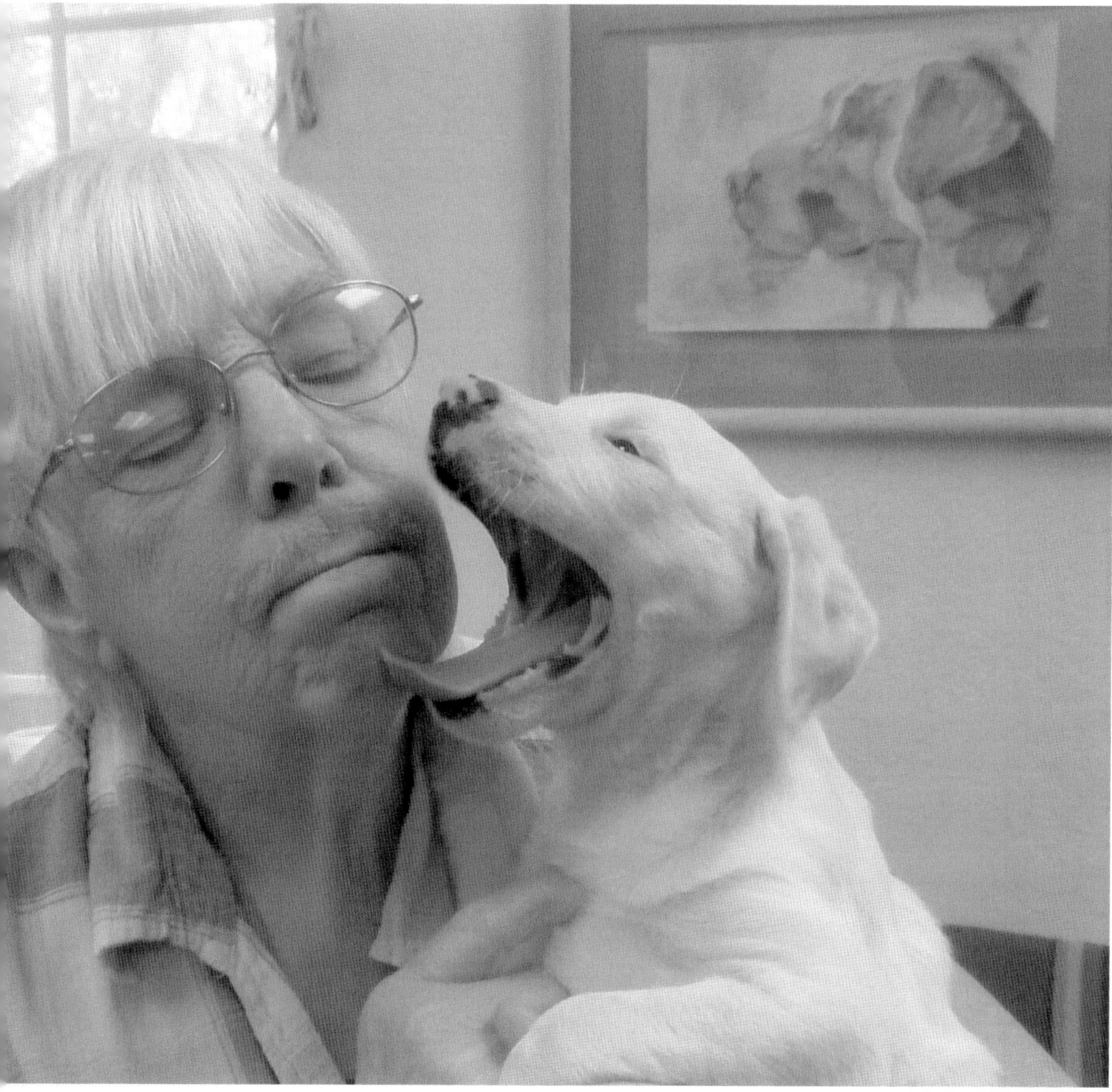

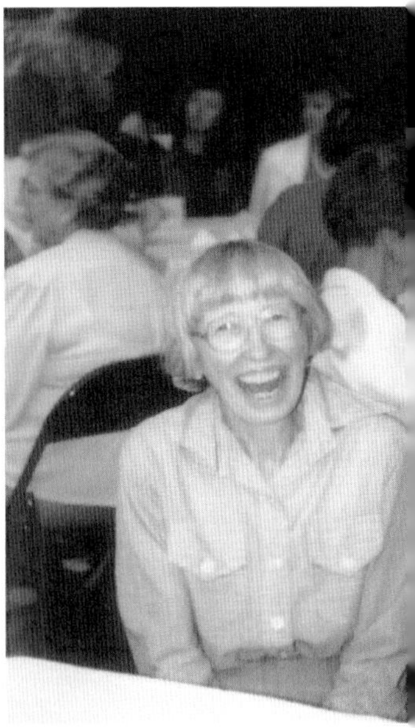

Elaine Dunn

A retired teacher, Elaine Dunn could always be counted on to volunteer for important jobs that no one else wanted. After her "official" retirement, she took a job as an in-home caregiver when she was in her late 70s. When asked why she didn't just take it easy, she said that having a job after retirement gave her the financial opportunity to donate to nonprofits. Not only did she donate money, but Elaine also devoted endless hours to preparing food for the homeless and gathering clothes for the people who needed them.

Every year at Christmas time, Elaine oversaw the Christmas Angel Project. This program was started to ensure that children who had one, or both, parents incarcerated would receive a present and not be forgotten. She prepared a list of each child's needs, be it a toy or a piece of clothing, and distributed the list to volunteers who made sure that every child got what they hoped for. Elaine was a true Christmas angel—doing what she did quietly and without any thought of receiving publicity for her efforts. (Courtesy of Dorothy Kauffman.)

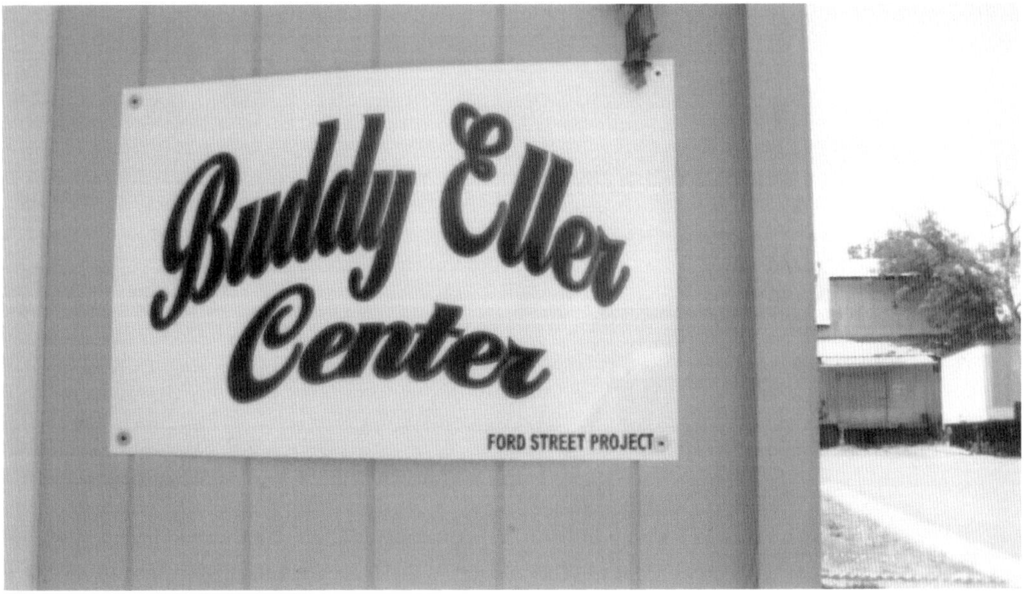

Buddy Eller

Don "Buddy" Eller was a man who had "been there and done that." Realizing that there was a large segment of the community that existed without resources or means to better their lives, Don "Buddy" Eller compiled the first ever report on homelessness in the valley. He worked with the Ukiah Community Center to ascertain the number of people needing assistance—obtaining information from law enforcement, local ministers, and other agencies associated with the homeless. His report was viewed as the first step in helping the community members realize the extent of the situation and what they could do about it.

He lived every day of his life helping others—operating with compassion and without judgment. The Buddy Eller Shelter in Ukiah is named in his honor and is a living memorial to Buddy and all he stood for. (Courtesy of Buddy Eller Shelter.)

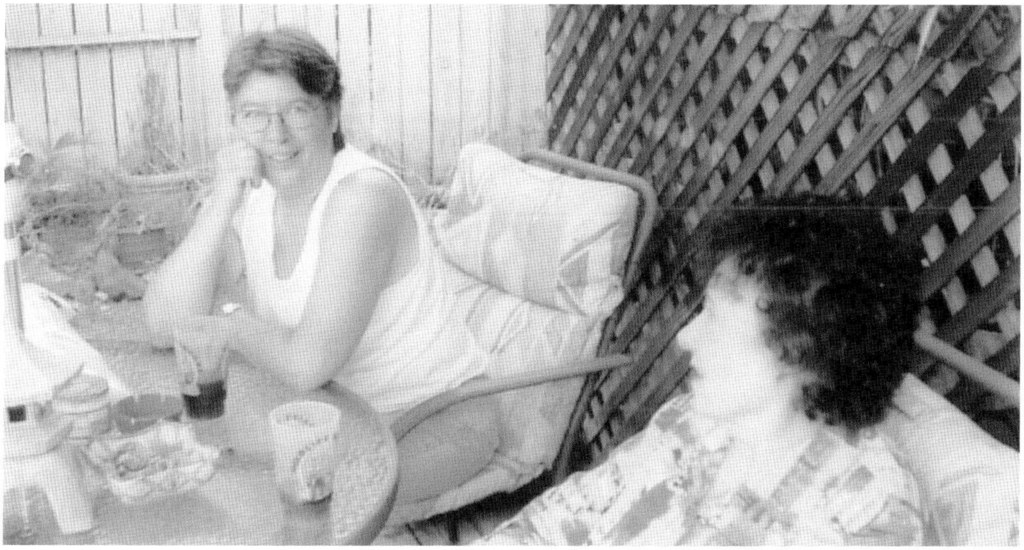

Jan Cox

Everyone knows the angst of having something that they need help with in their home. It could be a plumbing problem, a room that needs painting, or a fence that needs repair. The problem is finding someone to do the work without sending you to the bank for a loan. Everyone needs a fix-it person who is honest, reasonable, and shows up when they say they will.

For many in Ukiah, Jan Cox was that person. After she retired from Masonite, Jan taught herself carpentry skills and went to work. Soon, you could hear about Jan and her affordable, quality work just about everywhere in town. Many times, she even refused to charge for her work. After one local resident suffered a destructive home invasion, a neighbor called Jan and told her what had happened. Jan came over immediately and secured the house for the woman, saying, "Don't even think about paying me. You needed help and I was happy to do it for you." Jan Cox was a true good guy, helping people whenever and wherever she could. Her father, Kelly, owned a car dealership on State Street for many years. (Courtesy of Nancy Biggins.)

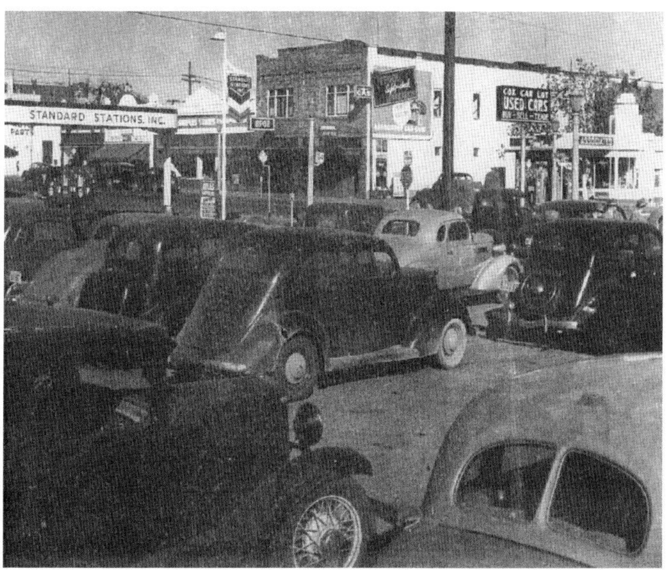

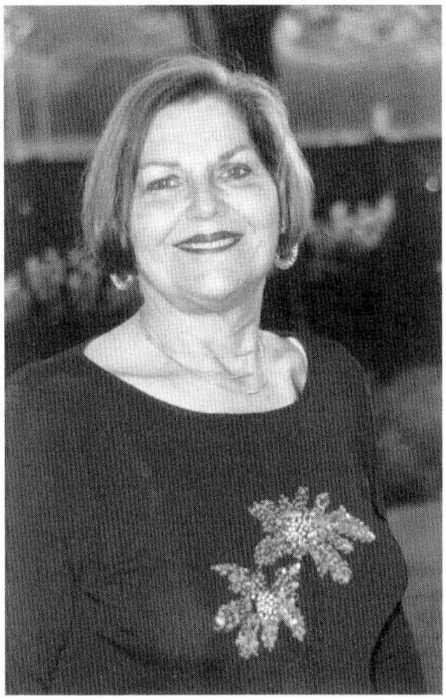

Kathy Davidson Reed

Over the years, Kathy Reed has served with, hosted, or chaired fundraisers that range from a women's film festival to a March of Dimes Bid for Bachelors, and has been a board member for over 20 nonprofit agencies. After retiring in 2008, Kathy tried to cut back on some of her nonprofit activities, but that didn't work out too well. When she discovered that no one was serving free meals on Christmas Day, she and her mother, Betty McGlade, created the Christmas Day Luncheon alongside local beautician Carol Cowles. Each guest was given lunch at a local venue and a bag with an extra meal to take home. The general public donates hats, scarves, and other items that available for those coming to the Christmas Day event.

Kathy credits her mother with teaching her at an early age how important it is to give back to your community. (Courtesy of Kathy Davidson Reed.)

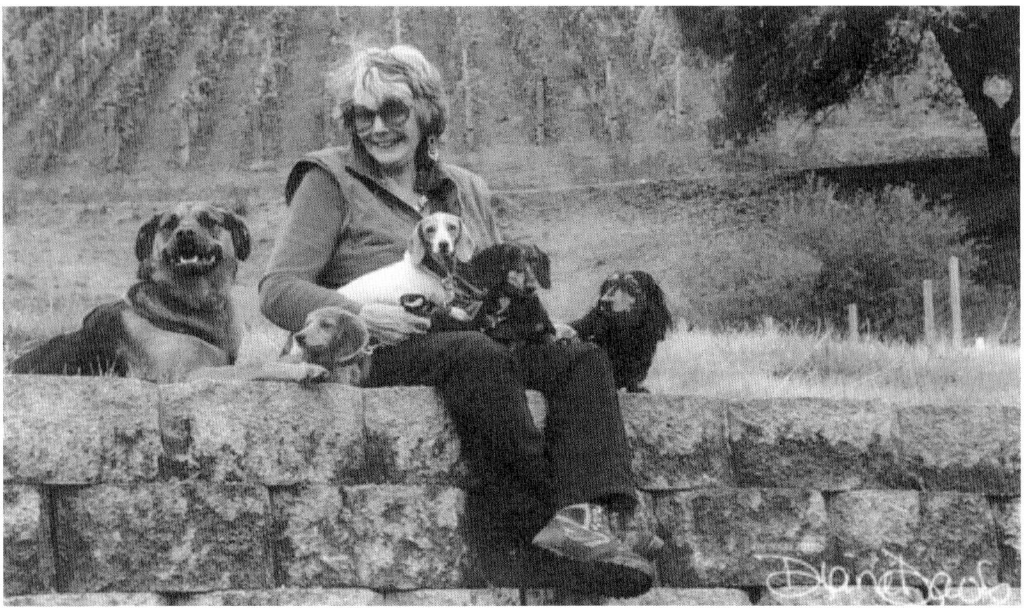

Eliza Wingate

Ukiah's branch librarian and her dog, Mccloud, have been constants at the Ukiah library for years. Eliza knows almost everyone that comes in, and everyone knows her. Patrons come to her for questions, guidance, and just to say hello before they head into the stacks.

Eliza has been responsible for many innovations that make the library the friendly, inviting environment it is today. She has overseen additions and programs in the children's area and is currently establishing a teen area. She has been instrumental in bringing more people into the library and reestablishing it as a gathering place for the community.

In 2003, the Aagaard family established the Mendocino County Historical Society's J. Earl Gardner Memorial Membership—an honorary membership given each year to someone recognized for his or her service to the community. The society voted unanimously to give the 2014 award to Eliza Wingate, due to her contributions to both the community and local society. (Courtesy of Eliza Wingate.)

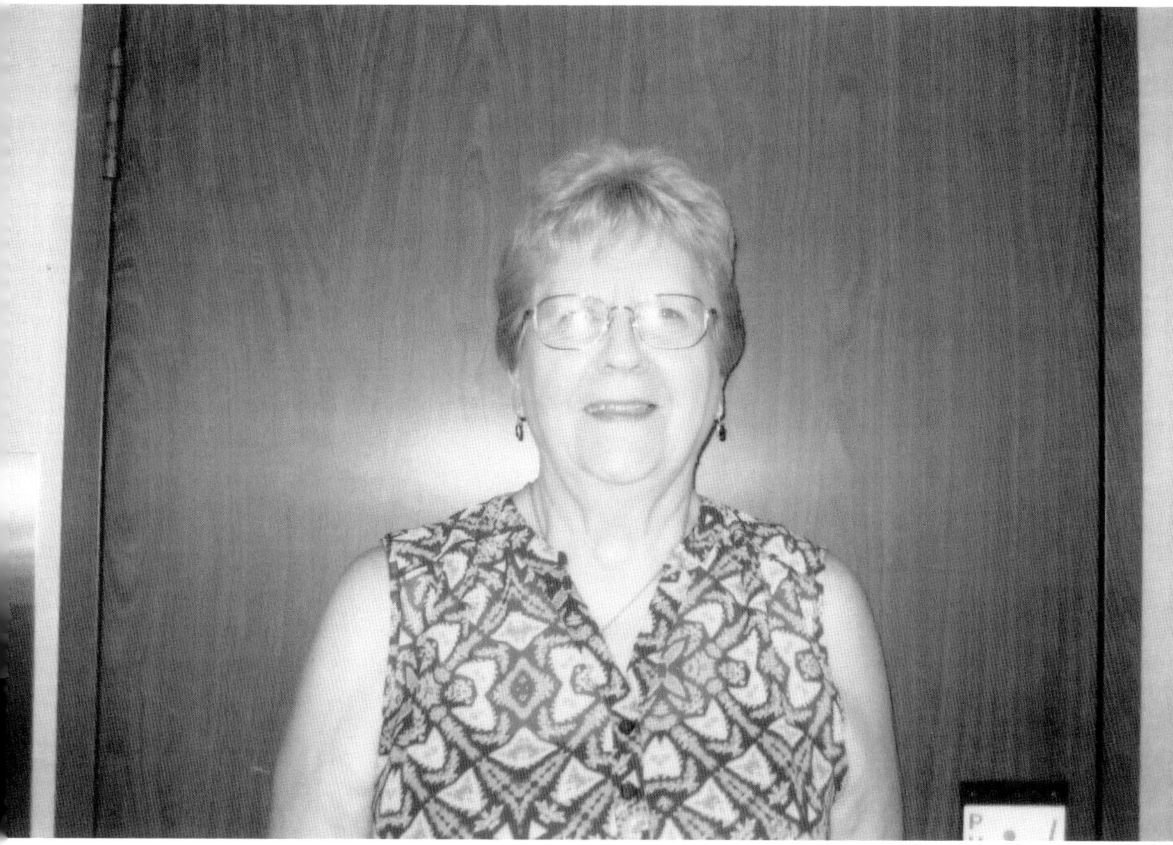

Nancy Trumble
Nancy has been the driving force behind the Friends of the Library book sales for almost two decades. While she originally started as a volunteer who worked only a few hours a week, the book sales have almost turned into a full time job for this woman.

Nancy is responsible for the coordination of the four-day sale held at the Veterans Memorial Building every year. She is also in charge of the monthly sales at the library, oversees the volunteer scheduling, sorts and prices books, and organizes online sales. Under her watch, the sales of the Veterans Building event increased over three times.

Her husband, James, also has worked as a volunteer for several years. The Friends of the Library and the library itself are deeply indebted to this couple. They have a deep understanding of how important a library is to a community. (Courtesy of Nancy Trumble.)

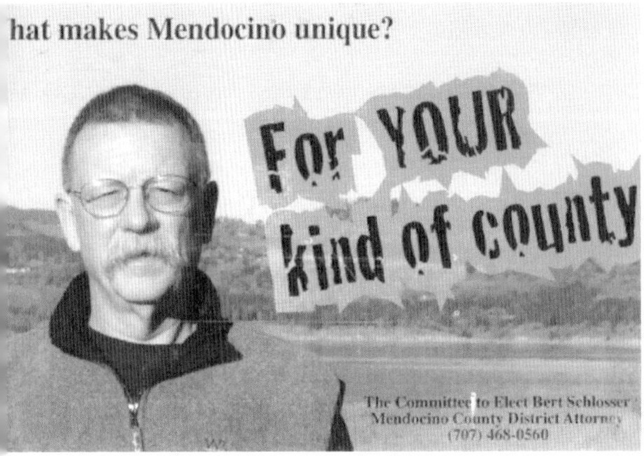

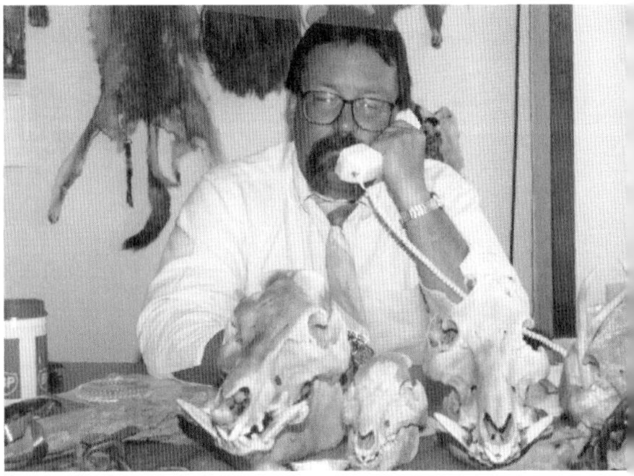

Bert Schlosser

This wild man also happened to be the best lawyer in Mendocino County's criminal defense attorney roster. When Bert passed away last year, one of his friends said, "Bert leaves a legacy unmatched and unmatchable." Bert loved being in the courtroom and fought brilliantly for his clients. He was tough, sharp, and didn't hold anything back when it came to representing his clients as a public defender. Bert represented people from all walks of life for every imaginable crime. When he represented a client accused of holding cockfights in his backyard, Bert wore a plastic rooster mask to court.

What few people know is that this rough and tough character collected first edition books, scale model airplanes, and old pocket watches. Just about anything that anyone could imagine was displayed somewhere in his office.

Bert was a man who could communicate with anyone, and if he couldn't get you to readily agree with his point of view, he wouldn't let up on you until he beat you into submission. An investigator who worked with Bert for a few decades said that defendants always expressed that, "The only good thing that had happened to them, no matter what they were charged with, was having Bert as their public defender." (Courtesy of the Schlosser family.)

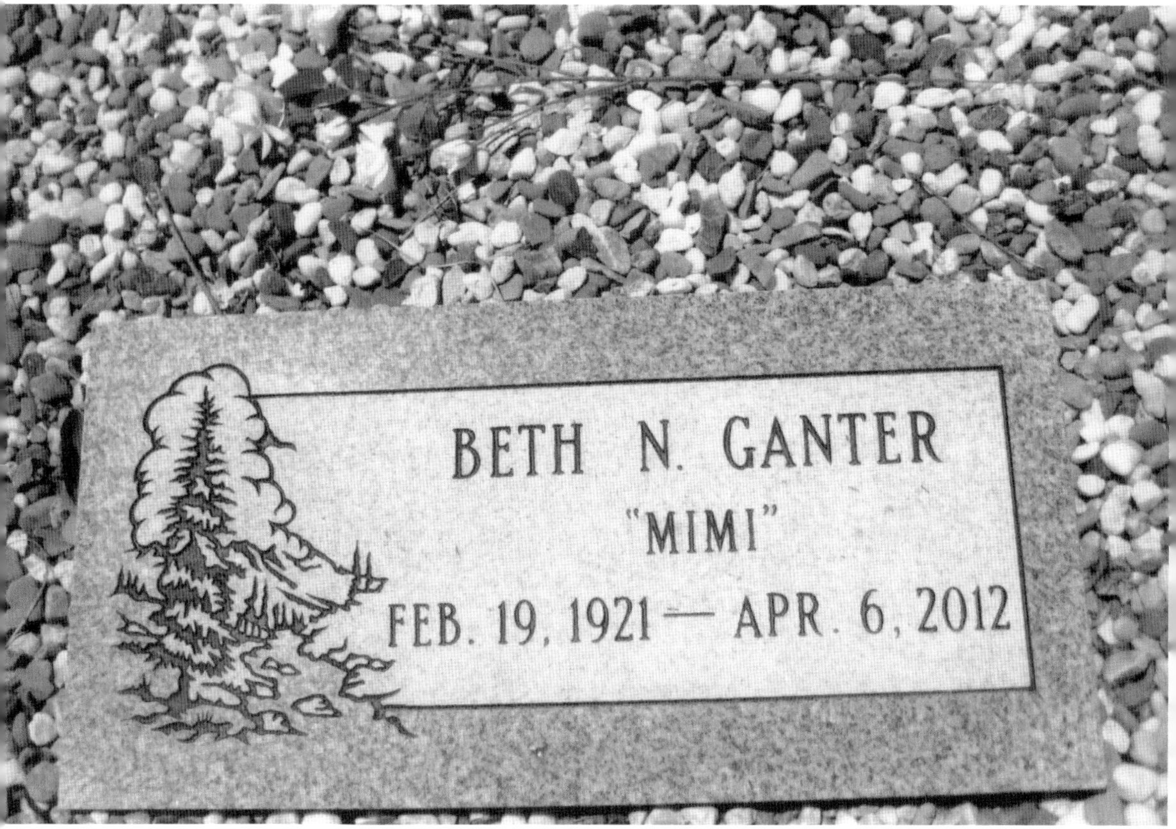

Beth "Mimi" Ganter
The State of California issued Beth Gartner a driver's license at the age of 13, due to her father's blindness and her mother's inability to drive. In high school, she was an outstanding athlete and was selected to be the editor of the yearbook. Her love of sports continued until her passing, and no matter if it was the Giants, the Warriors, or the 49ers, you could always find Beth watching the game.

As a young married woman, Beth not only raised her children but also helped her husband, Moose, with his service station business. After her husband's death, shortly before their 50th wedding anniversary, she helped her son with the service station until she made the decision to retire. After her retirement, she volunteered with local youth groups.

Today, one of Beth's daughters is a Mendocino County supervisor and one son is with the Mendocino County Probation Department. Always a lady and fashionably dressed, you could always find Beth at the beauty shop on Friday—getting "prettied up" for the weekend. (Courtesy of the Russian River Cemetery Association.)

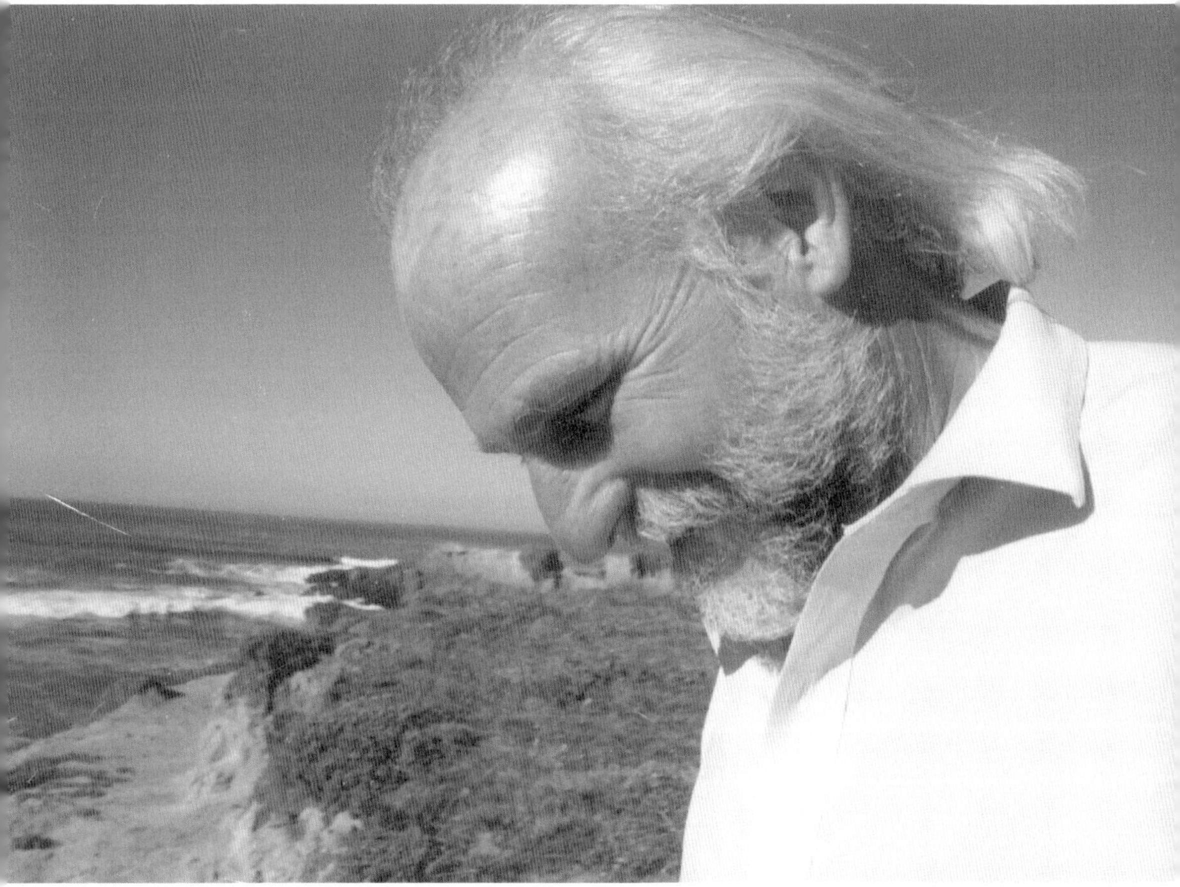

Richard "Rich" Petersen (ABOVE AND OPPOSITE PAGE)
Before the advent of cell phones, it was said that if the public phone in the lobby of the courthouse rang, it was for Rich Petersen. Rich was a much sought after criminal defense attorney, who spent more time in negotiations and trials than anyone in town. If it was a criminal case, everyone wanted to hire Petersen.

He was a colorful, personable man who always had time to greet everyone—always stylish in his Western clothes, custom made cowboy boots, bolo tie, and Western jacket. With his flowing white hair, from a block away anyone could tell that, "Rich was headed to the courthouse." It has often been said that people pass through life and are forgotten, but Rich Petersen—an avid hunter, fisherman, and camper—lived life to the fullest and will never be forgotten.

Several years ago, Rich appeared before a judge in overalls. The judge told him that he couldn't come to court without a tie, so Rich promptly went out into the hall, borrowed a tie from another lawyer, and strode back into court. The trial proceeded without further incident. Today, Rich's son Justin practices criminal law in the same courthouse where his father spent his life. (Courtesy of Justin Petersen.)

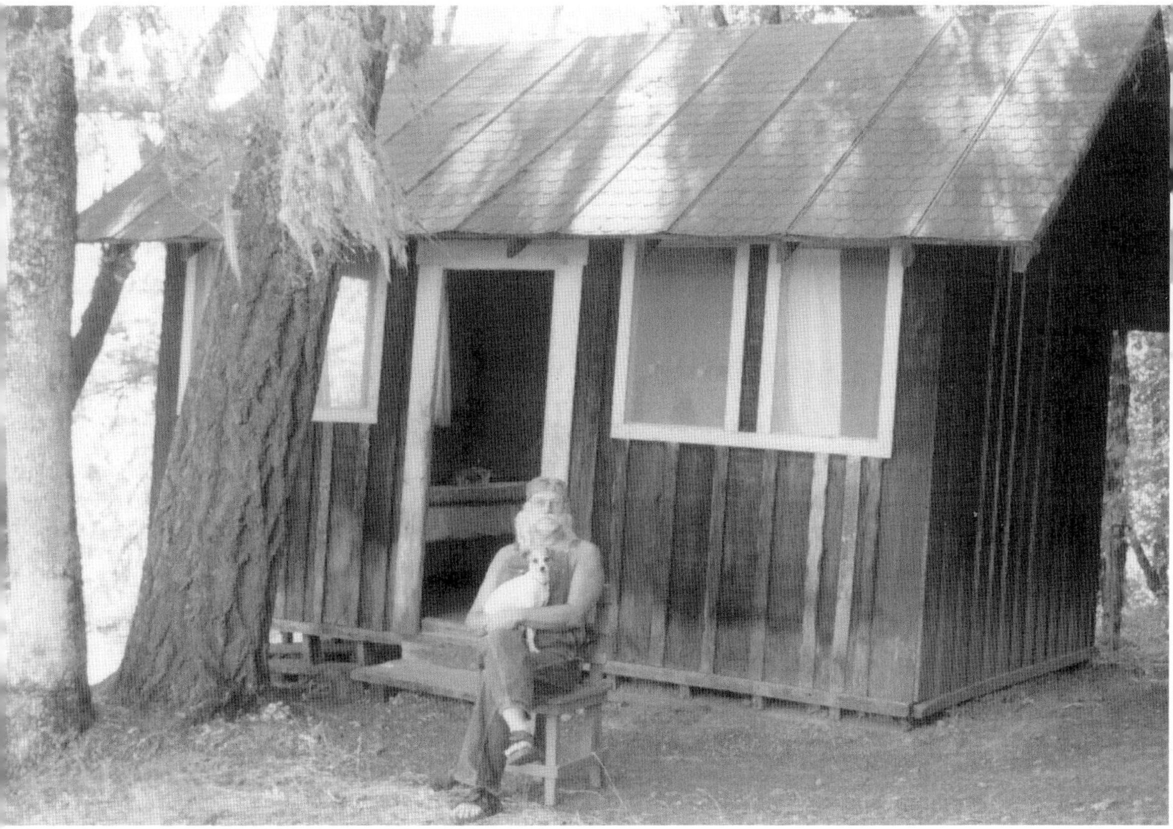

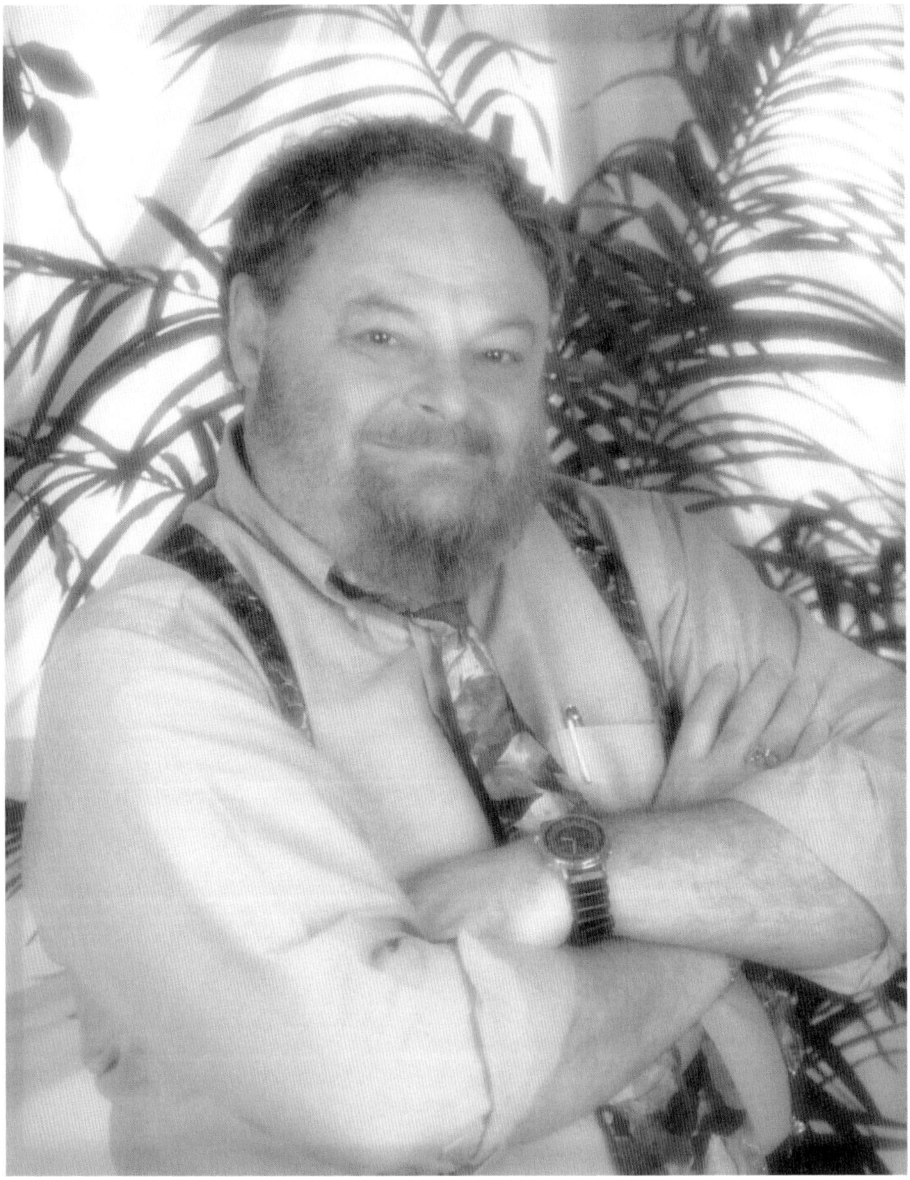

Sinet "Chuck" Simon

Chuck and his wife, Linda, moved to Ukiah in 1992 and promptly started SLP—working with insurance companies as brokers. Chuck was a man of many talents, ranging from insurance, to serving as a registered securities representative, to being in the real estate business. But aside from being a businessman, what Chuck enjoyed most was working with nonprofits. Any time he heard that a group needed help, he was there to lend a hand. He was a true believer in giving back to his community.

Chuck spent almost 50 years as a member of the Mill Valley Masonic Lodge and was once president of the Pomo Shrine, the Scottish Rite Shrine Temple, Leadership Mendocino, and the Mendocino County Airport and Land Use Commission. He was also an FAA safety counselor with the Ukiah Airport Commission and could always be found donating his time with the Ukiah Chamber of Commerce.

Chuck loved meeting new people and learning about their lives. Whenever he entered a room, everyone knew his personality was one larger than life. (Courtesy of Linda Simon.)

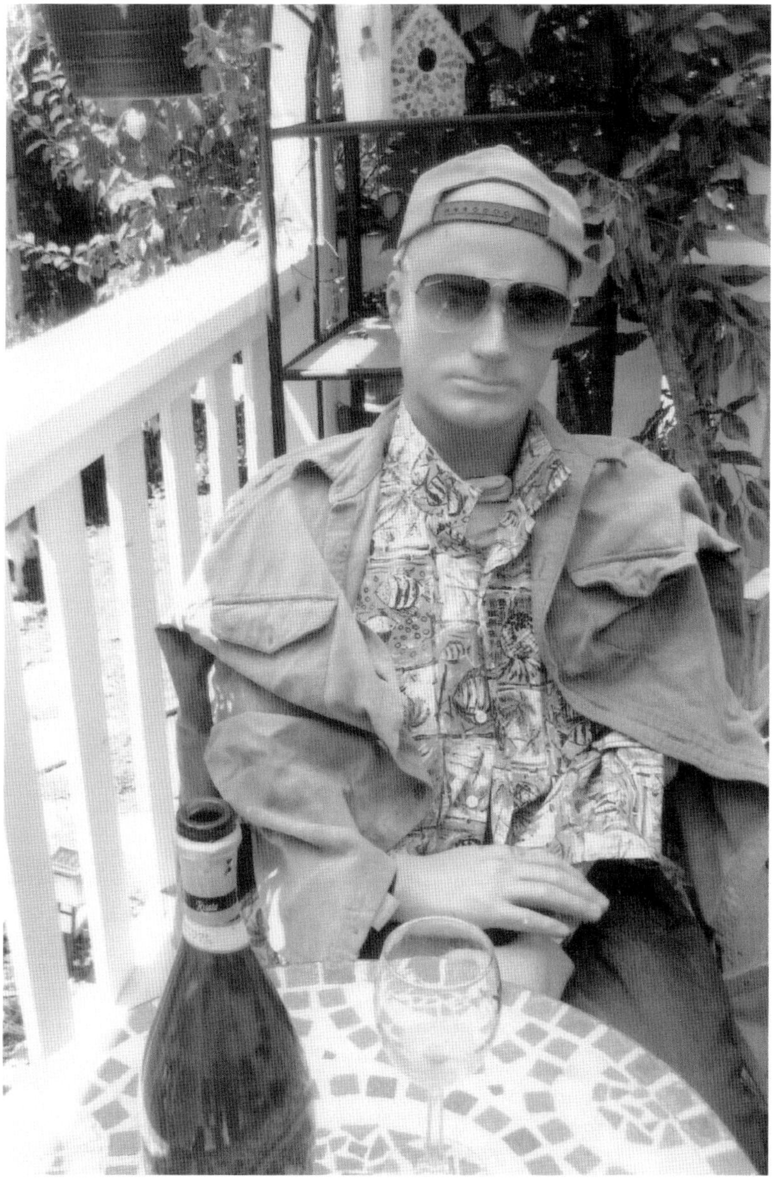

Mannequin Man

Mannequin Man, a well-known Westsider, moved to Mendocino County almost two decades ago. He retired after spending most of his life in Sonoma County and decided that a move to a greener environment would be to his liking. He can be found sitting on the porch of a west side home, just watching the world go by. He is always dressed to accommodate the season, and during the rainy season he keeps an umbrella with him on his covered porch—just in case of a wind driven shower.

Several years ago, he was kidnapped. The *Ukiah Daily Journal* printed the story, and the search went on for days. Much to the delight of his admirers, he eventually reappeared and has lived comfortably ever since. He did decide to spend more time on the side porch rather than out front, however, letting people know that he felt a little more secure in that sunnier location. If asked, Mannequin Man will hold a Happy Birthday sign for some lucky child. Over the years, he has made countless people smile when they see him, and many locals stop by on their daily walk to say hello. (Courtesy of M.D. Berger.)

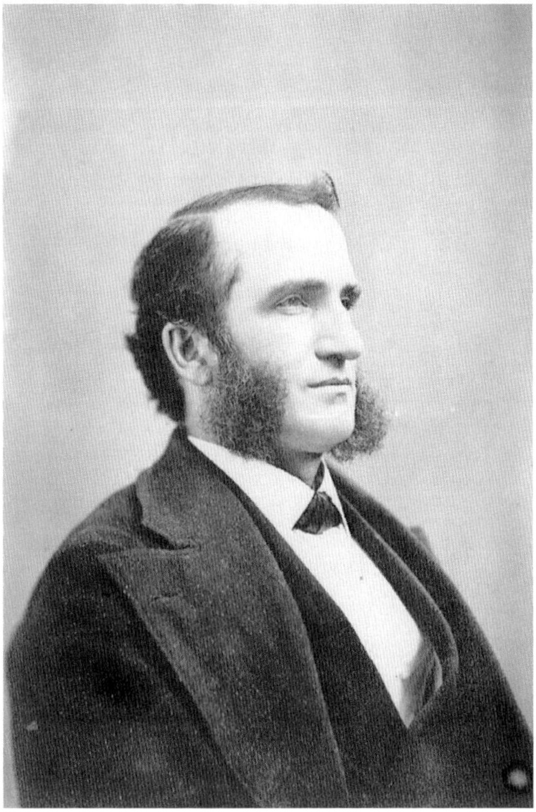

Myron Holley Beaumont (a.k.a. Thomas B. Edwards)
On February 7, 1878, Ukiah was shocked to learn of the suicide of Mr. Edwards, who was described as an up and coming member of the community. After his death, his background and life under a different name came to light. In reality, Edwards had been Col. Myron H. Beaumont, former commander of the First New Jersey Calvary during the Civil War. He was also the son of a prominent family in New York. His father was a doctor and his mother was the daughter of Myron Holley—the abolitionist and cofounder of the Liberty Party. His sister was married to an attorney who had been appointed by Pres. Abraham Lincoln as consul general to Germany.

Myron began a military career in the New Jersey Calvary, where he attained the rank of Major. A closer look at his service record revealed that much of his time in the military was spent in ill health and that he was a close friend with a doctor who was always ready to write him an excuse that got him relieved from field service. Later in his military career, he was wounded at Hatcher's Run, Virginia, and was eventually placed on disability so as to still receive a pension.

He moved to New York City with his wife, Mary, and within a few years of the marriage, Mary filed for divorce—charging Myron with numerous acts of adultery. There was talk that, to avoid paying alimony, he journeyed west with his brother-in-law's wife. The two ended up in Coos Bay, Oregon, where Beaumont became editor of the *Coos Bay News*. As his travel companion was dying, Myron became friends with a young woman who was visiting from Oakland, California. Upon the death of the second "Mrs. Beaumont," this young lady became the third.

Beaumont and his bride ended up in San Francisco, where he went to work in the Pension Office. He entered into business with a man named Samuel Schwartz and together they defrauded veterans of their pensions. Further swindles led Beaumont to leave the city, eventually reemerging as Edwards. Along the way, he found himself in Ukiah and married Aneta Grier. Six weeks later, as creditors were closing in, Beaumont committed suicide through a morphine overdose. (Courtesy of Held-Poage Library.)

INDEX